HUNTER KILLER

HUNTER KILLER

INSIDE AMERICA'S UNMANNED AIR WAR

LT. COL. T. MARK McCURLEY
with KEVIN MAURER

DUTTON
— est. 1852 —

DUTTON

— est. 1852 —

An imprint of Penguin Random House LLC
375 Hudson Street
New York, New York 10014

Copyright © 2015 by Thomas Mark McCurley

DUTTON—EST. 1852 (Stylized) and DUTTON are registered trademarks of Penguin Random House LLC.

LIBRARY OF CONGRESS CATALOGING-IN-PUBLICATION DATA
has been applied for.

ISBN 978-0-525-95443-9

Printed in the United States of America
1   3   5   7   9   10   8   6   9   2

Set in Granjon
Designed by Spring Hoteling

FOR MY CHILDREN

CONTENTS

Contents

Contents

AUTHOR'S NOTE

I am an operator.

I am not a door kicker. I do not fast rope, rappel, or jump out of airplanes. Never have I been called upon to assault any position, be it fixed or fluid, though I have been trained to do so. I do not claim to be like the SEALs or Special Forces. That wasn't my career path.

But I am still an operator. A fighter.

In 2003, more than a decade into my Air Force career, I faced a third consecutive assignment to a noncombat unit. I volunteered for the only combat job available to me at the time—the RQ-1 Predator. Dog, my squadron commander, looked sidelong at me when I made my request. A crusty, old-school fighter pilot, he shared the same belief as the rest of the Air Force, and even myself.

Predators were for chumps.

"Mark, are you sure you want this?" he asked.

Dog deeply cared about his people and would cheerfully work any assignment for me if I truly desired it.

"This won't be good for your career."

Careerism had never been my goal. I had long ago elected to deviate from the normal, expected path and bounce from aircraft to aircraft with each assignment. The Air Force expected officers to stick with one aircraft their whole careers. Each community told me the same thing. A change would be bad for my promotion opportunities.

"Sir," I said. "I just want to get into the fight. Do my part."

I had felt that way since September 11. I had been leading a T-6A formation sortie over Valdosta, Georgia, when the Federal Aviation Administration directed us to land. The controller was both curt and professional, but it was unusual since military often were exempted from such directives.

After we'd landed, our engines had barely spun to a stop before the excited crew chief ran up to us, asking if we had heard the news. Someone had flown an airplane into the World Trade Center. At first, we had reacted skeptically. After all, inexperienced pilots flew their little aircraft perilously close to the towers all the time. Sightseers did stupid things like that.

But, when I'd gotten to the 3rd Flying Training Squadron duty desk, I joined two dozen instructor pilots and students huddled around the screen watching clips of an airliner barreling into the first tower.

The video repeated and repeated. And then it changed. It was subtle at first, then nightmarishly clear. The "LIVE" icon flashed as the airliner plunged again into the tower. Another aircraft thundered into the second tower. We all knew one hit was an accident. Two was intentional.

Author's Note

We were in a war unlike any other fought by the United States. And I wanted to do my part.

Dog sighed.

"All right, I'll work this for you."

"Thank you, sir."

Hunter Killer is the story of an extraordinary group of young men and women with whom I had the honor to serve from 2003 through 2012. It is also the story of the Predator and its evolution from an aviation backwater joke to the tip of the spear in the war against terrorism.

In this book, I use only tactical call signs (nicknames) or first names to protect the identities of the pilots and crew. Certain senior leaders whose identities are already in the public domain are mentioned by name. Radio call signs for aircraft, units, or persons have been documented as accurately as my memory can manage. Some tactical call signs have been modified to ensure security of those entities still in harm's way.

I've taken great pains not to include details of any ongoing missions. I have also endeavored to protect specific tactics and procedures currently used by our crews as they continue to fight.

Hunter Killer is written from my point of view. This is a ground-level perspective of life in the remotely piloted aircraft community. I have strived to accurately portray events as they occurred, but the fog of war may have clouded how I perceived actions or remembered details. Any errors in the text are mine. Additionally, any opinions articulated here are also my own and do not represent the views of the United States Air Force, Department of Defense, or United States government. This story was written to honor the small cadre of aviators, the operators, who fought and continue to fight a war deep in the shadows.

Hunter Killer is their story.

We have just won a war with a lot of heroes flying around in planes. The next war may be fought by airplanes with no men in them at all. . . . Take everything you've learned about aviation in war, throw it out of the window, and let's go to work on tomorrow's aviation. It will be different from anything the world has ever seen.

General Henry "Hap" Arnold, US Army Air Forces, V-J Day, 1945

HUNTER KILLER

PROLOGUE
Retribution

The phone rang in the squadron operations center and I snatched it after the first ring.

It was my private line direct to the Joint Task Force based at Camp Lemonnier in Djibouti. We'd been tracking a high-profile target and I had a feeling this was the call we'd been waiting for, for weeks.

"Squirrel here," I said.

On the line was the Predator liaison officer, or LNO. He worked for the Joint Operations Center (JOC) commander. His job was to coordinate Predator missions in the region. My squadron provided the Predators to keep watch and strike suspected terrorists and pirates.

"Launch," the liaison officer said.

"How many?"

"All three," he said.

Three Predators equipped with two AGM-114 Hellfire missiles each waited on the ramp. The planes were in alert status, ready to take off at a moment's notice. The phone line wasn't secure enough to confirm it, but I knew one thing as I hung up the phone.

Today, the wolf pack hunted.

It was September 30, 2011. I was the commander of the 60th Expeditionary Reconnaissance Squadron at Camp Lemonnier, which was built by the French Foreign Legion in Djibouti. The country was a former French colony with oppressively hot weather and few assets save its location northwest of Somalia and across the Gulf of Aden from Yemen. It was prime strategic real estate for American counterterror operations.

Camp Lemonnier shares the single runway at Djibouti-Ambouli International Airport, on the outskirts of Djibouti City and close to the only major seaport servicing East Africa. Following the September 11 attacks, the United States leased it from the Djiboutian government for thirty-eight million dollars a year in order to establish a conduit for its humanitarian operations in the interior. The Marines were the first Americans at the base in 2002 and quickly established a small base capable of airlift operations. The mission of the Combined Joint Task Force–Horn of Africa quickly grew to include intelligence-gathering operations throughout East Africa. A few years later, the JOC stood up to address the growing terrorism threat in the region and across the Gulf of Aden in the Arabian Peninsula.

I hung up the phone and gave the order to launch. My director of operations called the maintainers on the ramp and passed the word. The single props on the backs of the Predators started to hum as the pilots in the ground control station—a shipping container with cockpits containing everything needed to control the aircraft—started preflight checks. My pilots slowly maneuvered the Predators off the ramp and onto the runway. Three crews eight thousand miles away in the United States scrambled to their cockpits, sitting at consoles in air-conditioned quarters at Cannon Air Force Base in New Mexico waiting to take control of the birds. My pilots in Djibouti would perform the takeoff and turn over control of the Predators to pilots in the United States to fly the mission. As a ten-year veteran of the Predator program, I'd been on that end of these missions countless times before. No other aircraft in the Air Force used two crews—one to take off and the other to fly the mission. It wasn't the only way our program was unique.

I went outside to watch the launch. The thermometer near the building hovered at ninety-five degrees as the three aircraft started to spin up. Heat was a worse enemy to the Predators than al Qaeda. The "heat window" was upon us. If it got any hotter, the delicate electronics within the Predators could overheat and melt before reaching the cooler temperatures at higher altitudes.

Back in the operations center, I could hear over the radio as the Djiboutian air traffic control tower cleared the Predators to take off. I watched from a concrete barrier as the Predators lumbered down the runway, barely able to lift off if not for the slight incline at the end of the tarmac. Once airborne, the Predators flew out to sea before turning for Yemen.

I checked my watch. We had several hours before the Predators would be across the Gulf of Aden and be on target. I returned to my other duties, but I made a mental note to head over to the Task Force in a couple of hours to watch the feed.

It was still hot as I walked into the Task Force's facility. The thermometer at the door now read a balmy 120 degrees. There were no comforting sea breezes in the summer, only a constant fifteen- to twenty-knot wind coming from the desert that felt more like a hair dryer. A wall-mounted air conditioner whirred as I walked inside the metal prefab building. The small unit strained to keep up with the stifling temperatures outside.

Six fifty-inch plasma screens lined the walls around the JOC commander's podium. Each showed the video feed from various Predators or Reapers flying around the region.

Some were in Africa.

Most were in Yemen.

The pilots and sensor operators flying the aircraft were based in numerous locations around the globe, digitally connected to our aircraft as if they were right down the hall.

The room buzzed with anticipation as I walked inside. The JOC commander was a short officer, standing on a central dais at the center of the room. From his position, he could see all six monitors. The Predator LNO stood at his desk a few paces to the right of the commander.

"That him?" I asked the Predator LNO, a tall Air Force major.

"Not sure," the LNO said. "We confirmed he was active about five hours ago."

The LNO didn't look away from the monitors showing the Predators' video feeds.

"We are still looking to get eyes on him right now."

Not having "eyes on" meant we couldn't see the target. The guys never said where the leads came from.

The target was Anwar al-Awlaki.

Born in New Mexico to Yemeni parents, al-Awlaki, thirty-eight years old, had been in contact with two September 11 hijackers and was in contact with Major Nidal Malik Hasan via email before

Hasan killed thirteen people in a shooting at Fort Hood in Texas in 2009. Al-Awlaki also inspired Nigerian student Umar Farouk Abdulmutallab to attempt to use an underwear bomb to blow up a Detroit-bound airliner on Christmas Day in 2009.

After being investigated by the FBI for his connections to al Qaeda, al-Awlaki fled to London and then to Yemen, where he worked as editor in chief of al Qaeda's English-language recruitment magazine, *Inspire*. The magazine featured an article on how to make bombs. The Boston Marathon bombers would eventually use the article to carry out their attack.

On the monitor, I saw the town of Khashef, a small village north of Sana'a, Yemen's capital. The village looked like a mix of mud-brick and cinder-block houses haphazardly thrown together. It was nondescript enough to serve as a hideout and close enough to the big city that conveniences were a short drive away.

"The target's active," said an analyst sitting nearby. "We are seeing indications he's on the move."

Two white Toyota HiLux trucks pulled up outside a house in the village. Both trucks had king cabs that sat about five people. The black-and-white Predator feed on the plasma screen locked onto the lead truck.

The officer gave al-Awlaki's coordinates and I checked the feeds. The two trucks sat very near the coordinates. My Predators were close enough to consider themselves on target. We all watched closely as eight men spilled out of a nearby house and quickly climbed into the trucks. They wore garb traditional to the area, white robes and head scarves. One wore all white and climbed into the lead truck. The doors barely shut before the driver of the lead truck took off, trailing a plume of dust and exhaust. The trail vehicle followed a moment later.

"Stay on them," the JOC commander said.

I watched the LNO type the command on his keyboard, sending the order through a secure Internet chat to the Predator crews in Nevada. Seconds later, the Predator's sensor operator smoothly shifted its cross hairs onto the lead truck, setting the camera underneath the aircraft's nose to track the truck. The crew was efficient, good. I knew a skilled team was important today.

"Sir," the Army officer said. "Awlaki just announced he was moving."

"Agreed, sir," another officer said. "Call came from the lead vehicle."

The JOC commander nodded.

"I want all eyes on."

Within seconds, the other two Predator feeds shifted to the two vehicles picking their way through the village's market. Vendors and shoppers clogged the road in the late morning, making final purchases before the noon heat made shopping unbearable. The crowd slowed the trucks as the drivers darted through breaks in the sea of people.

"Gordon is lead," the JOC commander said.

Gordon was the lead Predator's call sign. The aircraft was named after the Army Delta Force operator who was killed in Somalia defending a downed UH-60 Black Hawk crew in 1993. It was the only Predator call sign not based on an Air Force legend.

The goal was to hit al-Awlaki while in transit between the villages of Khashef and Marib. An isolated strike meant no witnesses and low collateral damage. It also kept civilians out of harm's way. Al-Awlaki simply wouldn't show up at the meeting.

"LNO, running ROE now," the JOC commander said. "Have the crews spin up their missiles."

The ROE, or rules of engagement, are a set of criteria that must be met to legally take a shot in combat. No Predator crew could strike until the ROE were satisfied. I knew we had to be careful and make sure the target was in fact al-Awlaki. We were not drones, but professional pilots and planners who scrutinized every target to make sure the shot was legal and just.

We couldn't shoot until he cleared the village. A Hellfire missile would obliterate his truck, but also send deadly shrapnel into the surrounding buildings. A miss in the village would be catastrophic.

This would be the biggest operation since the mission that had taken Osama bin Laden nearly five months prior. We were going after Washington's new number one target. This would be a high-profile strike, a signature mission that would likely cement Predator and the remotely piloted aircraft (RPA) community as one of the United States' premier counterterrorism weapons.

When I started flying Predators in 2003, we mostly watched and listened. We were looked at as second-class citizens next to the fighter squadrons. But over the decadelong war, we'd become hunters. Predators and Reapers were responsible for a significant number of air strikes in Afghanistan, Pakistan, and Yemen. By 2013, policy makers no longer needed to risk boots on the ground in exhaustive and costly expeditions. Predators and Reapers could slip silently across lines on the map to track and, if necessary, kill terrorists. The RPA gave US officials a long arm to directly attack US enemies abroad.

The LNO put on a headset so he could talk to the Predator pilots. Now the Internet chat would be used to document coordinates and clearances. With his headset in place, the LNO flicked a switch so all three Predators could hear his commands.

"Gordon," the LNO said. "You've got the lead, acknowledge."

A remarkably clear voice, tinged with only a hint of static, responded.

"Copy, Gordon's got lead," the pilot said. "Checklist complete in two mikes."

"Mikes" was radio lingo for minutes.

The convoy made it through the market and picked up the pace as they neared the edge of the town. We had only one shot at him. If we missed, al-Awlaki would go to ground. At best, it would be months before we found him—if we found him again.

The driver took his time in the village, knowing the civilians protected him and his passengers. But once he hit the open road, speed was his only security. After years of flying similar missions, I knew a shot in the open could be difficult. No one followed traffic laws, and cars raced down the region's highways at near reckless speed. Al-Awlaki's driver, I was sure, would be no different.

The convoy wound its way past the outskirts of town and onto the highway, driving a curvy track through smaller villages and open desert.

"Target's clear. Any word?" Gordon said.

The pilot's voice showed no emotion, no stress. The LNO looked at the JOC commander. He just shook his head.

"Negative, Gordon," the LNO said. "Still awaiting word."

"Awaiting word" was a euphemism for someone who couldn't, or wouldn't, make a decision. This one was no light decision. We were preparing to shoot an American terrorist in a foreign country. Only the president could authorize a strike of this magnitude.

"Copy," Gordon said.

"Try to maintain position so we can get a shot off quickly," the LNO said.

Gordon didn't respond. He didn't have time as he worked to

keep his aircraft in prime shooting range while anticipating any sudden turns by the target. Besides, the pilot didn't want to get into the classic "don't tell a pilot how to fly his airplane" argument. A few seconds later, Bong, another Predator flying nearby, scanned the landscape ahead of the convoy.

"Plain's leveling out," Bong said. "Looks like we're about to hit the straightaway."

"Copy," Gordon said.

The straightaway was the most logical place for the shot. The vehicles would maintain a constant speed on a predictable course. There were few ridgelines to block the missile or the targeting laser.

As expected, al-Awlaki's convoy hit the plain and immediately accelerated. Twin rooster tails of dust kicked up behind them as they raced through sand deposited on the road by recent wind- and sandstorms.

"Ten minutes."

Gordon's comment was more a query than a statement. We had ten minutes until al-Awlaki reached Marib. If the Predator was going to shoot, it needed to do so on this road. The JOC commander, headset pinned to his ear, shook his head in the negative. Each time the convoy passed a mile marker, it reduced the chances of a strike.

I watched the monitor as Gordon maneuvered into position. Flying faster than the trucks, the pilot executed S-turns to keep from passing the convoy. If al-Awlaki knew we were above him, he wasn't acting like it. The trucks sped straight down the highway.

"Gordon, say status," the LNO said.

"Checklist complete, awaiting clearance," Gordon said.

"Copy," the LNO said. "Bong, get into position for an immediate follow-up attack."

If Gordon missed, he would be unable to fire his second missile.

He would be so close at impact that a second shot would be impossible for the missile to negotiate. Bong would be lurking at a good distance to follow up or hit the second vehicle if the first strike was successful.

"Five minutes and the window closes," Gordon said. "Say status."

I watched as the JOC commander hung up his phone.

"It's time," he said. "Pass the 9-Line."

The LNO pushed "Enter" on his keyboard. He'd already typed the 9-Line, which spelled out the order to shoot in scripted lines. Each line passed specific information to the pilot. The Task Force's joint terminal attack controller (JTAC), an Air Force airman trained to call in air strikes, came online. He had been watching the feed in the operations center. JTACs were usually on the ground, but that was impossible in Yemen. We had no troops on the ground there. Instead, the JTAC monitored missions from his desk at the operations center, coming in only before a strike.

"Gordon, this is Badger Four One," the JTAC said. "9-Line is in chat. Call in with direction."

The video feed remained fixed on the two trucks. Occasionally, the picture would tilt and rotate as the camera adjusted to the Predator's maneuvers. Gordon didn't respond. The pilot was briefing his sensor operator, the second man in his crew, on the shot. The sensor operator was an enlisted airman who controlled the Predator's sensor pod near the aircraft's nose and fired the targeting laser. He was a second set of eyes, especially when preparing to launch a missile. Everyone in the operations cell started to get nervous because the brief was going long.

Uncomfortably long.

Why hadn't they done this already? I shifted my weight from foot to foot trying to burn off some of my nervous energy. The LNO shifted in his seat too, mirroring my discomfort. No one in the operations cell wanted to miss this chance. No one was sure when we'd get another opportunity. I checked the clock hanging over the monitors. Three minutes remained. The video tilted once more.

"Gordon's in from the south," the pilot said. "One minute."

The JTAC didn't hesitate.

"Gordon, you're cleared hot."

CHAPTER 1

Welcome to Predator

"Welcome to the Predator."

Chuck, a longtime instructor at the 11th Reconnaissance Squadron, stood in front of a Predator, giving us the welcome speech. It was my first day of Predator training at Creech Air Force Base in Nevada.

My class of twenty-nine new pilots and sensor operators crowded near the front of the aircraft as Chuck spoke. Up front, the newly enlisted sensor operators watched Chuck's every move as he pointed out the targeting pod, which hung below the chin of the Predator, and the different antennas used to control the aircraft.

I was standing near the back with the other pilots. At the time I entered the program in December 2003, there were few, if any, volunteers. Most Predator pilots had been forced out of other programs because they had damaged the Air Force's manned aircraft or failed to meet the technical or professional standards laid out for each aircraft. Some were there due to injuries that kept them out of manned cockpits.

Few were there because they wanted to be. I was one of only four volunteers.

Ever since I was a kid, I dreamt about being a combat pilot. Growing up in Mississippi, I was the second of two children. Independent by nature, I was fascinated with how machines were constructed. I had an Erector set that I used to design my own spacecraft. I imagined traveling to unexplored worlds, fighting in great space battles, or just discovering some lost civilization.

But it wasn't until my father took me to an air show at Hawkins Field, in Jackson, Mississippi, when I was five that I discovered my true passion. The Confederate Air Force, now known as the Commemorative Air Force, was reenacting a World War II air battle.

The ground vibrated with the rumble of the piston engines as German Messerschmitt and American Mustang fighters danced in a mad circle in the sky. Pyrotechnics erupted around the airfield, simulating bomb strikes and antiaircraft fire. The noise was tremendous, exhilarating, and wonderful.

But nothing compared to when my father bought me a ticket to climb aboard the B-29 bomber *Fifi.*

I scrambled up the crew ladder, with my dad's careful hand guiding me, and clambered into the copilot's seat. A massive dashboard spread out in front of me with an impossible number of dials and gauges. I cranked on the yoke and imagined what it would have been like to fly the plane.

I was hooked.

I worked hard in high school to earn a spot at the US Air Force Academy because of its guaranteed pilot training program. But after

I graduated in the class of 1992, my flight training was delayed because of the post–Cold War drawdown. Instead, I went to intelligence training at Goodfellow Air Force Base in San Angelo, Texas, where I became an intelligence officer.

Three years after I was commissioned, a "no-notice" slot in pilot training at Columbus Air Force Base in Mississippi opened. A fellow USAFA classmate had dropped out of training a week before it started due to family reasons, leaving an open billet the Air Force had to fill. The Air Force Personnel Center pulled my name off a list of alternates and served me "no-notice" to pick up everything and move to Mississippi. I accepted the spot without any reservations. Over the next eight years, I flew trainers and the E-3 Airborne Warning and Control System, which had a massive radar dish on its back. The plane provided command and control to fighters. I flew counterdrug operations off the coast of South America, I patrolled the skies off North Korea as the country's surface-to-air missiles tracked my every move, and I flew presidential escort in East Asia.

I was a good pilot, but my Air Force career had been derailed by my stint as an intelligence officer. My chances of becoming a fighter pilot were slim to none. After a few years as an instructor, it was time to return to the AWACS. I balked. I wanted to stay in the Air Force, but I didn't want to fly the AWACS again. I knew there was no chance it would deploy and I wanted to do my part. The planes had been sent home from the war and were not expected to return. They had become another noncombat assignment.

It was 2003 and the war in Afghanistan was already two years old. The war in Iraq was just beginning. When a slot opened in the Predator training pipeline, I asked for it. After some wrangling, I got it. It wasn't a fighter, but I wanted it because the Predator gave me a chance to stay in the cockpit and contribute to the war effort.

But looking at the Predator in the hangar, I still had my reservations.

I was thirty-three years old, and as Chuck spoke I pondered the prudence of my decision. Like every pilot in the Air Force, I still felt aviation was accomplished in an aircraft, not at a computer terminal on the ground. Trained professionals sitting in the cockpit flew airplanes. Pilots didn't fly from a box. No pilot has ever picked up a girl in a bar by bragging that he flew a remote-controlled plane.

One of my favorite T-shirts had a definition for "pilot" printed across the chest. It sort of summed up the pilot mind-set, albeit in a humorous way.

Pi-lot: n. The highest form of life on earth

To me, the shirt didn't portray arrogance as much as confidence. Flying was special. Few people got to experience the world from thirty thousand feet with a flying machine strapped to their backs and under their own control. From the cockpit, we could see the curve of the earth and watch the cars on the highway reduced to the size of ants. Every time I climbed into the sky, I felt the same exhilaration. Aviation wasn't a job. It was my passion. It was my calling. It was something I had to do to feel complete.

Most men identify themselves through their work, and I had the best job on the planet.

But flying high above the earth has its dangers too. That is when the confidence, often mistaken for arrogance, comes to the surface.

We trusted our skills, because when you're that high above the ground, no one can come up and save you. Unlike cars, aircraft weren't vehicles you could just pull over when they broke down. But that factor was taken out of the equation in the Predator. Unless the aircraft landed on top of the cockpit on the ground, its pilots were safe no matter what happened. I looked down on the Predator because of that fact. Flying it took away all the exhilaration of being airborne and all the adventure of being a pilot.

The first training lesson was Chuck's welcome speech. He delivered it with the cadence of a speaker who had given the same speech one time too many. He wasn't bored, but his tone lacked enthusiasm. His words came out flat and practiced. His insights into the aircraft came from experience, not theory.

Chuck had commanded the 11th when it deployed to Afghanistan to support the invasion. He'd seen the Predator in combat and knew what it could do. As he walked around the aircraft, he carried himself with the military bearing of an officer, even if he was dressed in only khaki pants and a golf shirt.

"This is a system unlike any you've seen," he said.

I had to agree.

It also looked like no airplane I'd ever seen. The pictures didn't do it justice. Until the Predator came along in 1994, typical unmanned aerial vehicles were not much larger than a remote-controlled hobby airplane. In my mind's eye, I figured the Predator would be about the same size.

Built by General Atomics, the MQ-1 Predator was about the size and weight of a Cessna 172 and looked like an angry gray bird with its inverted V-shaped tail resting lightly on the ground. It crouched as if yearning to launch into the sky.

Chuck invited us to come closer. The group of students crowded in. Up close, it was easy to see how the aircraft lacked durability. The thin composite body felt like dry paper. Its anemic landing gear was just springs that flexed with the weight of the aircraft. A converted 115-horsepower four-cylinder snowmobile engine, retro-fitted with a turbocharger, powered the slender white prop at the back. The aircraft could reach altitudes of up to twenty-five thousand feet and fly for more than twenty hours without refueling. The Predator was impressive in its simplicity.

Chuck finished with the specs on the aircraft and moved on to the history. The Predator was created in response to the US Air Force's call for an unmanned surveillance plane in 1993. General Atomics, based out of San Diego, originally presented its idea to the Air Force.

Neal and Linden Blue, oil magnates who own a lot of property in Telluride, acquired General Atomics in 1986 for nearly fifty million dollars. While living in Nicaragua, Neal had watched the country's ruling family, the Somozas, be deposed by the Soviet-backed Sandinista coalition. Unable to fight, he wondered what it would take to fly an unmanned airplane using GPS into the huge petroleum, oil, and lubricants (POL) tanks fueling the Soviet-backed army. He wanted to cripple the new regime. The acquisition of General Atomics offered the means for Neal to achieve part of his wish.

In 1992, he hired retired admiral Thomas J. Cassidy to organize General Atomics Aeronautical Systems Inc. Cassidy's mission was to research and produce unmanned aircraft. The company's first attempt was the Gnat. It was built with off-the-shelf parts and sported a camera turret similar to those found on traffic helicopters. It could stay aloft for nearly forty hours, but it was too small to carry weapons and its range was limited because the controller had to keep the Gnat in sight to control it.

Then came the Predator.

Using what their researchers had learned from the Gnat, the company designed the aircraft with an inverted tail and a massive video sensor ball under the nose. The Predator first flew in 1994 and was introduced to the Air Force shortly after. The pilots running the Air Force met it with skepticism, but Air Force intelligence saw its value.

The Predator could fly over targets and send back high-resolution imagery even on bad weather days. As an added bonus, the aircraft were cheap, at 3.2 million dollars per plane. Four airframes with a ground control station cost about forty million dollars to buy and operate. By comparison, each new F-22 Raptor cost more than two hundred million dollars to purchase.

The first Predator flight was in July 1994. By the time the war in Afghanistan started, the Air Force had sixty Predators, some of which had flown over Bosnia. In February 2001, the Predator fired its first Hellfire missiles and its role as a reconnaissance aircraft started to change. A year later, Predators destroyed Taliban leader Mullah Omar's truck. They also killed an Afghan scrap-metal dealer who looked like Osama bin Laden. In March 2002, a Predator fired a Hellfire missile in support of Rangers fighting on Roberts Ridge during Operation Anaconda. It was the first time a Predator provided close air support to troops on the ground.

The aircraft was valuable on paper, but it wasn't yet considered a key cog in combat operations or even aviation for that matter. The Air Force knew it needed it to fly intelligence missions, but the potential importance of the program hadn't reached the leadership. Flying a Predator was the last stop on most career paths, evident by the austere conditions of the training base. Guys didn't move on to other units to brag about their Predator experience. They left the service as soon as they could. I didn't know it at the time, but when I volunteered in 2003, that was all about to change.

———

Creech Air Force Base sat across US Route 95 from the little desert town of Indian Springs. Area 51 and the nuclear test range sat along the northern edge of the base. Indian Springs was the antithesis of Las Vegas in every way. The sleepy town consisted of mostly trailers, two gas stations, and a small casino that earned more in the restaurant than on the gaming floor. I drove by the local school and noticed an old Navy fighter parked out front. It was painted to resemble the Thunderbirds, the Air Force's demonstration team. Its shattered canopy played host to nesting birds.

The base wasn't much better. US Route 95 ran parallel to the old single runway, limiting the base's ability to expand. To the northwest was Frenchman Lake, where the military tested nuclear weapons in the 1950s. When I drove through the gate the first time, I entered a time warp. A few World War II–era barracks buildings existed at the base. They were made of wood, whitewashed in an effort to make them look new. As I passed them, I saw they had been converted into a chow hall, theater, and medical facility. The only new building was on the east end of the base, where the 11th made its home. For the next four months, I'd spend my days learning to fly the Predator in that building.

By 2003, the Air Force was acquiring two new aircraft a month. It now had to find pilots to fly the expanding fleet of Predators. There were nine other pilots in my class. We stayed in the back of the group as Chuck talked, somewhat aloof. It was an unconscious defense against something we didn't understand: RPA flight. Everything about the Predator was foreign. We were still trying to determine if the aircraft passed the smell test.

Never before had a Predator formal training unit class had so many pilot volunteers. The guys with me saw the little Predator differently. To them, it wasn't a dead-end assignment; it was an opportunity.

Another pilot, Mike, stood next to me. I recognized Mike from our school days at the Air Force Academy, but I had never really known him personally. Our careers hadn't crossed paths since graduation. He'd flown KC-135 aerial refueling tankers and F-16 fighters, while I flew trainers and the AWACS.

Mike was a couple of inches taller than me. He had a runner's build, and unlike my graying hair, his remained as black as when he'd entered the service. His eyes burned with an intensity I've seen in few officers. We caught up briefly before Chuck started.

"You volunteer?" Mike asked.

Volunteering was an important thing to us. One of the guys in the class had been assigned to Creech after being sent home early from a deployment. He'd knocked up an airman. The four of us who volunteered wanted it known that we chose this life. It was not foisted upon us.

"Yeah, I wanted to avoid a third straight noncombat assignment," I said. "You?"

Mike shook his head.

"I saw the writing on the wall," he said. "Late rated and late to fighters meant it was unlikely I could see a command." His career in aviation had been delayed, much like mine had been.

"Tough," I said.

"It is what it is," he said.

I nodded understanding.

From the back of the class, I looked at the young faces of the nineteen sensor operators who would train with us. These fresh-faced eighteen-year-olds would make up the second half of the crew. The pilot controlled the aircraft and fired the weapons. The sensor operator ran the targeting systems, cameras, and laser designators. Together, we had to form a tight, efficient crew.

As we walked back to the classroom, I took stock of the class. Raw recruits, washouts from other career fields, problem children, and passed-over fighter pilots yearning to prove they deserved a shot were building the Predator community. We all had chips on our shoulders. We all wanted to prove we belonged in the skies over the battlefield. It was the pilots who never forgot who would excel.

CHAPTER 2

Learning to Fly

All the pilots knew how to fly, but we learned quickly that that didn't matter in the Predator. It was a couple of weeks into the program and I was just settling into the "box," or cockpit, for my first flight.

The box was a modified Sea-Land container technically called a ground control station (GCS). The tan container had a vault-like door at one end that opened into a narrow walkway that led to the "cockpit" at the other end. The floor and walls were covered in rough gray carpet and the lights were dim to eliminate glare on the monitors.

Along one side of the walkway was a series of computer racks and two support stations. At the end of the container were two tan chairs in front of the main control station. A small table jutted out between the pilot station on the left and the sensor operator station on the right. A standard computer keyboard sat on the table in front

23

of each station, bracketed by a throttle and control stick. Below the table was a set of rudder pedals. Both the pilot and sensor operator stations had a throttle on the left and a stick on the right, but only the pilot's controls flew the aircraft. The sensor operator's "throttle" and "stick" controlled the targeting pod.

I shivered as I looked over my shoulder at Glenn, my instructor.

"It's cold in here," I said. "Is it always like this?"

"Mostly," he said. "You'll get used to it."

The HVAC system pumped freezing air into the numerous electronics racks to keep them from overheating. Temperatures could soar to more than one hundred degrees within five minutes if both HVACs failed. The performance of the Predators degraded under anything but optimal temperatures, so the ambient temperature for the crews ended up in the low fifties. The environment was ideal for the massive computers behind me, not the pilots controlling the Predators flying miles away. Crews often wore flight jackets even during the hot Las Vegas summers.

"Run your checks," he ordered calmly.

I rubbed my hands together for warmth and reached for the controls. I checked the instruments to ensure the aircraft was performing well. We controlled the aircraft through two data links that sent commands to the planes and received video feeds and telemetry in return.

Launch and landing, or recovery in Air Force–speak, used a line-of-sight transmitter mounted on a fifty-foot tower outside the GCS. It broadcast commands to the two football-shaped antennas near the front of the Predator. The line-of-sight link worked only if the aircraft could see the transmitter. Since few bases existed close to the fighting, mostly we flew using the beyond-line-of-sight system. That system used satellites in geosynchronous orbit that beamed the command signal to the Predators, connecting to a crew anywhere in the world.

When I first received word of my assignment, I envisioned stepping into a small office to sit at a computer and monitor the progress of the aircraft. I had no idea how similar things would be to a standard cockpit. I finished scanning the data readouts that replaced the more traditional dials and switches of a traditional cockpit.

"You ready?" Glenn said over the roar of two massive HVAC systems.

I nodded.

"Okay," Glenn said. "Let's practice some maneuvers."

Glenn sat on a rolling desk chair behind us as I flew the training mission. He'd flown in Vietnam, earning his credibility, in my opinion. He was like most pilots of the Vietnam era: bold, bright, cocky. He held us to the highest standards. He didn't allow us to cut corners. Glenn didn't care that the RPA community was still new and didn't have the same traditions as the fighter community. He expected us to live up to the same standards he'd achieved.

I grabbed the stick and throttle assembly and set my feet on the rudder pedals under the desk.

"Just like pilot training," Glenn said. "Check your airspace and let's make a turn back to the center."

He meant turn to the center of the small block of air to the southeast of Creech Air Force Base where we were assigned to train. The endless brown of the Nevada desert slipped sideways underneath the Predator. From the pilot seat, I could see the tracker display at the top of the rack with its Google Maps–like view of the world. We could mark targets, define restricted areas, and even watch a small pink airplane icon trace our flight path.

Under the tracker sat the heads-up display, or HUD. The pilot side had an artificial horizon, airspeed, altitude, flight path indicators, and engine instruments. The sensor operator HUD didn't have any of the flight instruments. Instead, it displayed a set of cross hairs to mark center of the picture and readouts to describe the targeting pod's position and target data. The camera, or "ball," on the nose of the aircraft provided both the pilot and the sensor operator with the only view of the aircraft's surroundings.

I pushed the stick to the side. On the tracker, a little pink carrot showed up on a compass dial and spun in the same direction as I pushed the stick. I stopped it on a heading to the southeast by releasing the stick. Then I pressed the "Trim" button at the top of the stick to command the aircraft to fly to that heading.

"Okay," Glenn said. "You'll notice that this takes a couple seconds."

There was a slight delay between the commands given through the flight controls and the aircraft's reaction. The distance between the aircraft and the GCS determined this delay. In line-of-sight mode, the response was near instantaneous. On satellite control, it could take up to three seconds. It doesn't seem like much, but when you're trying to fly a precise path or line up a target, waiting three seconds for your command to reach the aircraft can be maddening.

I counted silently.

One potato, two potato . . .

Flying the Predator was harder than flying a traditional aircraft. I wanted to feel the aircraft in flight, but there was no sound to indicate the speed or engine performance. No feeling of the wings that could indicate an impending stall or malfunction. All I had was spring-loaded feedback in the stick and rudder and a throttle that moved a little too loosely. I had none of the traditional senses beyond sight, and the ball was rarely pointed in the right direction to be useful. For most missions aircraft were trained on the ground, so flying was done using instruments. I had to abandon three thousand hours of experience in handling aircraft with traditional controls and relearn how to fly the Predator.

"Okay, what's next?" I said.

Glenn checked his flight data card.

"Last thing we got before heading back to the pattern is Ku."

Ku, pronounced *kay-you*, was the satellite frequency band that was used to control the aircraft. "Ku" rolled off the tongue a little easier than "satellite." It was essential to make sure we got the link correct and knew how to reestablish control if the link was lost.

"Bring up the Ku menu," Glenn said.

At the top of the tracker display was a menu bar. I ran the mouse to the right tab, clicked it, and opened a dialog box. It asked me for the frequencies, polarization, and a few other bits of information to set up the link.

"Find the frequencies," Glenn said.

I scanned the data card and typed in the right numbers and clicked "Send."

The screen devolved to static. Confused, I looked back at Glenn. He shook his head.

"Nice job. You just jammed CNN."

"Wait, what?" I looked up at the dialog box and down at the data card. The frequencies were right.

"Check your polarization," Glenn said. "The dialog defaults to horizontal. Our assigned frequency is in the vertical."

I felt stupid as I corrected my error. Immediately, the picture came back. The aircraft had entered a tight circle in the center of the area. The tracker display confirmed that the aircraft had executed its emergency mission. The Predator is programmed to fly home if the command link is broken.

"Well," Glenn said in his best deadpan, "I guess we don't need to bother with the lost-link demo now." There was a syllabus requirement to show how the aircraft flew home if it lost the communications connection with the cockpit.

After my first flight, I met the guys from my carpool and headed home. Most mornings, we met at a parking lot on the outskirts of Las Vegas and carpooled the forty-five miles from the city to Creech. The rides to and from the base were a good time to catch up on gossip and grouse about the training.

I arrived at the parking lot a few weeks into the training and started complaining about the program before we even got into the car. I had just completed a tour as an instructor, so I was overly critical of the program. I also harbored some pilot arrogance since we all still considered the Predator an abnormality. I forget what I said exactly, but one of my classmates, Oaf, called me out.

"Okay, time-out," Oaf said. "I've had enough. You're now Grumpy."

"No, I'm not," I said.

The moment I fought back, Oaf called me "Grumpy" at every opportunity. There was no way I was going to let them give me "Grumpy" as a call sign. Squirrel was my tactical call sign. I'd gotten it on the first day of pilot training. Coming from my intelligence background, I couldn't tell the class anything about my old job. So I tried to play it up by saying my job was classified. The whole deal was immature and poorly executed. The class leader decided then and there I should be known as "Secret Squirrel." Once we started flying, the class started calling me "Flying Squirrel." Later, it was truncated to just "Squirrel." Now, that call sign remains my identity. After all, how many guys end up with the name Squirrel?

But I'd complained enough about Creech that my new class-mates wanted to rename me.

Etiquette surrounding call signs is one of those unwritten rules of combat aviation. Many military units give call signs that are tied to an embarrassing story. There were a lot of guys in the community with call signs like "Crash," "Skid," "Divot," and anything else that suggested they'd damaged an aircraft, or themselves. No one gets a call sign like "Maverick" or "Iceman" unless it is done in jest. Most pilots get a few call signs over a career as they transition to other aircraft or squadrons. There's a way out if you don't like your new call sign, though. It's tradition that you can buy back your old name with liquor, and no one can take a call sign from you if you used it in combat.

Lucky for me, I'd been "Squirrel" in combat, so I was safe. But Oaf was really making a bigger point with the new call sign: Stop being a dick. We were all battling our years of flying experience to learn how to pilot the Predator. A lot of the pilots were there under protest. Much of the talk on the trip to and from Creech was about plans to return to our previous aircraft. Even volunteers like me had no plans to make a career in the Predator community.

After the first few weeks, I was near the top of the class. Mike and I were competing for the coveted "distinguished graduate" honor. Several of the pilots in class busted a ride, which was Air Force lingo for failing a training flight. Only Mike and I hadn't and maybe a couple of others. We both knew one mistake was all it would take to wind up second. I didn't plan on failing.

The sixth training flight is the most dreaded sortie in the quali-fication phase. By that time, pilots are far enough into their training that they often feel comfortable enough with the aircraft to fly it on their own. However, our skills were still underdeveloped. Ride six was historically the most failed sortie of the program.

The GCS was its usual arctic cold, but by now I was used to it. I had one hand on the stick and the other on the throttle as I dropped into the pattern around the airfield to land. Landing the aircraft was the single most challenging aspect of learning to fly. Every pilot got humbled at some point on an approach.

"Tower," I said. "Deadly One One, point Whiskey at sixty-five hundred feet."

The control tower came back immediately.

"Deadly One One, enter downwind for runway two seven, altimeter two nine nine seven."

I typed in the barometric pressure. The altimeter jumped a few hundred feet, showing we were closer to the ground than I'd thought. Sweat beaded on my brow. The drops ran down my back between my shoulder blades despite the chilling temperature inside the GCS. I could feel Glenn's eyes on my instruments as he watched my every move.

A misstep now could easily result in a crash.

The HUD showed a wildly bucking aircraft. Winds flowed down from the surrounding Spring Mountains range, creating unpredictable eddies and currents at low altitude. The turbulence tossed the two-thousand-pound Predator around. The aircraft's long wings were perfect for high-altitude flying, not landing. Even the slightest terrain change at low altitudes could result in wild lift changes. If you weren't careful, the airplane could soar or crash without a moment's notice.

I flicked off the autopilot. My stick and throttle now acted like those in any manned aircraft. Push stick forward, cows get big. Pull stick back, cows get small. Push stick to the side, world tilts. Almost immediately, the aircraft bucked. I tried to maintain altitude, but the air currents tossed the Predator like a rag doll.

"Don't fight the drafts," Glenn advised. "You'll just end up making it worse."

"Like a PIO?"—a pilot-induced oscillation.

"Yes," he said.

In heavy turbulence, pilots often set the throttle and a known pitch angle where they can maintain altitude. The airplane bucked up and down but generally stayed somewhere close to the desired altitude.

"Good," he said. "Start off with a standard overhead."

"Copy," I said. "Before landing check."

The sensor operator, an experienced instructor, came to life. During this first phase, we had little interaction with the sensor operators except when landing. He read off the checklist items.

"Gear down," he intoned.

I checked the gear. It was already down, having served as my main form of drag to help the aircraft descend. Three little icons glowed green in the HUD, indicating the gear was safely down.

"Down and three green," I said.

We didn't trust that indicator, though.

"Clear to move the ball?" the sensor operator said.

On the early flights, the sensor operators rarely touched the ball while the pilots learned to fly. One of the few times they did move it was to check the gear. We always considered a visual check more reliable than the green indicators. The ball swung about, pointed straight down at the nose wheel.

"Nose wheel steering, sir."

I kicked the rudder pedals, and the wheel in the image moved left, then right.

"Brief," the sensor operator said.

As pilot, it was my job to talk the crew through the landing plan.

"Okay, crew, this will be a normal landing using the ball; call out any limits [from the instruments]; if we have an emergency, I will land straight ahead, anyone on the crew can call 'go around' if you see something dumb, different, or dangerous develop. Our approach speed will be seventy-four knots with a climb/glide of sixty-eight," I said. "Questions?" The briefing was short and meant to prepare the crew for issues before they were encountered.

"No questions, sir," the sensor operator said. "Checklist complete."

The sensor operator set the camera to look straight ahead. I lowered the nose and started a turn toward the runway. Once lined up, I put the cross hairs on the near end of the runway, my aim point.

"Tower, Deadly One One, gear down."

"Deadly One One, cleared for the option."

Tower had cleared me to land, make a low approach, or practice a touch-and-go. The mountains outside slid to the left. A pair of prisons a few miles away flashed past. I picked up US Route 95 and adjusted my turn to roll out just inside it.

"Watch your parameters," Glenn said.

My glide slope indicator showed that I was close to my planned path, though a hair low. I added a touch of power. This had little effect, since the bucking nose sent the aircraft all over the place. I manhandled the Predator onto the best flight path as the plane slowed to seventy-four knots, just a hair slower than the traffic shadowing it on the interstate nearby.

"Don't fight it," he said. "Keep an eye on your glide slope. Sink rates are your worst enemy now."

The Predator soared upward as it hit the lip of the paved runway. Hot air rising off the concrete pushed the lightweight airplane away from the ground. I instinctively pushed forward on the stick to control its ascent. The plane careered downward.

"Go around," Glenn said.

His command was tinged with rebuke and frustration.

I could feel him over my shoulder, the disappointment seeping out like a fog. When I jerked the stick back, I didn't add power first. The Predator lacked speed to pull out of the dive.

"Power, then pitch," he said.

"On the go, crew," I announced, angry with myself.

As I banked the Predator around the airfield for another approach, I reflected on what I'd done wrong. I should have known better by now. Shoving the stick forward that close to the ground was never good. You either hit nose first and the spring-loaded gear would flip the airplane on its back, or you shot downward so fast you'd have to pull back on the stick so hard the nose would shoot up, striking the tail or prop on the ground.

As we worked our way back into the pattern, Glenn replaced me in the seat. The aircraft pitched and bucked like before. This time, he held it slightly high on the glide path. I watched the sink rate develop over the concrete just like before. The video showed nothing at first, and then a few seconds later I sensed a downward motion in the picture.

As the aircraft neared the runway, Glenn rode the glide path until it looked like we were going to hit the ground nose first. Glenn pulled back on the stick. As the nose tracked, the lift changed on the wings and slowed our descent. Glenn's hands twitched as he maneuvered the stick to keep the nose set in place and keep the wings level. Finally out of energy, the aircraft settled to the ground. Our only indication in the cockpit was a slight vibration in the camera's video as the stabilizing gimbals adjusted to the bump.

Glenn slowed the Predator, taxied it to the designated parking slot, and shut down the engine. I left the cockpit and after a necessary break went to join him in the debrief room.

The briefing room was just large enough for a standard picnic-size table and office chairs. Opposite the door was a drop-down screen and computer to work the projector. The sidewalls had whiteboards where the instructors could diagram missions.

Glenn was waiting for me at the picnic table. After I briefed the mission and the botched landing, it was Glenn's turn to speak. We both knew I would no longer be eligible for the coveted "distinguished graduate" honor.

"Squirrel, I'm sorry, but I have to bust you," he said.

"Sir," I said, "I don't deserve to pass. I would have asked you to bust me had you tried to pass me."

It was actually the truth. My integrity wouldn't allow me to accept a pass after I had so clearly failed. I wasn't sure which of us was more embarrassed. Glenn nodded and I left the briefing room.

Mike was still in the flight room as I left. He was getting ready for his mission.

"Squirrel," he said, "how's the second-best pilot in Predator?"

It was a bad joke between us to accuse the other of being second-best. It kept the competition, as all military aviation is, civil.

"Looks like he just moved up to number one," I shot back.

I wasn't angry with Mike. He had no idea I'd busted the ride. I was angry with myself. Mike seemed surprised and pulled me aside.

"What happened?" Mike asked.

I told him about the busted ride.

"Hey," he said. "It happens. We all are getting crushed in this program."

"Thanks," I said.

I knew other guys were busting rides, but it didn't happen to me. As I walked out, I tried to let the bad mission go. I knew tomorrow I'd have a chance to redeem myself. As I walked into the desert sun, I reminded myself that some days the knight gets the dragon.

But today, the dragon had squashed me into ketchup.

CHAPTER 3

Fight's On

The blue van raced down the black asphalt road. I turned the Predator on a parallel course so we could track the van once it cleared the security checkpoint. We didn't know who he was or where he was going.

Today, our mission was to find out.

He was probably just a range worker checking on a variety of the targets on Range 63. For today, we considered him a simulated insurgent. This was an intelligence, surveillance, and reconnaissance, or ISR, mission, the most basic skill set we learned in the mission phase of our training. These were the skills we'd use to track insurgents in Baghdad or in the mountains of Afghanistan. This was also how we provided the troops on the ground with a bird's-eye view of their objective.

Once we learned how to find and track the enemy, we got to

simulate engaging them with the two Hellfire missiles hanging under the wings. The weapons portion of the training worried me. Flying an ISR mission meant keeping the aircraft close enough to the target so the sensor operator could keep the camera trained on the individual or compound or car. Simple enough.

But delivering a missile was a whole different skill. The Predator's primary weapon was the AGM-114 Hellfire missile. Originally designed as a helicopter-fired antitank missile, the Hellfire had a small, seventeen-pound explosive warhead designed to penetrate armor. Later variants were scored like a grenade, which produced a wall of shrapnel on impact, converting the missile into an effective antipersonnel weapon.

Weapons didn't show up on the Predator until the introduction of the MQ-1B in 2001. The targeting pod had been upgraded, which enabled the crew to lock onto a target. Before the upgrade, the sensor operator tracked targets with the camera by hand. This setup wasn't ideal, since a tired sensor operator could relax at the wrong time, pulling the cross hairs off a target at a critical moment, causing a miss. Raytheon responded to the requirement and designed a tracking system to lock the targeting pod on a target.

I had no close air support experience, which could derail the second half of my training. I was still a close second to Mike in the rankings, and I wanted to stay that way, so I went hunting for the Predator's 3-3 tactics manual. The three-dash-three, as we pronounced it, was the baseline tactics guide that told us how to accomplish each of our assigned combat missions.

The manual would typically be found among a series of mostly unclassified documents for every weapons system in the Air Force. Searching through the squadron's library, I couldn't find anything. I did unearth an outdated article from the Gulf War, written by an

Army helicopter pilot about the A model of the missile, used only on helicopters. We were shooting the modified K model.

I started asking around, hitting up the instructors for any information or a copy of the manual.

"Where is the 3-3 tactics manual?" I asked.

My request was met by a shrug each time. Even Glenn didn't know where it was. The Predator had been in the Air Force fleet for nearly ten years and I realized it still didn't have a manual. I was flabbergasted. How could you have effective training without a tactics manual?

I decided to write my own.

At home, I had my old T-37 manual from my flight instructor days. The first part of the manual dealt with basic pilot skills. All Air Force pilots learned the basics on the T-37 in the 1990s, so the manual proved valuable as a model for what I was trying to do. But I had no idea how to write the tactics portion, so I approached Mike. He was a fighter pilot and had the tactical experience I needed.

"So what have you got?" he asked me as he sat down at my roll-top desk in my home office.

I handed him the folder of papers that made up my attempt to write a Predator 3-3.

"Well," I said. "I couldn't find any 3-3s from tactical aircraft."

Mike nodded. A 3-3 tactics manual for any fighter was restricted, even if it was unclassified. Squadrons didn't let outsiders have them on a whim.

"I basically formatted this based off the T-37," I said to Mike.

Mike flipped right to the tactics page.

"I see you finished your Hellfire section."

"Yeah, it's rough," I said.

I pulled up the appropriate file on my computer.

"I've got the basic diagrams in place," I said. "I used them as a template to describe how to employ a missile. Everything from 9-Line to post-strike procedures."

Mike reviewed the section quietly.

"It's not how a fighter would do it," he said.

"But we aren't fighters," I said.

Mike looked up.

"Every fighter trains a certain way, but the overall procedures are the same," he said. "To do it any other way is unprofessional."

He was right. The RPA community was in its infancy and the manual was an attempt to instill some professionalism into the ranks. Most people called the aircraft a drone, but, as Chuck said in his welcome speech, we didn't care for the term because it took all of the professionalism out of the job. The aircraft didn't fly or fight by itself. It was not autonomous. We might not be sitting in the Predator, but that shouldn't be mistaken to mean the Predator lacked a cockpit or pilot. We were in control of everything, including the weapons.

"Well, tear it up," I said.

For the next several days, Mike improved the tactics section. In all, drafting the document took a bit more than a month. Without the pressure of competing for "distinguished graduate," I concentrated on writing, with Mike's assistance. My flight skills and fighting techniques developed rapidly, thanks in part to the work I was doing on the manual.

But there was no substitute for hands-on training. My first weapons ride was a disaster. I had no idea how to even pull up the weapons menu on the tracker. Without a simulator to practice on, I had little way to understand what I needed to do in flight.

I had to confess to my instructor that I had no idea what I was doing. His expression mirrored the one I would have given students I flew with during my instructor tours. I got the dreaded "You didn't do your homework?" expression. He slowly walked me through the checklist, pointing out each switch and menu. With his patience and Mike's help with the 3-3, I quickly picked up on how to fire a missile.

When I reached the final phase of training, I was still in the top five in the class. But that final phase was even more difficult than learning to fire the Hellfire. This phase—three sorties in all—had us acting like forward air controllers. The mission was called strike coordination and reconnaissance. We stacked fighters in orbits and fed them targets. Basically, we were like a flying control tower. It took a lot of concentration and coordination to keep all the moving pieces on track.

The Texas Air National Guard sent several F-16s to support our class. I was on my last sortie and only a few missions away from my final check ride. The scenario had me searching for several Scud missiles hidden in the desert. Once we found them, it was my job to talk the F-16s onto the target. We had a two-hour block to complete the mission.

In the mission phase of training, the sensor operators and the pilots trained together, but not as an organic team. On this day, Sarah was in the seat next to me. I'd flown with Sarah in the past, so we were familiar with each other. She'd joined the Air Force at eighteen after graduating from high school in New York. She was a petite woman, and the control rack dwarfed her. But she had a keen eye and a reputation as one of the class's best sensor operators.

The rest of the class took the full two hours to find and eliminate the Scuds, but we found both them and the supporting surface-to-air missile (SAM) batteries within minutes. Our fortunate find gave us nearly a whole hour to build our talk-ons, a series of photographs and sketches to accompany the 9-Lines we built. They made it easier to describe a target to another pilot. It took only fifteen minutes to eliminate all the targets. I sat back, scenario complete, and looked at Glenn. We still had forty-five minutes of flying time.

"Anything you want to do?" I asked. "We've got the time."

Glenn looked up from his clipboard, where he made notes.

"Whatever you want; your requirements are complete," he said.

He wanted me to come up with more targets, but I didn't want to take the time creating a couple while the F-16 just waited. I radioed the F-16 to let him know we were finished. I wasn't sure if he had anything he wanted to do.

"Viper Two Two, Deadly One One," I called over the radio. "Scenario complete."

I was Deadly One One and the F-16 was Viper Two Two. A few minutes later, Viper came back on the radio. He suggested working some air-to-air engagements. I looked over at Glenn sitting between my station and the sensor operator's station.

We hadn't briefed air-to-air engagements and I wanted to get his approval before I responded. In the Air Force, we don't deviate from the plan, because aviation is cruel to those who make mistakes. Even a slight misjudgment when we mixed it up could mean crashing a multimillion-dollar fighter, or death.

Glenn nodded approval and I got on the radio with the F-16 pilot. We quickly agreed on some safety rules using the same altitude restrictions from the previous scenario.

This was unique.

Predators didn't engage in basic fighter maneuvers or dogfighting. RPAs had a losing record when it came to dogfighting after an Iraqi MiG famously shot down a Predator orbiting Baghdad during the invasion of Iraq.

That Predator was loaded with a pair of Stinger missiles. The Iraqi pilot overshot his first pass, but the excited Predator pilot fired a Stinger outside its maximum range. The Stinger was designed to take down aircraft from the ground, not from under the wing. The missile had little chance to hit the mark and failed to track the MiG as it came around for another pass. The Iraqi pilot didn't miss the launch. He tracked the Stinger's smoke trail and fired a countervolley of two missiles at the Predator. The Iraqi MiG's missiles tracked just fine.

I didn't like my chances over the Nevada desert.

"Deadly One One, Viper Two Two. Fight's on."

I looked up at the map over the HUD and saw the F-16 about twenty miles north of me. Viper Two Two turned inbound and started toward me.

"So what are you going to do?" Glenn asked.

"See what he sees," I said, not feeling as confident as I tried to sound.

I turned the Predator north toward Viper Two Two. I assumed the Predator's radar signature would be small and difficult to detect.

I was wrong.

"Viper Two Two, kill one MQ-1, BRAA two seven zero, ten, twenty thousand."

He spotted me within ten seconds and simulated firing a missile. The BRAA call outlined my bearing, range, altitude, and azimuth from a specified spot on the ground known as the bull's-eye. I was west of our bull's-eye point at ten miles and twenty thousand feet.

Viper Two Two turned outbound to reset for another run.

Glenn chuckled.

"What've you got planned now?" Glenn asked.

"Any suggestions?"

Glenn shook his head. I think he enjoyed watching the virtual carnage.

"This is new to me," he said. "I'm just curious to see what you do."

I didn't know how to take that comment. He was a combat-tested fighter pilot. I was certain he'd forgotten more about fighter tactics than I knew. I wasn't trained in fighter maneuvers, just some very basic air-to-air tactics, so I tried to remember the basics from flight school. I wasn't going to give up.

"Viper Two Two inbound."

I gritted my teeth.

"Viper Two Two, Deadly One One. Fight's on."

Hey, if I was going to play with the big boys, I should at least use the right terminology.

Instead of heading toward him, I turned and put my wingtip on him. I cheated in a way, since I knew in what direction he traveled. This wasn't much of a stretch in combat since AWACS or ground control would tell me where a threat was. Sarah spun the ball around and switched to infrared (IR). She could pick up the fighter's IR flare.

"Put a track on him," I said.

"Roger," Sarah said.

I watched her spin the ball around until she picked up the heat signature of the F-16.

"Tracking," she said.

The track locked the targeting pod to Viper Two Two. I kept an eye on the screen and turned the Predator slowly, keeping the pod at ninety degrees to the F-16. I pulled the power back as I turned, slowing the Predator to just a couple of knots above stall speed. I had no idea what the actual characteristics of the F-16 were at the time, or the variant the guys flew, but I figured if I flew slowly enough it would be hard to see us on radar.

We watched as the fighter drew close. It was nerve-racking.

At twenty miles, he was an indistinguishable spot with a bright flare from his heat signature. The radio crackled with background static. At ten miles, he filled our HUD with his distinctive lines and large air intake under his nose.

I adjusted my heading to keep my wingtip on him. I kept a close eye on my airspeed. I was sure Viper Two Two had us on radar, but we were going so slow he'd have to slow too, limiting the fighter's maneuverability.

I dipped the nose of the Predator to pick up a little more speed and tried to hide in the ground clutter. I looked at the tracker map above my HUD. Viper Two Two was within two miles. He must've seen a momentary blip as he wrenched the aircraft into a hard turn to orbit near me. There was no outrunning him. My only defense was my slow speed. Any second I expected him to call in with my location.

Finally, I broke the silence.

"Viper Two Two, Deadly One One. Confirm visual."

I wanted to know if he saw me. He was close enough to read our tail number.

"Negative visual."

I was shocked. I had flown out of pure instinct and managed to defeat a proficient fighter pilot. A single comment came from behind me.

"Interesting."

Glenn hadn't expected that either. I smiled to myself.

"Copy that, we are at your two o'clock, two miles, low."

It took a few moments before he could see us. We did five engagements in all. Three times Viper Two Two failed to see us, meaning he couldn't achieve radar lock for a missile or gain visual contact for a gun run. I counted these as victories even though I posed no threat to his advanced fighter jet.

After my flight, I used my notes to write up what I'd learned for the tactics manual. Five engagements wasn't enough to build a true tactic, but I gave the Air Force Weapons School at Nellis Air Force Base enough to test it in detail later.

That was my final test. I performed well on my last training missions and aced my check ride. I was now an RPA pilot in the eyes of the Air Force. As I walked out of my last debrief with Glenn, my mind was on my next assignment.

There were two operations squadrons.

The 17th Reconnaissance Squadron was the special tactics unit for the Predators. They were the guys who worked in the shadows. Their mission was operational test; they designed the tactics we used on new weapons. Only the best crews from each class were selected for the 17th. It was the most coveted job in Predator at the time. The rest of the crews went to the 15th Reconnaissance Squadron at Nellis Air Force Base. Mike was the only one who seemed somewhat unconcerned about where he would go. He had the top spot in the class and would likely be going to the 17th. For my part, I worried a little. The idea of working in the 17th fascinated me, and I wanted nothing else. But the busted ride early in my training haunted me. I feared my name was too far down the ladder to make the cut.

On the last night in training, we all met at the squadron bar. Part lunchroom, part snack bar, part watering hole, it was the center of the squadron's social scene. The commander was going to give us our orders. Afterward, we'd all depart for the operational squadrons and the war.

The bar itself was equipped with a keg dispenser and fridges full of beer. The counters behind the bar were jammed with snacks. The ceiling of the bar was littered with tiles painted and signed by each class. A single tile was missing where ours had been removed prior to the ceremony. In one corner, a cardboard Hellfire missile was suspended.

The room was packed with squadron aviators and their family members. We were waiting for Batman, the commander, to arrive. Tradition held in the Air Force that a student class presented gifts to the squadron and any instructors they chose as a means of saying thank you for the quality training. I helped carry the yellow-and-white mottled boa constrictor into the squadron bar. The boa was our gift, since the squadron's mascot was a snake. The snake stayed in the squadron bar ever after. Each class was given the responsibility of caring for and feeding the animal. None of the career aviators in the squadron had ever seen such a gift presented to a unit. Most were usually signed pictures or plaques.

The snake appeared unimpressed by it all.

Lastly, our class leader, Oaf, presented gifts to the instructors. We passed out the regular plaques—Best Instructor Pilot, Best Instructor Sensor, and the Purple Helmet. Glenn seemed nonplussed when Oaf called him forward. Oaf said every class had an instructor who offered such a profound impact on the team that a simple award was not sufficient. The class's decision was unanimous. Glenn earned the Purple Helmet award, a child's plastic army helmet painted purple, because he had a reputation as a dick.

I never thought he was a dick. Glenn rode me hard, but his intention was clear to me—he wanted to make me a better Predator pilot. He had no ulterior motive or need to feed his self-esteem. He simply wanted pilots to perform better. Glenn proudly displayed that one gift on his desk for many years after.

After presenting the mementos, the commander stood up and announced the assignments. To my surprise, Mike was going to the 15th. He was clearly the number one student in the class. When it was my turn, I was tense.

"Squirrel," the commander said, "you're going to the 17th."

Two other classmates joined me in the 17th. It was an unusual assignment since the 17th took only one pilot from each class on other days.

After the ceremony, we gathered in one of the flight rooms with the commander. He wanted a minute to speak candidly without the eyes and ears of our spouses. Gossip had its place in the military, just as anywhere else. Talking personnel decisions in front of civilians wouldn't have been right. When he opened the floor for questions, I had the first one.

"Why so many assignments to the 17th?" I asked. "Don't they usually take only one?"

The commander nodded.

"Yes, they do," he said. "However, they asked for more than their usual number in this assignment drop."

"Any idea why?" I asked.

"I'm sure you will find out when you get there," he said.

After the meeting, I hung back with Mike as the others left to rejoin the party. He asked the question I had wanted to ask.

"Why did I go to the 15th?" Mike said.

The commander paused for a moment.

"Normally, the number one graduate gets his assignment of choice," the commander said. "You would have gone to the 17th. But think of it this way: The 15th deserves the top graduate from time to time."

In truth, the 15th got the top graduate every other class. Mike took the answer in stride. He was the class's best pilot and his input on the tactics was invaluable. The RPA community was small and I was sure we'd have a chance to fly together at some point.

Before I out-processed, I dropped off the draft tactics manual with the instructors and recommended they push it forward for publication. The weapons officer looked skeptical, flipping through the folder.

"It's not formatted correctly," he said.

"I wanted to leave something for the weapons officer to do," I said, leaving before I put my foot any deeper into it.

I ran into Glenn as I left the squadron. He stopped me as he walked from the simulators to the briefing rooms with a student from the next class.

"Squirrel, don't pack any uniforms," he said. "You won't need them in the 17th."

He was right.

CHAPTER 4
Tier One

The mountains in eastern Afghanistan near Tora Bora wrapped protectively around the small mud-brick house.

Flying above, I watched the house rotate lazily in the HUD. There was no activity, not even a stray dog looking for scraps. The fire-pit coals, which had glowed a few hours before when the sensor operator switched to the infrared camera, had cooled, leaving no hint of heat.

We were looking for a courier, a lackey, really. He was a small part of an operation meant to track down one of al Qaeda's top facilitators. The cross hairs centered on the window of his bedroom, or living room for that matter. From the size of the house, it had only one room.

The missiles were cold. We weren't here to shoot. We were here to watch.

It was May 2004. We'd deployed to an undisclosed location to be close to the JOC running our operations. The JOC acted as the clearinghouse for high-level operations. They coordinated our operations with teams in the field to hunt terrorists around the globe.

Even from twenty-five thousand feet, the mountains of the Hindu Kush looked massive. The mountainous region of western Waziristan sat along the border between Afghanistan and neighboring Pakistan. Only a few routes existed between the towering peaks and deep valleys. In the winter, these passes were buried in snow, cutting off access between the countries. The only road was one hundred miles south, where the Hindu Kush petered out into a pimply brown landscape.

People living in the region hunkered down to hibernate in the brutal winter. Al Qaeda and their allies, the Taliban, came out of hibernation in April when the first pass opened. Now we were tracking them as they started to build networks and move fighters into Afghanistan.

This was an opportunity to thoroughly document the courier's actions. We were building a pattern of life so we could anticipate where he would be if or when the JOC decided to roll him up. Our mission was to capture, not kill. Alive, captured terrorists allowed us to piece together enemy networks. We wanted to pull intelligence from these guys, then use it to work our way up the chain until finally reaching the top.

The president's ultimate goal was finding Osama bin Laden.

Videos continued to surface with Bin Laden dressed in his camouflage coat with an AK-47 resting behind him. It looked like the videos could have been filmed in southern New Mexico. The only way we were going to find him was to map out his network. So we watched the little house, hoping the courier would lead us to the bigger fish.

And we watched. It was the interminable hell of being.

"So we never shoot?" I asked Wang, my instructor pilot.

Like Glenn had, he sat behind me in a rolling desk chair. I was the new guy and it was Wang's job to make sure I knew what I was doing before they let me fly a mission solo. I never asked where he got his call sign. He was a midlevel captain, soon to finish his two-year stint in the Predator. Originally from California, he carried himself with a mellow detachment, rarely allowing himself to become excited about anything. I imagined him surfing in his off time.

"Most of the guys here will finish their two-year tour without firing once in combat," he said.

My heart sank.

I'd signed up to make an impact on the war effort. I wanted to do something productive to help keep Americans safe. Just watching a blacked-out hut in the middle of the night didn't exactly fit that bill. Shooting was why I wanted to be a fighter pilot in the first place. It wasn't like I wanted to kill people. But it felt like we were being productive if we destroyed something.

But the intelligence missions had to be done before the exciting ones could happen, I reasoned. Tracking and mapping al Qaeda's network led to targets in the future. It was the only way I could focus on the mind-numbing missions.

The next crew came out to the box to relieve us at the end of our two-hour shift. I briefed them on our orbit, airspace clearance, guidance from the JOC, weather, and anything else that was important. After they took control of the Predator, we slipped out of the back of the GCS and stepped into the bright sunshine.

Light filtered through the camouflage netting strung from the GCS to the massive oak trees surrounding the compound. The netting both shaded the compound and dappled the ground around me with golden blotches. The early summer humidity blunted the chill of the box. I hurried past the squadron's other GCS and ducked into the ops center, hoping to avoid breaking a sweat.

"We'll grab the launch in a couple hours," Wang said. "Get something to eat."

Wang left the ops center, but I lingered for a moment. The difference between the outside and inside was startling. We were in a new kind of war, one fought not on a battlefield but from a secluded spot thousands of miles from the action. The room felt sterile, cold, and medicinal. Conversations were always muted. It was like a library.

My attention was immediately drawn to the two fifty-inch plasma monitors mounted on the long wall. The flat screens—labeled "Blue" and "Green"—showed camera feeds from Predators overseas twenty-four hours a day. The house I had been watching for the past two hours rotated in the middle on the Blue-line screen. The Predator was still tracing its tedious circle about the house. The Green-line screen showed a column of camels being led along a trail. The Green line was heading back to the base for landing and was just scanning the ground for targets of opportunity.

Beneath the screens were two workstations occupied by intelligence officers who monitored the feed and supported the crews in flight. The analysts made sure pilots had up-to-date information on a target and monitored the chat rooms used to pass messages.

At the back of the room, the mission commander and the weather officer sat behind a bank of four computers each. The monitors displayed Internet chat rooms, email, and mission briefs.

One monitor showed a scaled map of Afghanistan. We could use it to zoom all the way in to see imagery of each village and base. Three little Predators ticked across the screen in real time.

I stood in the back and watched the feeds. I wasn't the only person to start watching and get mesmerized by the scenes.

"How was the flight?"

Mongo, a pilot sitting at the mission commander station, shook me out of my funk. Named after the character in *Blazing Saddles*, he was built like a football player. He was six feet five inches tall. Time had softened him, but he still looked fit. He wore a perpetual gap-toothed grin.

A former F-16 pilot, he was a class ahead of me. He planned on doing two years in the Predator before going back to the F-16 community.

"They always that boring?" I asked.

"Mostly." He smiled, showing the gap between his teeth. "You'll get used to it. Hours of boredom . . ."

". . . interspersed with moments of sheer terror," I finished for him. "Got it."

Mongo explained the unit's mission as part of my squadron in-processing. He scribbled his name on my checklist as he talked.

"You've seen the two GCSs," he said. "We fly two CAPs [combat air patrols] in Afghanistan, all by satellite from here."

I nodded at the monitor.

"I see three birds."

Mongo considered the twitching icons on the map.

"The Blue and Green are our lines," he said. "The yellow one—that's Pacman. He's with the 15th."

The 15th—Mike's squadron—was tasked with supporting the conventional units. Based at the Predator Operations Center at

Nellis Air Force Base in Nevada, they had two CAPs that split their time between Afghanistan and Iraq. The 15th provided imagery and video to commanders on the ground. They also chased the Iraqi leaders posted on the deck of playing cards. These cards were a standard set of playing cards with images and names of the Iraqi leadership being hunted after the invasion. Occasionally, the 15th fired on targets, but mostly they just watched.

"Don't they have two CAPs as well?"

Mongo scaled out the map to reveal both Iraq and Afghanistan. A fourth icon was superimposed over Baghdad.

"They're splitting theaters today," Mongo said. "Don't worry about them so much. They don't get close to us. Usually, we only cross paths when we land."

I looked at the monitor a little closer.

"We get the flight data from the Link, correct?"

Every friendly aircraft over Iraq and Afghanistan transmitted its location data to the Link. Like *The Matrix*, the Link provided a snapshot of every aircraft in the area. But the monitor showed only the four Predator flights.

"Yes," Mongo said.

"Shouldn't we be seeing the other aircraft out there?"

Mongo shrugged.

"I am afraid we haven't cracked that nut yet," he said.

He paused for a second.

"Sorry, Squirrel."

I shook it off. Jokes about my namesake really didn't bother me. I found it rather amusing that the other pilots were self-conscious when describing an aircraft malfunction to maintenance as "squirrelly." They always apologized for offending me, for any inadvertent slip of the tongue, though they never really meant it. A chance to make fun of a fellow pilot was always a welcome source of entertainment.

All pilots knew this and had to develop a thick skin and an ability to fire back.

Mongo smiled as he returned to the day's flight schedule.

"Hey, you should get some lunch," he said, noticing a change. "The plane's delayed."

"How long?"

"An hour maybe," he said.

I nodded.

The Launch and Recovery Element (LRE) was mostly maintenance troops and a few flight crews. We didn't take off or land the Predators except during training. Crews stationed overseas alongside the aircraft in theater did that for us. Taking off and landing were specialty skills because of how difficult it was to fly the aircraft. We took control once the Predator was at twenty thousand feet and cruising toward the target. So the delay was on their end. They had their hands full keeping the little birds working around the clock in the harsh Central Asian environment.

I ran into Lieutenant Colonel Stew Kowall in the hallway on the way out of the operations cell. The commander was a short man with a thin build and thinner hair. His close-cropped scalp gave him the look of Captain Picard from *Star Trek*. His bearing was a bit meeker, though. He was an intelligent man, but he rarely flew.

Stew was a career officer. He'd flown one tour in the F-15C before transferring over to the "executive officer" track. He'd abandoned flying for staff work and the face time needed to make the higher ranks.

I was surprised to see him, since he usually sequestered himself in his office or back at Nellis Air Force Base. The 17th was rotating back to Nellis in a few months. The wing commander wanted to regroup all the Predator units together. I could see the point when I considered the need for oversight of the entire program. But I rather enjoyed the autonomy of being separated from the leadership and driving to work every day in an isolated base.

He looked at me as I greeted him, eyes narrowed as he worked out my identity.

"Squirrel, right?"

"Yes, sir."

"How do you like it so far?" he asked cryptically.

"It's okay," I said evasively.

I wasn't about to complain to the boss. It wasn't wise to complain at all.

"Hmm," he said with a grunt, and kept walking down the hall. "Well, welcome to the squadron."

I stepped aside to let him pass.

"Oh, Squirrel," Stew said. "I heard you wrote a 3-3. Is that correct?"

He was referring to the tactics manual I had written back in training. My mind raced as I worked out how he had found out. I hadn't told anyone in the squadron about it.

"Yes, sir," I replied. "I saw a need and filled it."

It felt like a lame pickup line or, worse, brownnosing. I regretted it as soon as I said it.

"Hmm." He nodded again as he started toward the ops cell. But then he paused to think a second and looked back at me.

"You're a mission commander now," he said. "I need that kind of initiative."

With that, he turned and disappeared into the ops cell. I stood there stunned. Pilots didn't become mission commanders after four days in the squadron and one sortie under their belts. Most took three to six months to be selected, and then only if their track record was good enough. How was I to run a mission if I wasn't even certified to fly one?

I suddenly had no appetite.

After the initial surprise wore off, the encounter energized me to get back in the seat. A few hours later, I was back in the GCS watching the Predator lift slowly off the ground and climb into the night sky.

All I could do was watch. The JOC wanted to keep an eye on their assets and required us to be in our seats before takeoff, even though we weren't in control during the ascent. I watched the downlinked video feed as the launch crew raised the landing gear. I felt like a voyeur peeking through the curtain into another pilot's cockpit. The Predator banked to the right and started a lazy circle around the airfield as it climbed. Airspace around the base was limited to a fifteen-nautical-mile circle. The host government was reluctant to give us too much leeway or else the local tribes might think we were hunting them.

In the summer months, temperatures in the high desert soared. The air became so thin we were lucky to generate lift at a measly one hundred feet per minute on a hot day. The plane just didn't have enough power. It took us twenty minutes of circling to climb to twenty thousand feet. Finally, the pilots downrange turned the Predator west and entered a narrow air traffic control corridor that led to the targets in northern Afghanistan. Once the Predator was established in the corridor, it was our turn to take over.

"Watch for the warning," Wang said.

"Loss of LOS Uplink" flashed on my warning screen. It indicated that the crew had cut their line-of-sight (LOS) radio command of the airplane so we could take over. The Predator gave precedence to the line-of-sight transmitter. Once the link was severed, the Predator would maintain its course via autopilot until we established our link.

I reached up and clicked the link button next to my HUD. The screen flickered and I pushed my stick over to the right a touch to verify that I had control. A couple of seconds later, the plane banked to the right.

"Nice job," Wang said. "Now you've got a while to wait."

It took several hours to reach the target. In the meantime, we decided to practice Hellfire runs. The sensor operator was a veteran of the squadron. It was my first time flying with him, and I didn't catch his name. We didn't talk much, since I was concentrating on Wang's commands.

He fired up the pod's laser illuminator. It acted like an infrared flashlight. It would shine down like a finger from God pointing out a target.

"Don't shoot the base," Wang said. "It freaks out the guard tower."

The sensor operator spun the ball around and started to search the valley for a target. Three dry wadis ran about ten miles southwest of the base. When Alexander the Great had passed through, the area was a lush, verdant valley. The wadis were major tributaries that combined into a larger river heading toward the distant Indian Ocean. Alexander had built a fort at the juncture to guard the strategic waterway. I could just make out the ruins on the monitor. Only a single square tower remained of the once impressive fort.

The sensor operator put the cross hairs in the middle of the ruins. It was a perfect target because it was static and unoccupied.

"Okay, call comes in from a foot patrol," Wang said. "They've been hit by a sniper and are taking casualties. They report that incoming fire appears to be coming from the northeast corner of the fort."

The sensor operator shifted his cross hairs to the appropriate spot. A north arrow, superimposed on our HUD, showed him in which direction he needed to slew the pod.

"Okay," I said. "We've got eyes on."

We spoke casually together in the cockpit. Wang played all the roles of the foot patrol, JOC, and JTAC.

"What do I see?" I asked.

"You see two figures, prone in the corner against the wall," Wang said. "You see a bright flash."

"Hostile fire observed," the sensor operator said.

I asked the ground commander, and Wang confirmed for him. They were receiving incoming fire.

"Copy," I said.

I turned to the sensor operator.

"AGM-114 prelaunch checklist."

The AGM-114 prelaunch checklist was a cumbersome thirty-step process to activate and test the missile before firing it. The launch checklist that followed added another twenty steps. The whole process could take five minutes to complete for new pilots.

The sensor operator and I worked our way through the checklist. It was a great distraction while waiting to reach our target but a real pain in the ass when lives were on the line.

When I was ready to shoot, I told Wang.

"Copy, call in with direction," Wang said.

He wanted us to inform him when we started our missile run and to tell him from which direction we were flying.

I rolled in and pointed the nose at the target.

"Wildfire is in from the northeast, one minute."

I had one minute until I fired the missile.

"Wildfire, you are cleared to engage."

"Cleared to engage" allowed me only to practice firing a missile. I couldn't employ any ordnance until a real controller cleared me "hot." We were flying now with real missiles. For safety, every member of the crew ensured we did not accidentally launch a live weapon while practicing.

"Copy, cleared to engage."

I watched my run-in line. The winds pushed from the west, making my aircraft drift left. I turned the aircraft about ten degrees to the right to crab into the wind.

"Thirty seconds, laser on," I said.

The sensor operator hit his trigger and the "LTM Firing" message appeared on the screen. We used the illuminator, or Laser Target Marker, instead of the targeting laser to avoid accidentally injuring someone on the ground. This laser acted more like a flashlight and could not guide the weapon.

"Lasing," he said.

"Lasing," I said to Wang. "Thirty seconds."

"Copy," Wang said.

At twenty seconds, I adjusted my course again, ensured that I had the right switches set, and concentrated on the target. At ten seconds, I depressed the "Release to Consent" button. A "Ready to Fire Right Missile" showed on my HUD.

"In three, two, one . . ."

I simulated pulling the trigger. We never pulled the trigger on practice runs.

"Rifle, twenty-five seconds."

I warned Wang, acting as the ground commander, to expect impact in less than thirty seconds.

I monitored the GPS clock and counted down the time.

"In five, four . . ."

Wang called out "Splash" to indicate that the missile hit in our field of view. I nodded.

"Cease laser, safe laser, master arm safe."

The sensor operator read back the orders and switched off the illuminator.

"Nice job," Wang said. "We've got the altitude; let's head north."

It took us nearly four hours to reach our target area. I was back on station over the same mud hut. I set the Predator into orbit and circled the house, waiting for the courier to move or get on his phone. When he did, the analysts watching from the ops center and the JOC went to work. Analysts documented activities and saved screen shots of the target. All the value of the flight happened around us as we sat for eight hours in the seat, bored to tears.

Things didn't get interesting until a few months later.

It was a night mission and I'd just taken control of the Predator from the launch crew. Wang no longer flew with me. I was a mission commander with two hundred hours in the aircraft and I knew just enough to become comfortable with the aircraft and mission.

Next to me sat Dani.

We rarely flew as a two-person crew. Pilots and sensor operators swapped out frequently based on schedules and breaks. Unlike in movies like *Top Gun*, pilots and sensor operators weren't partners who flew the same shift. We also didn't play volleyball together in our off time. Flying the Predator was shift work. We lived at a hotel.

I got up, drove over to the compound, shifted my mind-set from family man to combat pilot, flew my shift, went back to the hotel, and tried to shift back to a family man on the way home. Do that for weeks on end and flying the Predator was more like working in a factory. All of the sexiness of being a pilot was gone.

As for the volleyball in blue jeans? That was never cool.

I turned the Predator toward the coordinates in the secure chat room and started toward the target. Our mission was to find a new facilitator we'd seen referenced in intelligence reporting. We still had about thirty minutes before reaching the Jalalabad area where he lived.

I liked Dani. She was a very experienced sensor operator, one of the senior members of the squadron. She typically gave check rides to the younger sensor operators and occasionally flew with the new pilots like me. During the long missions, we mostly argued about our football teams—my Steelers, her Bengals.

Dani spun the camera around and started to scan the ground as we flew. Too often, the real action happened far from where we thought it would be. So we watched the ground go by and hoped to see anything of interest.

By the time we arrived near the target area, the sun was making its slow, graceful debut. I could make out the streaks of warm light peeking between the tops of the mountains. I kept my eye on the instruments—highlighted in green on the HUD—but the image of the ground was slowly graying into an unrecognizable mass, with Rorschach blotches indicating hot spots.

At sunrise and sunset, some infrared cameras struggled to maintain a passable image as the ground warmed or cooled to match the ambient temperature. Dani adjusted the camera to compensate and the countryside beneath us came back into view. Within minutes the rocks were once again projected in sharp relief on my HUD. The trees swayed a bit as the morning's breeze flowed down the mountain.

I watched our pink line on the tracker map above the HUD as we skimmed the Afghanistan-Pakistan border near Tora Bora, a cave complex south of the Khyber Pass. Three years before, American special operations forces had almost captured Osama bin Laden there. Officials said the complex was his headquarters and after the battle he escaped to Pakistan. A ridgeline that paralleled the international boundary on our chart filled the monitor.

"I've got a fire," Dani said.

I could see the flames and hot spots on the screen. The fire was like a white-hot finger snaking down the length of the ridgeline. The camera was in IR mode, making anything with a heat signature glow against the cold gray background.

"Reporting the fire," I said, typing in the chat room.

Dani swung the camera across the ridgeline and spotted two caves. The mouths of the caves were well concealed from aircraft, but the fire was illuminating the entrances.

"I don't see any pax," Dani said as she zoomed in closer to the caves. "Pax" was our term for people.

Then we saw the camp. It was three or four pup tents. A small campfire simmered between the tents, a makeshift rack and pot suspended above. Next to the road, a small cart was abandoned in a rut. Dani kept the camera on the camp for several minutes before it disappeared behind another mountain. Dani flicked the camera about, pleased that she once again had a good picture to work with, when we saw movement.

"Hey, what's that?" I said.

Dani trained cross hairs where I pointed on the HUD screen.

The trees were still. I held my breath. Had I seen anything? Was it a trick of my imagination? Did they hear us and hide?

A moment later, four spots emerged from behind the clump of trees.

"Zoom in."

Dani didn't need to hear my command. A great sensor operator, she anticipated my command. She had already centered the cross hairs on the walkers and started the zoom. The mirror inside the ball flexed and twisted as it adjusted, making the picture flash, invert, invert again back to normal, and then settle on a wide, rocky escarpment.

The four figures were making their way up the jagged slope. It looked like three of the men were guarding the fourth. The fourth man was much taller than the others, wearing dark brown robes with white sleeves and headdress. He used a long walking stick to help him climb. The others were dressed in black and carrying AK-47s. They walked at a respectful distance from the taller man. Two of the guards flanked the taller man and the third walked in front of him. None got within five yards of the man.

"Dani?"

"Yeah," she said.

"Is that who I think it is?"

"Who?" Dani squinted at the screen.

She stared at the video as if straining to see more detail.

"UBL," I said.

There is no universal standard for translating Arabic to English. The FBI spelled Osama bin Laden's name "Usama bin Laden," shortening it to UBL. We just adopted that acronym.

Dani shot me a sideways glance.

"I can't tell."

"You know that video that came out a couple months ago," I said. "The one with him climbing down boulders with his body-guard."

"Yeah," she said warily.

"I think this is the area that was filmed."

I pointed at the screen.

"Look, the area is full of those kinds of boulders. Besides, who else has a bodyguard in this region?"

In my mind, the taller man looked like Bin Laden. He carried himself with the same arrogance. My heart raced. The man had the mannerisms, the physical description, and even the suspected target area. For a second, I wondered if I had the world's most wanted man in my sights.

"Hey, LNO?"

Our intercom was connected directly to the JOC. One of our pilots sat at a desk near the analysts and acted as an LNO. He could answer questions and relay information from the JOC in our language.

"Go ahead."

It was Tony, a former C-130 driver from Texas.

"Can you get the analysts online? I think we got number one in sight."

There was silence on the intercom for a moment. I could tell Tony was trying to process what he'd heard. It sounded strange to say it.

"Uh, okay," Tony said. "Hold on."

A few seconds later, Tony told me to stay on the walkers. Al, the JOC director, wanted us to forget our previous mission for the moment. This told me they took the finding seriously. I knew the analysts back at the JOC were glued to the monitors trying to figure out if we had Bin Laden. I put the Predator in orbit near the walkers, and Dani set the camera to track them as they continued to walk up and over the slope.

The wait lasted a long time. I'd expected to hear something pretty quickly. At the very least, we knew the guys in question had guns and were likely fighters.

We were getting impatient.

"Tony, any news?"

"Not much," he said a moment later. "Al's on the phone with upstairs. Been there since you called."

Upstairs was the chain of command. Al was seeking permission to do something. He couldn't make autonomous decisions for a target like this, if it was Bin Laden. A potential missile strike required a lot of coordination. I looked at the clock imprinted in my HUD. We'd already tracked the men for more than twenty minutes as they walked calmly along the ridge.

"So what's your read, Tony?"

I had no idea what was going on in the JOC. I wanted to get a feel for the mood.

"The analysts are pretty excited," he said. "They've been running confirmations for a while."

Confirmations were always the problem. Short of Bin Laden waving at us or giving us the finger, we had only a few protocols remaining that could confirm the identity of the man below with any reasonable amount of certainty.

Protocols or rules of engagement defined how, when, and if we could engage a target. Unlike fighters, directors at the JOC all the way up to the president had to weigh in on every Predator shot. Bin Laden meant a call to the White House. A "no" at any level stopped the shot.

In case we got the thumbs-up to shoot, I started to discuss options with Dani. I also started to spin up the Hellfire missiles so we would be ready to go.

"The guards are irrelevant, expendable," I said. "Only one target matters."

But the rocks could be a problem. They provided some cover for the men. At impact, the Hellfire buried itself before the contact fuse detonated the charge. The shot could fail if it hit behind a rock.

"We could aim for the high rocks and maximize the frag pattern," Dani said.

I agreed and started thinking of attack headings.

Tony broke up the meeting.

"Al's off the line," he said. "He doesn't look happy."

After a long silence, Tony came over the radio.

"I'm posting coordinates in chat," he said.

I plotted the coordinates. We were headed to a random area far to the west. It was nowhere near our original target, which was still about thirty miles to the north of us.

"Tony," I said. "This is in the middle of nowhere."

"Go to the coordinates and wait."

Tony's response was terse, devoid of the friendly personality he'd had a few minutes before. It felt like he was being told what to say. Someone upstairs didn't want us to go after this target. They were so against it that they were willing to force the JOC to drop their planned operation for the day, punching a large hole in the pattern of life we were building on our main target.

I took the Predator out of orbit and flew to the coordinates. We returned the missiles to their dormant state. Dani put the cross hairs of the camera on the spot and we stared at rocks for the next three hours.

I never understood why we were forced out of the area. The JOC should have cleared us to our original target. Someone didn't want us looking at UBL enough that they were willing to destroy a pattern-of-life operation. Like chain of evidence in a criminal investigation, pattern of life had to be constant, without breaks, in order to build a clear picture of the target's life without the chance of accidentally following the wrong person. This frustrated me because I knew the impact watching rocks would have on our current mission.

I wanted to know who that guy was and why someone felt the need to protect him.

When the new crew finally came in to relieve us, I drove over to the JOC to chat with Al. The JOC was in an office building near our compound.

The JOC had a sterile smell. A table filled the center of the main room. On top were dividers sectioning the table into about a dozen stations, each with a phone and a shelf for binders. Colored cables snaked from the ceiling, down a corner, and across the floor to jury-rigged LAN stations. Analysts sat in front of computers around the room's walls.

Two sixty-inch plasma screens hung on opposite walls. Each showed a Predator feed. Beneath each monitor sat one of our pilots, a liaison officer like Tony.

"Al around?" I asked the nearest analyst.

"His shift is over," the analyst said. "He's gone for the day."

"Who is in charge now?"

"Carly," the analyst said, pointing to a thin, athletic, thirtysomething blonde.

She'd flown fighters in the Air Force prior to joining the JOC.

I took a deep breath and reached back to my intelligence training. I remembered a thing or two about teasing information out of people. I was technically the oncoming mission commander now that my flying was done for the day. It would be my job to help coordinate flights and crews for the rest of my twelve-hour day.

I used that to break the ice.

"I heard there was some excitement earlier."

A mission commander would naturally want to know about this sort of thing. Of course, I was taking the chance that she didn't know I was the guy in the seat.

"Why'd they call it off?" I asked.

If Al had given her a thorough briefing before leaving, he had left out my participation. She was frustrated the shot had been called off too.

"Politics."

"Excuse me?" I said.

"Politics," Carly said. "Management between us and the boss called it off."

"They give a reason?" I asked.

"Don't have to," she said. "It's their call."

I didn't have to be an interrogator to see her negative assessment of that office.

"Was it him?" I asked.

I had to know if I'd actually found Bin Laden.

"We think it was him," Carly said.

In 2002, a Predator fired a Hellfire missile at three men near Zhawar Kili in Afghanistan's Paktia Province. One of the men was tall and he was mistaken for Bin Laden, but they were just local tribesmen searching for scrap metal to sell for food.

I looked sidelong at her.

"So it was real?"

She paused for a second.

"We think it was."

I was having trouble keeping my frustration from boiling over.

"Then why cancel the shot?"

Carly sighed. I had got her this far and I hoped I hadn't pressed her too hard.

"There's a manager who won't let a shot like this go through," she said. "He stops everyone."

Now I was really mad.

"That's treason," I said.

"No." She shook her head. "That's politics."

CHAPTER 5

The Shot Heard Round the World

Bam. Bam.

I knocked twice on the door of the GCS. The echo rumbled down the length of the container, alerting the crew that we were ready to take over. I waited for a reply.

One knock in response meant to stand by.

Two knocks was code to come in.

Three knocks told us to shut up and wait.

We were standing just outside the Predator Operations Center at Nellis Air Force Base. Today was my first day flying with the 15th Reconnaissance Squadron. The 17th had just moved back to Nellis at the end of August. Some of the crews were sent to help the 15th stand up a new CAP.

The Air Force moved both squadrons into a compound enclosed

behind a seven-foot cinder-block wall. Other than the ops cell, the other "buildings" were triple-wide trailers cheaply stapled together. A single Cadillac, which is what we called a portable bathroom/shower trailer, was in the back of the compound. A handful of GCSs belonging to both squadrons sat in the center of the compound.

I was back in a green flight suit and far from the humidity at our compound. It was midday and the high desert sun beat mercilessly down on us. Las Vegas was hot in September. The temperature hadn't dropped below 105 degrees for the whole month, but at least it was a dry heat.

The 15th had asked for additional help when they stood up another CAP. They didn't have the manning yet to fully support it, and the 17th had a few extra bodies waiting for the rest of the squadron to move back to Las Vegas. I didn't mind helping out. It beat sitting around. Plus, after spending a lot of time over Afghanistan, I wanted to help with the war in Iraq. That was the real fight at the time.

The knock had barely subsided when the rear door flew open.

The pilot, a medium-height blond man with a slight build, stalked out of the GCS. He looked angry, though I could see no reason why, since we were five minutes early. As he pushed passed me, I heard him mumble, "Plane's yours."

He disappeared around the corner before I could say anything. *What the hell?*

I ducked my head into the box and saw a panicked sensor operator looking back at me.

He mouthed the words "What do I do?" I ran to the seat and looked at the HUD and tracker. The plane was on a direct course into Iran.

That wasn't a big deal if the Predator was flying over Baghdad.

But this Predator was just north of Basra. The border was close. The aircraft would cross into Iranian airspace in moments.

There wasn't time for me to sit down. I pressed the button on the stick that shut off the autopilot and gently rolled into a steep bank back toward Iraq. With the black line of the border about to overlap my icon on the tracker, I edged the bank up to sixty degrees. Twenty degrees was the limit in the pilot's manual, but I needed to turn fast.

In the HUD, the world tilted as the aircraft attempted to match the bank I commanded. The pink tracker icon twitched and rotated. Data from the plane refreshed every couple of seconds, making the turn appear erratic on the tracker. The landscape slewed sideways.

Once the nose turned far enough south, I slowly relaxed the bank and let the plane roll out. I then reengaged the autopilot to ensure that we continued to track away from Iran. With the plane flying southwest, I sat down and put on my headset.

I saw a chat from the Roulette mission coordinator (MC). Roulette was our mission call sign.

ROULETTE_MC> Iran is calling on Guard.

Guard was the international emergency frequency. Air defense units from nearly every country used it to identify aircraft and to warn them against airspace incursions. Aircraft could get shot down if they didn't heed the air defense directions.

They don't have the balls to shoot me down, I thought.

The sensor operator still looked a bit shaken. He didn't want Iran to join the war any more than I did.

I took a deep breath and smiled.

"You guys can change out now," I said.

It was a quick changeover brief, and my sensor operator, a crusty technical sergeant who had been with the program since Bosnia, took over.

The 15th worked for Multi-National Force—Iraq. The command in Baghdad decided the priority each day and delivered our orders via email and mIRC chat. I checked in via the chat room and flew to the coordinates they provided. We spent most of our time tracking small time-bomb makers, couriers, and occasional insurgent cell leaders. The job remained tedious and boring. This was mostly because the Army was running the operation in Iraq and they didn't really know what to do with us.

I opened the Roulette mission chat room.

> *ROULETTE_33> Checking in, 5,000 feet.*
> *136_CM> c, proceed to target, pass ETA when able.*

I didn't recognize the unit. I mentally calculated my distance from the coordinates. We were close, so transit wouldn't take long. When we arrived, the sensor operator scanned the area. It was an open field and a single tree.

> *ROULETTE_33> On tgt, confirm location plz.* [On
> target, confirm location please.]
> *136_CM> confirmed.*

My sensor operator put a track on the tree. Black brackets on the HUD clamped onto the tree's image. The targeting pod jerked slightly as the brackets centered on the picture.

> *ROULETTE_33> What are our EEIs?*

EEIs, or essential elements of information, could be anything from an odd hot spot on the ground that could be a weapons cache or roadside bomb to a chance meeting between two individuals.

> *136_CM> Watch the target.*
> *ROULETTE_33> What cues are you looking for?*

I asked the question because knowing what he wanted was essential.

> *136_CM> Just watch the target.*

Eight hours later, the tree remained fixed in our HUD. We didn't get any subsequent messages from the Army unit. I heard two knocks as our scheduled replacements arrived. The sensor operator smashed his hand against the side of the GCS twice and the new crew walked into the box. We spent a few minutes briefing them on the mission and how the Predator was performing. As I climbed out of the seat, I was confident the new pilot knew exactly what needed to be done.

I walked back to the operations center to check out. I thought about how life in the two squadrons was so different. In the 17th, we enjoyed high morale because the mission felt important.

The 15th felt irrelevant.

The drudgery of twenty-four hour operations with little or no feedback from the field had taken its toll. There was no closure on a mission. The air crew didn't have any idea if their participation helped an operation. The Army didn't praise people for doing the job. The 15th got feedback only when mistakes were made. Silence meant they weren't screwing up.

It was difficult to sustain any motivation under those conditions. The lack of communication between the Army commanders and the pilots was an issue. Our pilots rarely checked in with the ground commanders in the field. My checkout pilot in the 15th told me to just announce I was on station in the tactical operations center, or TOC, chat room. The TOC controlled the ground unit's movements. The TOC would then let the ground commander know we were on station, and they'd get back to us when they needed us. It was a lazy and unprofessional way for us to conduct operations. There was no rapport between the Predator crews and the soldiers on the ground. It was like we were fighting two different wars.

That was still no excuse for the lack of professionalism I'd witnessed during that first changeover. I saw Mike in the compound later in the day walking from the 15th's trailer to the ops cell. It was the first time I'd seen him since training.

"Hey, Mike," I called out and jogged over to meet him.

I wanted to get his take on the episode.

"Hey, hey, Squirrel. What's up?" he said, smiling broadly.

"We need to talk," I said.

I explained what had happened during my changeover. I also gave him the pilot's name. Mike instantly changed from affable to serious. He shook his head, no longer smiling.

"That's not good."

"It's my first day flying with the 15th," I asked. "Is that common here?"

Mike sighed.

"Unfortunately, it's more common than not."

He didn't like breaches in flight discipline.

"We've got to fix this," I said.

We both knew I didn't mean just this particular pilot. Mike and

I had tried to fill a need with the training manual, and now we knew the community needed a shot of professionalism. The community as it stood was rotten to the core.

When Predator stood up, the Air Force designated 85 percent of the slots for fighter pilots, and the rest went to the other aircraft. The fighter community used Predator as an opportunity to unload deadweight. Any pilot who'd screwed up, was substandard, or was just not good was dumped into the program. The pilots knew why they were there. They also knew the fighter community would not take them back. That bred bitterness to the point where they ceased comporting themselves as officers. They showed up late, turned in substandard work, and apparently abandoned aircraft in flight. Given that kind of example, the enlisted sensor operators devolved into a similar professional death spiral.

We had a lot of work to do. It would take time, but it had to be done.

I was named chief of standardizations and evaluations for the 17th. My job was to enforce regulations and flight discipline by going on check rides with my pilots. Mike and I also started a grassroots campaign to bring up the subject in our pilot meetings. Usually, these meetings discussed new software loads and safety issues. We decided that it was time to inject actual piloting skills into the meetings.

I ran into Mike again transiting between buildings a few weeks later.

"Squirrel," he called out, excited.

"Hey, Mike. What's up?"

Mike's eyes shined with an intensity I hadn't seen recently. There was fire, purpose, pride even. My eyes narrowed.

"What did you do?" I asked with mock suspicion.

I thought he'd decertified one of the laggards. With the way some of them had been behaving, we both knew our troops on the ground deserved as much.

"It wasn't me," he said. "But it was Droopy."

Droopy was an F-16 pilot like Mike. Where Mike exuded intensity, Droopy appeared the polar opposite. The pilots in his first Viper squadron came up with the call sign because he also looked somewhat like the cartoon character.

Mike said Droopy was trained in close air support. He'd deployed before coming to Predator and knew the stakes for the ground units. It was his unit's primary mission before he transferred to Predator. It galled him to check in with the TOC and then sit silently watching the action for eight hours.

He wanted to get into the fight.

So earlier that day, troops were attacked in Droopy's sector. He pulled out an old mission card he'd saved from his Viper days. It was a close air support template printed on well-worn four-by-eight card stock. Droopy placed the card on the console behind the control stick and keyed the mic. Using his best fighter voice—an octave lower to sound more menacing—he called the JTAC, Bulldog Two One.

"Bulldog Two One, Roulette Three Three, ready check-in."

The JTAC probably expected another silly "we're here" kind of call from the Predator.

"Go for Bulldog," the JTAC said.

"Bulldog, Roulette checking in flight level one four zero, one by MQ-1, orbiting ten miles south of your position, two hours playtime, two by AGM-114, pod and self-lase capable."

Droopy told the JTAC his altitude (fourteen thousand feet), his position, his weapons load (two missiles), and the aircraft special capabilities (targeting pod and laser designator).

"Copy, Roulette," Bulldog said crisply.

He was talking to a fellow professional.

"We have a TIC in progress with troops pinned down," Bulldog said. "Clearance on my authority. Call when ready 9-Line."

TIC, or troops in contact, meant US forces on the ground were in a firefight. Bulldog wasn't going to wait for fighters to arrive. He wanted the Predator to engage. Droopy and his sensor operator looked at each other. They weren't expecting that response.

Bulldog paused for a second.

"Roulette, ready 9-Line."

Within five minutes, Droopy fired both Hellfire missiles and broke the ambush.

Mike was still grinning when he finished telling the story. It was a big day for our program and our community. Taking a shot in combat that saved American lives was something we could build on, the kind of thing that could flip morale 180 degrees, if we played it right.

This wasn't our first shot in combat. Not by far. However, it was an engagement where we acted like professional strikers.

Droopy's shot changed the face of Predator in both Iraq and Afghanistan. We had dipped our toes into the traditional fighter pilot's pool. Word spread quickly among the JTACs that real pilots were starting to fly Predators. In the weeks following, our crews noticed a slight increase in missile strikes.

Mike and I wanted to make sure Droopy's success led to a more professional RPA community. We wanted to start bringing that standard to all the crews. I took every opportunity to mention the shot to guys in casual conversation. Pilots are natural gossips, especially about women, airplanes, and tactics. It was arguable which was more important to an aviator at any given moment.

Probably airplanes.

Life in a Predator squadron was a lot different from life in other Air Force units. The bar in most squadrons was the center of life in the unit. Guys sat at the tables, ate lunch, finished paperwork, or just shot the breeze. Everybody was on the same schedule and flew in pairs.

Most Air Force squadrons buzzed with energy during the day as guys trained. But the Predator compound was quiet. We didn't have a bar, and the flight briefing rooms and offices were deserted. Only the operations center had any life, but even then, pilots just checked in and out. It wasn't a social scene.

Predator pilots and sensor operators worked in shifts. I remember going to the Christmas party one year and meeting guys in my squadron for the first time. They were on a different shift. But even then, I didn't have a lot of close relationships with the other guys because we rarely flew together, and even if we were in the same shift, working a dozen feet from each other, I might be flying in Iraq and the other pilot might be flying in Afghanistan.

Unlike the fighter community, we didn't fly in pairs. We didn't use wingmen or talk on the radio with each other. The conversations were with the guys on the ground and our sensor operators in the cockpit.

But even that relationship didn't extend past the cockpit, because I was an officer and the sensor was an enlisted airman. In flight, we tried hard to break down those walls so we could be a good crew, but in the office, there was a line drawn between the officers and the enlisted, just like there is in all the services.

Flying the Predator was isolating and unlike any other experience I'd had in the Air Force. But that didn't stop me or Mike from trying to take the professionalism of the other communities and instill it in Predator.

The 17th wasn't an easy sell. Most of our operations did not involve ground troops. We didn't need 9-Lines. When a raid was on the books, we flew solely in observation mode, so we didn't need close air support procedures. Still, I peddled it to the guys in the 17th as a necessity if they flew with the 15th or returned to the 11th as instructors.

I also focused on my own skills. After hearing about Droopy's mission, I studied every facet of close air support. I needed to be ready to shoot when my opportunity came. I also needed to be proficient so I could test the other pilots in the squadrons. It was my job to make sure the pilots in the 17th were meeting Air Force standards even if our day-to-day job was different from that of most other pilots.

After Droopy's shot, a shamal, which is a northwesterly wind, flowed out of Turkey and blasted its way across Iraq. The winds picked up small dust particles and turned them into a massive, choking sandstorm that blanketed much of the Mesopotamia Valley.

Nothing moved on the ground. Helicopters and cargo planes were grounded. But the Predators continued to fly. Our IR targeting pod burned through the dust cloud as if it didn't exist. The images weren't spectacular, but they were clear enough for us to fly.

I set the Predator in an orbit near a suspected safe house in Ramadi. The central Iraqi town sits along the Euphrates River about seventy miles west of Baghdad. Ramadi is the capital and largest city in the Al Anbar Province. The house was located near a main road frequented by American patrols, making its location an ideal staging point for launching attacks.

Whoever lived in the house hadn't made a move in hours. For all we knew, they were waiting out the storm. We watched for some time, observing only the occasional car or pickup pass. Iraqis hated dust storms nearly as much as we did. The dust from a shamal permeated everything, even sealed Ziploc bags and electronics. You tasted dirt, grit, and worse things with each tortured breath. I was running an ops check when a truck drove by. The aircraft's oil was a little low but otherwise normal. I only glanced at it while I typed my log entries into our spreadsheet.

"Sir," Sarah, my sensor operator, said. "Was that a technical?" A technical was a small vehicle, usually a pickup truck, modified to carry mounted weapons like machine guns. They were mobile, fast, and dangerous.

I had trained with Sarah at the 11th. We'd successfully outmaneuvered the F-16 together. It was nice to fly with a familiar face.

My head snapped up to the HUD. It was too late. The truck had already passed out of view. Sarah zoomed out so she could keep the house in the picture while looking for the truck.

"Stay on that house," I said.

I wanted to find the truck, but our target was the house. A moment later, the secure phone rang. I picked up the receiver.

"Roulette."

"Check your chat."

It was the mission commander in the ops cell. I scanned our mission chat room. A note from the Marine Air Traffic Control caught my eye.

DASC> Roulette, TIC in progress, cleared off tgt, get eyes on ASAP.

I hung up the phone, and Sarah plugged the target coordinates into the rack and tracked the targeting pod around to get eyes on the location. The whirling video behind my stable HUD was disorienting. I looked away and focused on something in the cockpit until the picture settled.

"Switching to day TV," Sarah said.

We usually flew in IR, but she wanted to see what the visible spectrum would give us. Seconds later all I could see was a solid orange glow. It was impossible to pick up any distinguishing images on the ground.

"Going back to IR," she said.

A snowy image showed the bridge and some vehicles, but not much more. The sand was at a uniform temperature and blocked the heat signatures of High Mobility Multipurpose Wheeled Vehicles (HMMWVs). Even when we drove in close, the image remained marginal.

The lead vehicle appeared to be disabled. An insurgent driving nearby had noticed the stopped truck. He gathered several other fighters and ambushed the HMMWVs. Unfortunately for the insurgents, this convoy happened to have a JTAC with it. A frequency popped up in the chat room.

I checked in with the JTAC, using the procedures I had been practicing. Secretly, I was a bit embarrassed that I felt nervous.

"Vengeance Four One, Roulette Three Three. Ready check-in," I said.

"Go check-in," the JTAC yelled into his mic. The loud *pop-pop-pop* of gunfire sounded close.

I rattled off my check-in, focused on sounding professional.

"Copy, Roulette," the JTAC called back immediately. "We are taking small arms fire from across the river. Unable to provide direction. Lead vehicle disabled and unable to move column at this time. No known friendlies across river. We see something south of the bridge, possible weapons fire. Scan and report. How copy?"

"Roulette copies," I radioed.

I looked over at Sarah.

"Shift right."

The bridge and the soldiers slid out of sight as Sarah tracked the camera down the river toward the truck.

"Stop there," I said.

We could make out block-shaped buildings emerging from the sand as she followed a road that paralleled the river. The truck was parked on the road. It was small, like a Ford Ranger with a king cab. It was probably white, too. Most vehicles were, except the taxis that had orange quarter panels.

"I can see some shadows," Sarah said. "Could be pax."

Seconds later, a staccato of flashes erupted next to one of the shadows. The hot gases from the burning gunpowder showed like deep black accents against the gray screen. It was small arms fire. We'd found the shooter.

"Whoa," Sarah said.

"Shots fired," I called out.

The JTAC had a ROVER kit, a small laptop device that could receive the video feed we transmitted from the aircraft. With it, he could see what we saw.

"Copy," said the JTAC. "I see it. Call when ready 9-Line."

I called ready.

"Roulette, this will be Type II control by Vengeance Four One," started the JTAC.

Type II control meant the JTAC could see me or the target, but not both. He likely used our feed to identify the target. I scribbled the note on my whiteboard. It was easier than messing with the paper data card on my knee.

"One, two, three—N/A."

The first three lines denoted a specific run-in for a target to include range and bearing. We didn't use these lines for Type II or Type III control.

The fourth line was the target altitude.

"Two one three four feet."

Line five identified the target.

"Personnel in the open."

The JTAC went off-line momentarily.

"Stand by for coords—I've got to change my designator battery."

We waited and watched the enemy while he swapped battery packs on his laser range finder. I wondered how accurate that laser would be through the sand. I made a note to myself to check my laser before engaging.

Once the JTAC was back online, he continued the 9-Line by compressing the last lines into one radio call.

"Self-lase, friendlies one hundred meters south, no remarks or restrictions."

Sarah and I ran our checks. Sarah plugged the coordinates into the targeting computer. The video shifted slightly. The bridge and the enemy truck overlapped and were too grainy to distinguish at this point anyway.

"You ready, Sarah?"

"Yes," she said.

The camera remained locked in place.

"You've got the target," I said. "Let me know if I am getting too far away."

I kept the Predator close because visibility grew exponentially worse the farther we flew from the target. There was no threat the insurgents would shoot us down and it was unlikely they even heard us over their own AK-47 fire. I wanted to keep eyes on the target. If we lost them in the storm, we'd have to reconfirm the target and go through the 9-Line again. That would take too long.

I turned outbound, away from the target to line up my run. By the time I could turn inbound, the picture had degraded so the bridge and vehicles were barely recognizable.

"Sarah, you still have the target?"

"Yes, sir."

She sounded strained. Her face remained fixed on the screen in front of her. Her forehead creased in concentration.

I was focused on the Hellfire's missile parameters. My bearing to target had to fall within four degrees of the aircraft heading. This proved rather difficult as the nose tended to track with the changing wind currents.

Firing the missile was a huge challenge with a light plane bouncing in the air currents. The Hellfire missile was designed for helicopters. Helicopters didn't shoot them on the move. They hid behind hills or trees and popped up with just enough time to stabilize and fire from a hover. The Predator aircraft had to remain in motion at all times. Airflow over the wings kept it aloft.

I used the rudder pedals to force the nose to track properly. Altitude was set at ten thousand feet. The autopilot would take care of that for me. I kept an eye on my range. I had to release the missile inside a one-kilometer window. Once I hit that mark, I'd have about thirty seconds to fire before I flew too close.

Release too early and the missile would fall short. Shoot too close and the missile might not see the target when it armed. If I overshot, the errant missile could hit a house.

Precision was key.

I looked up at the tracker, which showed my approach as a blue ladder that led into a little red cross hair embedded within a circle on the target. A small green box sat just forward of my aircraft on the screen. That was the expected weapons engagement zone (WEZ), or best place to shoot.

"Roulette in from the southwest," I said.

"Roulette, Vengeance Four One, you're cleared hot."

Cleared hot. I was authorized to fire the missile. This call also told everyone else on the net to stay quiet.

"Copy, cleared hot," I said.

I looked over at Sarah. She was still focused on her screen. I touched the rudder to align the nose. An indicator on my HUD lined up to show me angled properly. I selected the left missile.

"Ready to fire left missile."

I slid my finger over the trigger.

"In three, two, one . . ."

Sarah suddenly leaned forward, staring intently at the picture.

"ABORT, ABORT, ABORT," she screamed out.

My finger pulled away from the hot trigger. I was attuned to an abort call. Anyone on the crew could call it. We practiced it on every training sortie at the 11th.

"What's wrong?" I asked, eyes scanning the HUD. Then my eyes focused on the picture. The shadowy glob we had been tracking was the command HMMWV. When the JTAC changed the battery on his laser, it reset and transmitted his coordinates instead of the insurgent's truck. We had just about fired our missile into friendlies.

The JTAC asked why we aborted. I didn't want to tell him over the radio, but lives were on the line. He was decertified on the spot and a JTAC from the TOC had to come online, get updated, and pass the 9-Line again.

This time, when I turned inbound I could make out the small pickup truck. Sarah zoomed in so the truck filled our field of view. We were both careful to make sure we were shooting at the right target.

I checked the laser range data. The sandstorm could disrupt the laser to the point that it could not determine an accurate range. A bad data point could send the missile off target enough that it would never see the laser spot.

The data was good.

"In three, two, one . . ."

I pulled the trigger. A white fireball blossomed in the HUD. The bracket indicating our track flashed once, twice, three times and then settled once again on the truck as the plume dissipated. I could still see the fighters firing near the truck.

"Roulette, rifle, twenty seconds," I put in chat, monitoring the GPS clock.

I let the Predator drift in the wind so it would remain steady. Sarah needed a stable platform to guide the missile. Far below, the Army troops ducked for cover. The target was close enough that shrapnel might hit them.

The cross hairs twitched as we passed over the truck.

"Steady, ten seconds," I told Sarah.

She drew in a deep breath.

I focused on the clock.

"Five, four, three . . ."

I paused. The missile hit the truck dead center. A large chunk of engine flipped end over end. The rest was engulfed in a cloud of smoke. The missile detonated with such force that the fighters were obliterated. The bodies remained invisible in the sandy gloom.

"Cease laser, safe laser," I said.

"Good hit, Roulette," the JTAC put in chat. "Incoming fire has ceased."

The rest of the flight was a blur. I rode a high for the rest of the day. I had taken a shot defending American troops on the ground. What more noble cause was there? I couldn't think of one. I'd also proven to myself that I had the skills to carry out a strike mission. That wasn't an easy shoot. Besides the sandstorm that made visibility difficult, we'd also discovered the JTAC's error at the last moment and stopped certain fratricide.

Sarah's quick thinking only showed me what I already knew. The Predator community had the talent to be part of the strike team. Droopy's shot was the first real victory. Mine, I hoped, cemented it.

We were no longer just voyeurs.

CHAPTER 6

Sparkle

The compound in Iraq rotating in my HUD matched the pictures from the mission brief.

Circling above, I could make out several houses that served a variety of purposes. One was for the staff, one was for work, and the other was the main living quarters. The buildings were shoved against the north and east walls of the compound, leaving ample space for a courtyard. The gate was on the southeast side. A high exterior wall thwarted prying eyes.

Sometime prior to my shift, the high-value individual, or HVI, had arrived. The lights in the compound were out, indicating that the target was asleep, or at least in the process of bedding down for the night. There were no hot spots, tracks, or motion to indicate any activity outside, other than a pair of dogs darting erratically about the courtyard. For all intents and purposes, the site was primed for the raid.

It was 2005 and I'd fallen into the steady rhythm of the war. The 17th was now based at Nellis Air Force Base with the 15th. We shared a compound, but not the mission.

By 2005, Predators were integrated into the operational scheme. In both Afghanistan and Iraq, the Army realized the utility of having an eye in the sky watching over them. Predators watched the compounds pre-raid and then moved on to the next target just as the raid started. The teams wanted up-to-the-second intelligence just before going in, and with a Predator on station, we could provide it.

Video feeds popped up in most of the bases in both theaters. Troops watched with rapt attention missions we considered dull. We called it Pred porn. I admit it sucked me in at times. I always had the feeling that something was about to happen, and most people watched hoping to see a Hellfire missile flash onto the screen.

As we monitored the compound from the cockpit, I reviewed the plan. Three UH-60 Black Hawks would insert the assault force in and around the compound. Space allowed for only one helicopter to hover over the courtyard. The other two would land just outside and Rangers would breach the main gate. Once inside, they would clear the buildings. Three chalks, three buildings.

I flipped through the briefing posted by my intelligence coordinator on one of my monitors. My sensor, Jack, and I watched intently as we waited for the assault force to arrive.

Jack was an experienced noncommissioned officer in the squadron. I didn't know him well, as we had never flown together before tonight. Unlike on some missions, we were busy, so I didn't have time to get to know him during the flight. We were both focused on the monitor and any signs of movement. We took being the Rangers' eye in the sky seriously. Like shooting, this kind of mission always felt worthwhile because there was instant feedback. If the Rangers caught the target, it was like we caught him too.

I checked in with the TOC. The JTAC was not on the ground for the mission. The only way we could communicate was in a secure chat room. His call sign was Brigham Two One, or BR_21 in chat.

ROULETTE_21> BR_21, on station.
BRIGHAM_21> c, watch for any activity.
ROULETTE_21> c.

I sighed. We worked to keep the chat rooms efficient. "C" meant copy. The chat room's messages came in streams like in *The Matrix.* You had to watch it closely or risk missing vital information before it was pushed off the screen. Typing while flying was a pain in the neck. I was as likely to do something stupid with the aircraft while typing on a keyboard as I was if I were texting behind the wheel of a car.

My eyes tracked from the HUD to the tracker and back to the chat room. Then I saw it.

BRIGHAM_21> Drummer 44 airborne, eta 30 mikes.

The raid was on. Drummer, the Black Hawk helicopter, was thirty minutes out.

ROULETTE_21> c.

My focus went back to the compound. Anything we picked up now—movement, squirters (people escaping the raid), more fighters— would be valuable information for the troops heading toward us.

Half an hour later, the three Black Hawks slipped underneath us. A plume of dust emerged below the helicopters as they flared out and started to land near the compound. One helicopter was supposed to hover above the compound as the soldiers fast roped into the courtyard, but that had been called off. I wasn't sure why.

Instead, it circled protectively overhead.

The other two choppers landed outside the west and south walls. Their rotor blades couldn't have been more than twenty feet apart. Tight formations of soldiers raced under the whirling blades and headed toward their breaching points. One group arrowed for the main gate. The other aimed for a small side entrance. As the soldiers moved toward the compound, the helicopters lifted off and disappeared, maintaining an orbit nearby.

"Watch the doors," I said.

Jack shifted his cross hairs to the center of the courtyard. From there we could see the doors of all three buildings and the men approaching the gates.

Nothing moved inside the compound.

"Breaching," Jack said.

I focused on the gate.

Jack zoomed in as the soldiers stuck explosive charges over the gate's lock. We could see small flashes as the charges blew. The Rangers streamed into the courtyard. Everyone moved with a purpose. The soldiers knew their targets and moved quickly to their assigned positions. I admired their precision.

One small group peeled off to search a building.

I inwardly cringed. A few months back, I'd watched as a similar raid, led by conventional troops, assaulted a suspected weapons storage facility. The line of men gathered outside and then slowly entered the building. A moment later, a massive explosion obliterated the building and took the men with it. There was nothing I could do to save those men then, and there was nothing I'd be able to do now. I silently prayed for their safety.

Each of the three chocks paused briefly outside the three buildings and then filed quickly inside. I held my breath a moment, but nothing happened. There was no firefight, no explosions. The TOC chat room remained silent. Jack kept the targeting pod fixed on the compound as we flew an orbit nearby. The autopilot allowed me to concentrate on the image. Jack was a seasoned sensor operator, but another set of eyes didn't hurt.

Jack saw them first. It looked like two figures—men by the way they were dressed—coming out of the northernmost building. They crawled out of a window at the back and jumped the east fence.

When cornered, the insurgents usually fought while the leaders escaped. These two ran, which meant one could be the target, leaving his fighters to die. It was cowardly and pathetic.

"Rabbit," Jack said, as the cross hairs tracked the two men as they cleared the wall.

"Follow him," I said.

Jack broke his track, and the targeting pod's cross hairs followed the men jumping the gate. The men were deep ebony against the cooler vegetation around them. I had a second thought.

"Try to keep the compound in sight."

Jack zoomed out. The wider field of view allowed us to see the compound on one side and the black dots fleeing on the other. We took the initiative to follow the rabbits, even though our mission was to watch the compound. Normally, we would have stayed on the scene until the troops finished the raid, collected any intelligence like papers, maps, and computers, and eventually departed. The runners were too suspicious to pass up.

To the east of the compound was an open field. We could see the night breeze blow against a crop of some kind, but we couldn't determine what type or how tall it was. The pair separated at first and then merged their paths about half a mile from the compound. They continued to run together for a little more than half a mile.

I typed in chat.

> ROULETTE_21> BR_21, we have two squirters east of the compound.
> BRIGHAM_21> c.

Was he watching the feed? Usually, the collection managers or JTACs got pretty riled up if you unilaterally pulled off target.

> ROULETTE_21> Did we get the jackpot?
> BRIGHAM_21> neg, not home.

The raid from the Army's standpoint was a dry hole. That's when I thought we might have the target in our cross hairs.

> ROULETTE_21> c, rabbit under the cross hairs, came from main building.
> BRIGHAM_21> say loc.

He wanted our location. I passed the coordinates and waited. Finally, Brigham came back online.

> BRIGHAM_21> Stay on target. Vectoring QRF to intercept.

The Rangers set up a blocking position a few miles up the road. They would act as the quick reaction force, or QRF, and capture any squirters from the main target. The TOC alerted them, and the soldiers climbed into their HMMWVs and headed toward the compound. The TOC came back to us, asking for assistance locating the squirters.

I remembered that a pilot—Travis—had used the Predator's IR pointer to light up some insurgents so soldiers on the ground could locate them.

Travis had been conducting route scans over Baghdad. He was searching the road for bombs when insurgents ambushed a convoy. The Army patrol reported fire from what appeared to be apartments in the distance. Between them was an open field obscured by a raised earth berm.

The Predator's sensor ball could see three bright objects on the other side of the berm. Then one of the objects rose and threw something toward the soldiers. A moment later, a small explosion blew sand and dust into the air above the soldiers' heads.

Travis told the soldiers he had eyes on the target, but the soldiers still couldn't see the insurgents. Travis's sensor operator turned on the IR pointer and shot it like a flashlight at where the insurgents were hiding. The Predator was at an angle where the IR beam overlapped the soldiers. The ground commander was convinced that the Predator was targeting them, so Travis directed the soldiers to drive one hundred meters forward. Anyone left behind was a target.

The soldiers pulled forward and the little black dots remained on the earth berm lobbing grenades and unloading their AK-47s in the direction of the soldiers. A few minutes later, Travis ended the threat with a Hellfire missile.

We called it "sparkle." The beam was invisible to the naked eye, but under night vision goggles it looked like the finger of God stabbing accusingly at the ground.

ROULETTE_21> BR-21 say pos of QRF.

We saw nothing in our HUD and we didn't want to zoom too far out for fear of losing the targets in ground clutter.

BRIGHAM_21> They are near, unable to see targets with nogs.

The QRF's night vision goggles, or nogs, couldn't see the squirters.

The two men huddled together in the same spot. Maybe they were catching their breaths. Then it occurred to me. If they were sitting, it was possible the HMMWVs couldn't see them through all the crops.

ROULETTE_21> We'll mark the tgt, stby sparkle.

"Go ahead, Jack," I said.

The squirters were resting. They had run about a mile in a short time and were gased. There was no way those guys could see the laser, but the soldiers looking for them could see it in their night vision goggles. Jack turned on the IR pointer and fired it at the two squirters.

BRIGHAM_21> Good sparkle. QRF en route.

Time passed slowly and I was concerned because the soldiers from the blocking position still hadn't found the men. There was no communication in the chat room. I scanned our data readouts; the IR illuminator was starting to overheat.

Though a low-power laser, it was still a relatively high-energy device. Temperatures in the targeting pod slowly increased until reaching the warning region. Only the cool winter air kept it out of the red for now. I pulled the keyboard into the middle of my table and started to type.

ROULETTE_21> confirm QRF has targets in sight.

Even without our IR illuminator pointing at the target, the soldiers' night vision goggles should have been sufficient to pick out the two men in a field.

BRIGHAM_21> affirm, package is secure.

I looked back at the HUD. They hadn't reported anything and we hadn't seen any movement. The two black dots were frozen in place. Jack zoomed in a little closer to the two men. I noticed the motion first. It was subtle, then more pronounced as I made out our soldiers walking around the prisoners. They were almost invisible to the targeting pod in IR mode because their body armor contained their body heat. In contrast, the two prisoners radiated a deep black glow on the camera.

"Jack," I said. "Zoom out one."

Jack did. Just outside the original field of view was parked a handful of brightly glowing HMMWVs.

"Cease laser."

We circled the target until the troops left. The rest of the flight was uneventful and we changed over with another crew soon after.

Leaving the compound after my shift, I noticed a news crew setting up outside the turnstile leading to the operations center. A public affairs officer stood with them.

"What are they here for?" I asked a buddy leaving with me.

"I don't know," he said. "But it can't be good."

As a practice, we didn't talk to the media about our work. The Office of Special Investigations, the Air Force's counterintelligence network, told us al Qaeda was looking for members of the Predator program.

Letters recovered after Osama bin Laden was killed in 2011 showed how paranoid he was about our ability to monitor the tribal areas of Pakistan and track al Qaeda operatives.

"They can distinguish between houses frequented by men at a higher rate than usual," he wrote to Atiyya Abdul Rahman, al Qaeda's top operational planner, in 2010. "Also, the visiting person might be tracked without him knowing."

He urged Rahman to move al Qaeda's leaders out of Waziristan. He said the best place to hide was on the outskirts of cities. Meetings should be limited to once or twice a week and "the leaders" should move only in bad weather.

"A warning to the brothers: They should not meet on the road and move in their cars because many of them got targeted while they were meeting on the road. They should move only when the clouds are heavy."

Despite denials and covers, the enemy knew someone pulled the triggers. They just couldn't pinpoint who we were. That was a status I wished to preserve. As far as my neighbors knew, I was just an Air Force guy. Even if they saw me in uniform, they still didn't know exactly what I did while I was gone. It wasn't uncommon to see Air Force uniforms in Las Vegas, since there were two bases in the area.

I also understood the need for publicity. Good press sells a product, and every service was battling for a bigger slice of the budget. But the reporters were broadcasting from our front door. I wondered why they didn't do the interview at a more generic place. Maybe it was my intelligence training, but I never understood giving up information, even basic stuff, when it wasn't necessary.

Do the interview. Explain the aircraft. But don't stand right in front of the building where we went to work. Go out to the gate or something.

The 15th's squadron commander emerged from the turnstile dressed in a green flight suit and a big smile. The lights came on and the reporter asked a question. We turned away as he started to talk. There was nothing we could do but make sure we didn't get caught in the shot.

But as I walked out to my car, I thought back to the two runners in Iraq. They'd had no idea we were watching and they'd had no chance of escape. On the flip side, I knew they also had no way of knowing where we were as we controlled the Predator circling above. We had anonymity and security that other units didn't have. We were never face-to-face with the enemy, but when the lights from the camera went on, I was sure the enemy knew where we lived and where we worked now. It was one thing to say we were based at Nellis or Creech, but another to show exactly where on the base. For the first time, I felt like we were in harm's way.

CHAPTER 7

Pattern of Life

The motorcycle raced down the dirt road.

The HUD cross hairs sped across the terrain to keep up with it. There were two men on the bike. Our target, an al Qaeda captain, was riding on the back behind his driver. Like almost all of our targets, he wore the traditional clothes of the region and had a thick black beard.

Our intelligence analysts believed he was rising fast in al Qaeda's chain of command. His current focus had been to control the group's US and UK operations. He fled to the area after pushing his luck with the local government.

Our analysts believed he knew where Bin Laden and Ayman Muhammed Rabie al-Zawahiri, al Qaeda's second-in-command, were hiding. If Osama bin Laden was the head of the snake, the Captain was the fangs.

The driver darted in and out of traffic as the target clung to the back of the bike. Periodically, we passed coordinates to the JOC, who sent them to the guys on the ground. The twists and bends in the road made tracking him a challenge.

We'd been trying to link the Captain to Osama bin Laden for months.

The 17th was now at full strength in the Nellis compound and we had started to pursue midlevel al Qaeda leadership.

Someone high in the government shifted our pursuit away from Bin Laden and al-Zawahiri, an Egyptian physician. They both had run to ground, and that made it difficult to recruit sources. We kept our ears open for tips and information, but we no longer combed the mountains looking for them.

Al, one of the JOC's managers, changed our focus to the next link in the chain of command. Over the next year, we hunted mid-level facilitators and even Bin Laden's main courier, Abu Ahmed al-Kuwaiti. The courier would eventually lead American intelligence officials to Bin Laden's compound in Abbottabad, Pakistan.

But at the time, we were still years away from finding him. What we did know was that al Qaeda facilitators operated in the mountains around northeast Afghanistan. Most of the fighters fought there alongside their Taliban brothers. The Taliban and al Qaeda weren't really allies. That was a relationship forced upon them by the Americans.

The hunt started months before I had the Captain in my cross hairs.

We gathered in the squadron briefing room where intelligence briefed us on the mission change. Maps of the target area showed a shift from the region on which we had been concentrating. We were headed into the Hindu Kush to find the Captain and use him to lead us up to the next link in the chain.

The next day, I was in the cockpit. I noticed the change in terrain on my first flight. I marveled at the mountains. Deep valleys cut through the region like unhealed wounds. Small settlements spotted the terraced slopes at odd intervals. Dirt roads snaked through and around the ruined landscape, providing the only means of contact with the villages. Seasonal rains or snows frequently cut off areas for weeks or months.

I surveyed the ground as we slowly passed over Kunar Province. Houses started to expand in our HUDs to uncomfortable proportions. The land rose to meet us and we had to maintain an altitude of twenty-five thousand feet to minimize the chance of alerting people on the ground to our presence. We had to be careful. The sound of the aircraft engine would give us away.

The little pink Predator icon on my tracker merged with my target indicator. It was well after sunset when we got to the area and started our search. The small village was high in the mountains. A low-level facilitator was supposed to meet with a courier after sunset. We knew from experience that his meetings usually happened around ten P.M. and concluded by midnight.

I checked the HUD against the satellite imagery. The photo was taken from about three hundred miles up, which gave us only the God's-eye view. We flew to the side of the village and saw only the sides of the buildings.

"Tony," I called into my mic once I was convinced of our location. "Wildfire is in the target area."

"Roger," came the immediate response. Tony was sitting LNO for us at the JOC.

The HUD jerked from side to side as Jantz, the sensor operator, searched the village for the target house. I set up a circle around the target area to help him. The top-down photo left a lot to be desired. We both searched for identifiable features like the house's fire pit, water storage, trail, or animal pen.

"Sir, is that it?" Jantz said.

I compared the imagery displayed on my side monitor. The features seemed to match.

"Looks right," I said.

Jantz and I had flown together a lot over the past month. I was in charge of the squadron's standards, so it was my job to meet all the new pilots and sensor operators and give them the welcome brief. Jantz graduated the training course on a Friday and got his welcome brief on Saturday. That Sunday, he was flying his first real combat mission. Ours is the only Air Force career field where the day after you graduate training you're in combat.

Jantz wanted the weekend off. He'd earned it after five months of training for the war. We needed the bodies. He made it a point to let folks know he didn't care for the early report. I finally had to pull one of our senior sergeants aside and get him to counsel Jantz.

Since I was the senior guy flying that day, I had to fly with the problem child. It is common practice to pair a new crew member with an experienced counterpart. That way a new sensor, like Jantz, could learn the tricks of the trade from a "graybeard." I didn't mind being labeled a graybeard since I enjoyed teaching, but I was annoyed to see myself paired with him at first.

For the month I flew with him, I challenged him with difficult practice shots against moving targets. The first couple of shots were rough, but he quickly developed a rhythm in the seat, a sense of where he was and what needed to be done without spoiling a shot. He excelled to the point that I wanted him in the seat if we had to shoot.

He was also good company in the cockpit. Our missions were often boring, so we'd all become skilled at staying engaged. Jantz and I played hangman on the whiteboards mounted to the walls or just talked about his upbringing in Oregon and his wife. He was recently married.

We were less rank conscious in flight. It started in training. We pushed the enlisted sensor operators to forget that the pilots were officers. We were just "two crew dogs" doing a job. I didn't want the sensors to be afraid to point out something if I was doing it wrong. That kind of rapport was key, especially when it was time to shoot.

Jantz and I had an epic game of six degrees of separation. After setting up to watch the house, we started to play. He worked hard to stump me. The game was simple. He'd pick two actors—in our game one of them didn't have to be Kevin Bacon—and I'd link them within six movie roles.

"Arnold Schwarzenegger and Alyssa Milano," Jantz said.

I almost laughed.

"*Commando,*" I replied.

It took me less than a second to come up with the 1985 cult-classic action thriller. Schwarzenegger played Milano's father, who had to rescue her after she was kidnapped by mercenaries. The plot of the movie didn't matter as much as the action.

"What movie?" Jantz said.

He looked bewildered. He'd never seen the movie and had no idea both actors were in it. Jantz, born well after the movie was released, didn't know Milano was a child actor. He was about to call foul until he typed the title into the computer.

Jantz never stumped me. I guess all those nights watching bad eighties movies paid off.

The games kept us mentally engaged. I could monitor the feed and the radio while we played. A shift could last eight hours, so we brought water and snacks into the GCS despite regulations banning both.

Before one flight, I stopped on the way at Boston Market and got a dinner tray. It was during the NBA play-offs and I had the game on one monitor and the tray propped on the table near the keyboard. The Predator was on autopilot orbiting a target. The radios were silent and the chat room was quiet. I was a few forkfuls into my dinner when the commander poked his head into the GCS. I watched as his eyes tracked down to my dinner and then up to the monitor showing the game. He just shook his head and closed the door.

It was common to eat in the AWACS and other heavy aircraft in the Air Force, but the GCS was governed by OSHA regulations. The federal agency tasked with workplace safety said the cockpit was a computer station on the ground. Under their regulations, food or drink was banned in the cockpit.

OSHA didn't take into account that a person at a regular workstation could get up to take a break. We could not, due to the need to maintain positive control of the aircraft. Food was a necessity over an eight-hour flight, just like in any other cockpit. There were some times that empty bottles were filled in flight too.

There was another problem. I had failed to exhibit the professionalism the commander expected.

The next day, we got a memo from the commander reminding us not to eat in the GCS. That didn't stop us from taking in snacks and bottles of water and soda. But I never stopped at Boston Market for takeout again before my shift.

Jantz and I didn't have time to eat or play games on this mission.

Mountains and ridges obscured the target from certain directions. I flew the mission by hand. I needed the extra maneuverability so I could keep the target in sight. At times, I had to edge closer to the target so I could look straight down and see the road. I couldn't do that with the autopilot limiting my bank angle to avoid a stall.

Wind was also an issue.

It was the change of the seasons, and this high in the mountains, drafts could reach one hundred miles an hour or more. The wind could push you miles off target if you weren't careful. I kept the Predator in a tight bank angle to minimize the effects of the wind.

We set up to the north of the house, where we could see the winding road that led into the village. We needed to keep the approach in sight or risk missing the courier's arrival. The house was perched precariously at the edge of a terrace. Thick wood beams supported the sections of the mud house that hung over the side. The loss of a single truss could spell disaster. I briefly imagined the house slowly toppling over the edge and landing on the house below and starting a cascading effect that would eliminate the entire village.

Tony, sitting LNO, shook me out of my strange daydream.

"Hang right there," he said. "The analysts want you to watch for activity."

"Roger," I said.

The waiting was the worst part. I checked the clock. It was ten P.M. The meeting should start soon, give or take half an hour. Everyone in the region ran on his own clock. We spent the next several hours flying a ground track that resembled a bent Q-tip. It wasn't difficult, but it required a lot of concentration to keep track of the variable winds. I was happy the house wasn't moving or it would have been impossible.

The compound remained dark. The only bright spot in the IR feed was the fire pit. It had long since faded into the background. We saw a dog run around the compound's courtyard area for a while. It beat a quick retreat into the warm house as the temperature rapidly dropped.

I checked the clock. It was midnight now and there was still no sign of the courier. Terrorists changed their tactics with frustrating regularity, but one consistency was the timing of meetings. They didn't happen after midnight. The courier was not coming today.

He showed up a couple of nights later, when another crew was flying over the house, and they followed him to a new safe house in the valley. Within a couple of weeks we had followed the courier and mapped out an intricate network of contacts and potential targets. At one point a crew spotted the courier talking with a man on a motorcycle.

We knew from other sources that the Captain rode the motorcycle. It was allegedly the only one in the province. He used it to make his rounds. The Captain was an arrogant man, convinced that he was untouchable. He figured the Predators were far to the south chasing ghosts. The main American force was far to the west tied up with the Taliban.

He was safe.

Our next missions focused on the bike. We couldn't identify the Captain yet. Facial recognition was difficult using the targeting pod. We needed to get too close to get a clear picture of a face, and secrecy outweighed confirmation. While we kept watch, intelligence officers on the ground worked their sources trying to confirm that the Captain was the man riding on the back of the motorcycle. Within days we received confirmation.

Next started an awful sixty days of trailing him across the

countryside. We watched and monitored as he started his rounds early in the morning, just after sunrise. He visited the same houses in the region, stopping for just a few minutes to pass messages. We flew circles around him, always prepared to strike if called.

I climbed into the box a few weeks after my first mission and flew the Predator to his house. I'd been doing it for the better part of a month, and I already knew what I'd see during my shift. Around seven A.M., the Captain's driver showed up on the motorcycle. The Captain was already awake. He rose around dawn and ate breakfast while he waited. He was punctual, rising at the same time every day.

The cross hairs in my HUD were fixed on the pair as they bounced down the dirt tracks to the paved roads and his daily route. The first stop was a gas station. This was a typical corner filling station, not unlike its American counterparts, minus the overhang above the pumps. An orange-and-white circular sign identified it. Like the other Pakistani buildings, this one was walled in with two metal gates that were opened during business hours.

The gas station stop took five minutes. We made one circle above him as he dismounted the bike, went into the office, and emerged promptly at the five-minute mark. He never bought gas.

I knew his next stop was a facilitator's house nearby. I turned the Predator and headed eastbound into the valley. I flew close enough to keep the Captain in sight, but I already knew where he was headed. The house was modest, with a gate and small court-yard. As he had at the gas station, he hopped off the bike and went straight inside, leaving his driver to tend to the bike.

I looked at the clock. We had thirty minutes to wait. I put the Predator into an orbit and settled in. Half an hour later, the Captain was back on the bike and headed to his last stop of the day. This third stop was a small shack on a dirt road. We could see him in the

HUD sitting on the back of the bike, a notebook in his hands. I knew from experience that he wasn't getting off the bike. Instead, we watched his contact walk up the dirt driveway and take a pouch of papers or money from the Captain.

The contact stood at the end of the driveway and watched as the bike sped off. This activity happened every day until dinnertime. The Captain didn't meet anyone at his home. Whatever he wanted accomplished was spread out around the world via those couriers and facilitators.

While I followed the Captain, a second Predator watched his house. His wife left at midmorning, the same time every day, to go to the market. The kids, those old enough to attend school, walked to the madrassa down the road. His wife returned a couple of hours later with the evening meal. She did the laundry and hung it to dry by midafternoon. Then she stoked the outdoor fire pit and prepared dinner in the kitchen.

After about thirty days, we could look at a clock and tell where the Captain would be. Even a glance at a feed in the ops cell could tell us the location without looking at a grid reference. We didn't need annotated charts and maps to give us a sense of where he was going.

We knew his every move.

After tracking him for forty-five days, we knew the exact time he arrived at any station along his daily route. If, for example, we lost him in weather, we would not bother trying to relocate him. We calculated the time he was missing and shifted the camera to a new spot just to see the little motorcycle flash into view. If weather delayed a launch by hours, which happened sometimes, we could go to a specific location knowing he would show within minutes of our arrival.

He couldn't fart without us knowing about it. For a total of sixty days, we watched the same thing over and over again. But the mission wore on our nerves. There was no variety, no new targets, and no disruption of his routine. For the first time, I started to dread flying. I was becoming a zombie. It was like stamping an endless line of widgets at a factory. I knew before the chill of the GCS hit me what I'd see or do. I'd either track the bike or sit over his house and watch his wife do chores.

For the past sixty days, the daily brief was always the same too, which only added to the drudgery of the job. Imagine listening to the same song every day at the same time. It got to the point where I could lip-synch the whole brief. We sat in chairs around a conference table as the intelligence guys went over the PowerPoint slides and maps of his suspected but always accurate route. At the end of the first month, some joker in the intelligence shop overlaid an animated icon of a guy on a motorcycle blitzing around the map. A photo of the Captain's face was pasted to the rider's head. The first time I saw it, I chuckled. It was a nice break from the monotony of the brief.

Then things changed one day.

The morning brief was different. The cheesy graphic the intelligence shop had developed wasn't there. A concept of operation, or CONOP, brief replaced it. We weren't watching any longer. Today, the JOC intended to roll up the Captain.

I could feel a tingle of excitement shoot through my body. Finally, we were ready to act. I felt alert and engaged as the intelligence staff explained the plan. A team on the ground was going to ambush him outside the village during his daily run. I knew the village. It was seared into my mental map, since I'd flown over it for weeks now.

"Squirrel," the major from the intelligence shop said. "You're primary."

It was my mission to track him on his rounds and make sure he ended up in the right place. If for some reason he changed his route, I would track him to the new location.

It felt strange to be flying what we hoped was our last mission against this target. There was an intimacy about following someone for months. We spent so much time with the family that I knew what the Captain's kids looked like and what roads they took to school. I knew how his wife did the family laundry and where she shopped for dinner. In the back of my mind, I knew the Captain was a terrorist and plotted to kill Americans. But it was hard not to see him and his family as very human. He wasn't a James Bond villain plotting from a massive mountain hideout. But his job was to kill Americans. On a visceral level, I wanted to return the favor. This guy was responsible for planning attacks. He was the very reason for our presence in Central Asia.

A few hours after I took control of the Predator, I was high above him as he dodged between cars. As usual, he was on time and on the correct route.

"Wildfire Eight One on target," I announced to the JOC.

"Copy," Tony said.

As I flew lazy S-turns to stay with the slower bike, I secretly wished he would change his schedule and take another route. Based on the brief, the team didn't have a good backup plan. If the Captain escaped, I was confident the JOC would give me the thumbs-up to shoot.

We were approaching his next turn and I hoped he'd go straight.

"Right turn," the sensor operator said into the mic and passed the coordinates.

I checked his reference against the readout on the HUD. He was on track.

"Wildfire, target on route Yellow."

Yellow was the color of the predicted route overlaid on the CONOP map. The Captain was dressed in the baggy shirt and pants of the region and a wool Afghan *pakol* hat pulled over his dark hair. I could see the tails of his shirt flapping in the breeze as the motorcycle raced along the dirt road. He was headed straight into the trap. I cursed his arrogance and predictability. I really wanted a shot at him.

As he made the last turn, I could see the impromptu checkpoint in my HUD. It was in a remote area far enough between stops, or villages, that no one would miss him until it was far too late. Hidden on the side of the road was another team. They were disguised as locals traveling along the road. After he passed, they blocked the road with a barrier.

The road was no bigger than two lanes, with broken asphalt and no markings. Cars drove up and down, and people with bikes and carts traveled along the shoulder. The Captain didn't notice the checkpoint behind him.

"Wildfire, target passed first checkpoint."

It was only a matter of minutes before the team would spring the trap. I focused on the HUD and made sure we kept the cross hairs on the target. If he suspected something, he wasn't showing it. Just ahead of him, I could see the team huddled near a graveyard. They were hidden under head-to-toe burqas. At a glance, they looked like a group of women visiting the family plot.

When he got close, I watched as the team rushed out from the graveyard and surrounded the bike. They had their pistols and sub-machine guns drawn. The Captain's driver turned and attempted to flee. On the back of the bike, it looked like the Captain was trying to destroy his notebook. In the HUD, I could see the backup team from the block position close off the road and start running toward the bike. From more than twenty thousand feet, it looked like a baseball rundown.

The Captain leapt from the bike and ducked into a wheat field. The two teams took off after him. I could see some of the men ditching their disguises.

"Stay with the target," I said.

I reported the Captain's location and direction to the JOC.

The cross hairs followed his path into the field, finally catching up to him as he ran. He made it across the field and dashed into a one-story mud house.

"Target is in the house," I reported to the JOC.

The response I wanted was authorization to strike the house. I almost spun up my Hellfire missiles just in case.

"Stay on the house," Tony said.

"Roger."

On the ground, the teams surrounded the house. One man crept to the front door and tossed a tear gas canister inside. Gas started to billow out of the door and the windows. Seconds later, the Captain stumbled out and surrendered. We stayed on station for a few minutes before peeling off.

On my way home that night, the Captain's capture was on the news. When I heard the report, I had to smile. The next morning, I was excited to be back at work. The halls were buzzing about the capture of the Captain. It was another small victory for Predator.

It was nice to see two months of work take a terrorist off the street. But as much as I had wanted a shot at him, it was even better that the Captain was alive.

According to reports, he spilled his guts to the interrogators.

The intelligence shop gave an out brief from the operation. Those of us on shift at the time attended. I sat next to Mongo. The brief ran as expected. Intel issued a laundry list of actions from our aircraft, supporting units, how the roll-up went down, and finally results.

Intel claimed that the Captain told his interrogators that he saw and heard us following him. Evidently, each morning he would go outside for his morning constitutional and watch the sky for his followers. To the west, every day, our wings reflected against the morning's rays. A bright flash of light let the Captain know we were there. Unbeknownst to us, we were directly stroking his ego, since he believed he was untouchable.

The revelation set me back. We had been so convinced of our stealth that we had shown our hand to the enemy. While we played games, he watched us and reveled in the attention he received. His arrogance grew epically, its flames stoked by our miscalculation.

In the end, I didn't know who was monitoring whom. The enemy had stared back.

"Not much we could do about it," I said to Mongo.

Mongo agreed, saying, "There was no way we could get to the other side of his house."

All pilots learn in training that flying with the sun at their backs makes it hard to spot them in the sky. In the mornings, we tried to set up orbit east of a target so he'd have to squint to see us. It didn't change our sound signature. For that we had other techniques. Unfortunately, the limited airspace forced us to fly west of the target. That made us easy to detect, even if the Captain couldn't hear us.

"I think we just got the topic for our next training day," I said.

Every pilot made a note of the mistake, because the Captain was only the start. We vowed the Captain's replacement would have a more difficult time finding us.

CHAPTER 8

Strike

The weather forecast over the Afghanistan-Pakistan border looked like a Rorschach diagram. Winter had thrown out one more storm before finally giving way to spring.

It was my Saturday shift and I knew for the next eight hours I'd be fighting storms with a HUD full of gray clouds. It was with that vision that I stomped out into the warm sun of Nellis Air Force Base. On my way to the GCS with Jantz, I wished the weather was as good over the target. I knocked twice on the door and got two knocks in return. Securing the door behind me, I waited a second to let my eyes adjust to the darkened room.

Mongo was in the pilot's seat.

"Squirrel!" he crowed.

"Hey, Mongo," I said. "Any news?"

Mongo shook his head. A quick glance at the HUD told me the whole story. Everything was white or gray. It was impossible to see the countryside.

"No," he said. "I haven't seen the ground all day and the target's been quiet. Nothing in the chat room either."

My heart sank. It looked like another dull day. After the last mission, our focus had shifted to the Facilitator, a known planner and bomb maker. After the Captain's capture, the Facilitator was the next man up. We'd spent the past six weeks mapping his pattern of life. We set up orbits near his last reported location based on intelligence and waited for him to do something.

The Facilitator was expanding his operations and the JOC officials were concerned that he would soon go into hiding.

But tracking the Facilitator was harder.

His house was near Afghanistan's rugged border. It was a four-hour flight from our home base to his location. We couldn't maintain twenty-four-hour coverage. We had only two GCSs but needed three aircraft in order to maintain a "constant stare" over the target. To accomplish this, we would have to let one aircraft fly uncontrolled back to base. No pilot wanted to do this, because if the uncontrolled aircraft crashed, it would mean the end of someone's career.

Thankfully, "General" John was in charge of the JOC that day. His solution provided the right balance. The squadron used its two cockpits to fly to and over the target and released the returning aircraft to fly home alone. This way, we could fly one aircraft over target with the first GCS. The other GCS would control an aircraft en route to the target. The crews would sever the link to the third Predator, and it would fly itself on autopilot to the landing and recovery unit in Kandahar.

As soon as the JOC and the 17th leadership signed off on the plan, we set up a steady stream of aircraft to the target area.

While the Facilitator's movements didn't adhere to a pattern, his meetings did. He concluded each meeting with a phone call to his wife. So he had a habit of walking outside. After the call, he disappeared for the night. We'd watch the house until the next day, when he'd emerge for his next round of meetings and travel.

We were motivated after the success of the previous mission, but after thirty days we sagged a little in the seats. *Groundhog Day* weighed heavily on us again as we tracked him each day. The tedium of following the same actions became mind-numbing until I climbed into the seat to start my Saturday shift.

"All right, I'll take it from here," I said, patting Mongo on the shoulder.

We swapped seats and I took five minutes to run a few status checks. Mongo and his sensor headed to the back of the GCS, on their way out. I happened to glance at the chat room as Mongo hit the switch to unlatch the door.

Written in red: *Spin up your missiles.*

"Son of a bitch!"

Mongo and Jantz looked at me.

"What?" they said in unison.

"AGM-114 prelaunch checklist. Go," I said. "Mongo, you're safety observer."

Mongo sent his sensor back to the ops cell, then rolled up a chair behind the crew seats. Safety observers were required in the 17th to ensure that all shots were executed according to the rules of engagement. It never hurt to have another set of eyes to make sure we did everything perfectly.

I felt the adrenaline race through my veins as we ran the

checklists. I looked at the HUD and made sure I wasn't going to hit the other Predator in the area. The missiles flashed a "green-for-go" icon. All I needed was clearance and a target.

"Hey, Pusher," I said into my mic.

"Go ahead," he responded.

Pusher was the LNO deployed to the JOC. He was a career special operations helicopter pilot recently transferred into the Predator program.

"What's going on?"

"Target's active," Pusher said. "Looks like he's sending the execute orders for strikes. I'll get back to you."

I checked the HUD. A solid deck of clouds below the aircraft extended out to the horizon. I couldn't see the ground at all.

"Okay, man," I said. "You know I can't see anything right now, right?"

"Yeah, we're working that."

The adrenaline faded into a calm born of resignation and frustration. An essential skill in any military organization is the ability to hurry up and wait. After getting the order to spin up our missiles, we waited for the order to move for the next three hours. Mongo sat quietly in the back of the GCS as Jantz and I dodged clouds, rain, and ice. We had our hands full just keeping the bird in the air.

The thick, layered cloud decks meant icing. Temperatures remained frigid at altitude even if the terrain far below had thawed. We still couldn't see the ground and I wasn't sure how much longer I could stay airborne before the threat of ice sent us home. The Predator had no way of de-icing.

I kept pinging Pusher for information. I wanted to start thinking ahead if I was asked to attack. I'd need to find a path through the clouds, and I figured it would be smart to start finding a way without the stress of setting up the shot.

But Pusher didn't have anything for me.

"Yeah, we're working that," he said over and over again.

Jantz was scanning the clouds when he spotted a hole. When we got to it, we could see all the way to the ground. In our cross hairs was a man walking in a field and animatedly talking on what appeared to be a phone. My eye flicked up to the tracker above the HUD to check to make sure the coordinates matched.

This had to be the Facilitator. Jantz tried to zoom in closer, but the clouds closed in again and we lost visual. The weather just wasn't cooperating for an air strike.

"Hey, Squirrel," Pusher said. "We don't have a lot of time."

"I can't help the clouds," I said. "How's the checklist?"

We still didn't have clearance to engage, even if I could see long enough to shoot.

"Working it," Pusher said, his familiar refrain.

Of course, I thought sarcastically.

"ROE is done, just awaiting final approval," Pusher said a minute later. "I need you to get below the clouds."

That shocked me. ROE complete meant only the final decision authority remained. Right now I guessed staffers were calling the White House for the go-ahead.

"The weather is kind of in the way," I said as I searched for another opening in the clouds.

"It's bought," Pusher said. "We got you clearance. We need you down now before he gets away."

"Copy," I said.

I pushed the stick forward and slid into the cloud bank. The move went against everything I'd been taught, but the JOC was afraid the Facilitator might go to ground. After six weeks, I was willing to push it a little.

A thin layer of ice coated the aircraft. The delay from the satellite already made the aircraft hard to fly, but now the controls were even more sluggish. I hoped the air was warm enough below the clouds to melt the ice. No one spoke in the GCS as I concentrated on the HUD. My eye moved from gauge to gauge, checking my heading and altitude. It was tense and I could feel the stress in my jaw as I waited for the cloud cover to thin. I had no idea what to expect at the bottom of the cloud bank.

The Predator finally broke through the clouds, and a mountain filled my HUD. The slopes jutted upward into the overcast. I could clearly make out the scraggly brush on the slopes. The brush was not as far underneath as I would have preferred.

The canyon walls pressed in like a flytrap.

"Zoom out," I told Jantz, hoping that I could get a view of the terrain around me.

I glanced up at my tracker and saw some open space to my right side. I immediately put the Predator into a turn to stay in clear air while I looked for a route to the field. Jantz rotated the ball as we both looked for a path to the target. As we scanned, I checked the tracker.

"Over there," I said. "That canyon mouth."

A nearby canyon followed an arcing path directly to the field. It was our only chance, but once I started down the canyon I couldn't abort. There wasn't enough room to turn the aircraft around and I couldn't climb into the cloud bank for fear of crashing because of the ice. If we went down the canyon, we would have to overfly the target and burn it if we didn't shoot. I didn't want to waste six weeks of work.

"Squirrel, we need you to get closer to the target."

"Pusher," I said. "I can't. Terrain is blocking. I'm committed once I start in."

"Well, everyone in here is getting a little nervous," Pusher said, indicating the JOC ops room. "You are on the edge of the airspace."

I knew he was right. I had descended fairly far to the east to punch through the thinnest part of the cloud layer.

"I will do what I can, but I need clearance to get closer."

"Get closer," he said.

His persistence revealed the tension at the JOC.

Clouds flashed through my picture and I could see the brush close underneath as I turned to fly up the canyon. Just as I was turning inbound, I heard the door of the GCS open, and Alan, a more experienced sensor operator, walked up behind Jantz and me. The squadron commander maintained a shooter list, and new guys were never on it. Jantz was still too new to take such a critical shot.

Alan's arrival took me by surprise. I shot Jantz a look to stay put. Stew, sitting mission commander today, hadn't said anything to me about the change. Alan was a kid from somewhere in the Midwest, I think. He and his brother had joined the Air Force shortly after September 11. Now they both were Predator sensor operators. Alan had joined the 17th after training and had been with the squadron since the beginning.

I was frustrated. Flying in this weather was hard enough. Crew changes should have been coordinated with me well before we made the turn into the canyon. Changing a crew member just before the shot increased the chance of a miss.

"MCC, pilot," I called the squadron's mission commander.

"Go ahead," said Stew, speaking in his calm monotone.

"Sir," I said. "Why is Jantz being pulled?"

"Because I want Alan in the seat."

"Sir," I reasoned, "Jantz is spun up. We've got this wired. I don't think it's a good idea to swap sensors just before a run-in."

"Put Alan in the seat," Stew said.

The discussion was over. The squadron commander's word was always final. This was the one time aircraft commanders did not have the final say. I watched Jantz unplug his headset and climb out of the seat. I will never forget the look of anger, betrayal, and loss of confidence on his face.

I looked away and refocused on the mission. I put the Predator into a turn and waited for Alan to get comfortable. There was no way I was going to fly the canyon until Alan was briefed on the target.

Alan was a small, blond kid with delicate features. He looked as if he still belonged in junior high instead of in the military. He was eager to improve his skills and we talked a lot about tactics. When he wasn't flying, he was quiet and never brought a lot of attention to himself. But he was respected in the squadron as one of the most competent sensors we had.

Alan had watched the video feed play out from the op cell, so he just needed the target brief and a minute to ready the controls. Alan gave me a thumbs-up, and I guided the Predator into the canyon. We were seven miles out when Pusher came back over the intercom.

"Squirrel, you are cleared to engage," he said. "How copy?"

I couldn't answer for fear of losing focus on the canyon. Mongo jumped on the radio.

"Copy that, Pusher, cleared to engage."

The Facilitator was still on the phone. The call was key. When the Facilitator hung up, he'd get back in the van and disappear into the village. We had to strike now. Mongo patted me on the shoulder.

"Okay, Squirrel, the checklist is yours."

"Copy," I said.

I felt a sudden calm descend over me. The stress of waiting for approval was gone. Now I had only to concentrate on putting the Hellfire missile on target. Alan, the new sensor operator, rolled the ball so that it was pointed right at the man.

I banked left and angled the aircraft deeper into the canyon. Because of the shot, I had the targeting pod displayed on my HUD. I couldn't see ahead of the aircraft to see the weather. I knew the clouds were low. Wisps of white cotton flitted through the targeting pod's picture.

Canyon flying was one of the things most pilots think would be cool until they do it. Air Force history is littered with the wreckage of men who flew too close to the rocky walls. From day one, pilots are cautioned not to fly into a canyon since they don't know what's on the other side. This canyon was really a valley, I told myself. It was the only way I could fight off the claustrophobic feeling as we got deeper and deeper into it.

I concentrated on the tracker, watching the ever-tightening contour lines of the chart. The walls were growing steeper and closer. My eye skipped from the HUD to the tracker and back. Scrub brush flashed close by and my natural impulse was to climb. I couldn't do that because of the clouds. Just when I thought the walls were closing in on me, the mouth of the canyon emptied into a plain. We could see the van waiting for the Facilitator. He was still on the phone and disappeared behind the van as we cleared the canyon.

I turned to the left, hugging the canyon wall.

"What are you doing?" Pusher asked.

"I need to get to the other side," I explained. "To see the target."

"We don't have time."

He was right. The Facilitator appeared to fiddle with his phone. I turned back and pointed at the van. The Facilitator wandered back to the front of the vehicle. The HUD in front of me became my world as I looked at the man. He walked at a slow, relaxed pace, unaware of my approach. The pixels on the screen sharpened and I could make out the folds in his clothes.

"You ready, Alan?" I asked.

"Yes, sir."

We had only moments before entering the launch window.

"One minute, laser on."

Alan pressed a couple of buttons and the aircraft laser fired. I reviewed the HUD. A bright red "Laser Firing" flashed prominently. Satisfied, I focused on the target. The Facilitator gave no indication that he heard us. I wondered how he didn't hear the Predator. I figured the hum of the prop was echoing across the valley. He must have been very confident in the bad weather to actually ignore his surroundings.

"Thirty seconds," I intoned without inflection. When I reviewed the tapes later, I was surprised how dead my voice was.

Pusher broke in over the radio.

"We need you to hurry, Squirrel," he said. "He's almost gone."

"Shut up, Pusher," I said.

The target showed large on our screen now. We were almost to the minimum range when he disappeared behind the passenger side of the van. I selected both missiles to maximize the frag pattern.

"Twenty seconds."

I checked my instruments. My alignment was good. I was still in the weapons engagement zone. I pressed and held the "Release to Consent" button. "Ready to Launch Both Missiles" flashed on the HUD.

Clouds flashed through my screen. I prayed that the ceiling wasn't dropping. I couldn't go any lower. As we sped toward the Facilitator, the Predator broke into clear air.

"Ten seconds."

Alan flexed in his seat. The target was so close the camera became extremely sensitive to motion. Any adjustment was overly exaggerated. Alan kept the cross hairs locked on the al Qaeda leader, tracking him as he moved around the van.

"Three, two, one . . ."

I pulled the trigger. Twin white-hot flashes erupted into the HUD as the missiles left the rails and raced toward the target.

"Rifle," I said, indicating I'd fired the missiles.

The Hellfire's icons disappeared from my HUD. I watched the first missile's trail as it went into the clouds following Alan's laser marker. I continued the countdown.

"Five, four . . ."

The Facilitator's head snapped up. His cell phone was still pressed against his right ear, but he'd heard the twin sonic booms of the missiles. In the HUD, it seemed like he was looking right at us. His gaze was locked in the targeting pod for a brief moment before he ran.

"Follow the runner," I said.

Alan pressed the stick and the camera's cross hairs started to move. The Facilitator ran for a nearby gully. It was his only chance at cover. The cross hairs jerked to life and lagged the man by a few feet. He got three steps before the first missile entered the camera's field of view, arcing to follow the moving laser spot.

A split second after I saw the exhaust trail, the missile detonated in a blinding flash that whited out our screen. About a second later, another almost imperceptible flash blotted out the screen again. It took a few seconds for the HUD to clear as the heat of the explosions subsided.

"Cease laser, safe laser," I said to Alan.

Alan shut off the laser and engaged the safety. I returned the weapons panel to safe as well.

"Okay, guys," Pusher said. "Let's get some BDA."

Pusher wanted us to conduct a battle damage assessment to confirm that the missile had killed the Facilitator.

Alan was already scanning the wreckage. Smoke still hung in the air. The van was a scorched chassis and engine block. The missiles had vaporized the rest. Streaks of debris radiated out of the impact crater near the van like compass points. I studied the debris field, looking for a body.

"Zoom out," I ordered. "Look for the target."

Alan pulled out. I noticed something dark about thirty yards from the shredded van.

"What's that?" I pointed at my monitor.

Alan leaned over to see where my finger indicated.

"A body?" he said.

His cross hairs moved over to the spot I marked.

"Guys, we need to find the target," Pusher said.

"I think we found him," I said. "Under cross hairs now."

"You sure?"

"Yeah," I said. "It's the only thing around here hot enough to be a body."

The Facilitator's sightless eyes stared up at us as we passed directly overhead. His body was burned and unrecognizable. The driver, a regional warlord, was so badly mangled that local authorities identified him by association.

"Pusher," I said. "We'll climb back up to altitude."

I wanted to get to clear air and away from the ground.

"Uh, you guys are cleared to RTB"—return to base, Pusher said. "We have to vacate the airspace."

"Copy."

We climbed out and headed back to base. The weather remained bad, so we rotated the targeting pod in a circle to ensure that no storms were building around us. On each rotation, we paused on the empty rails, naked without their missiles.

In a way, we were happy we took out the target. We had had our chance, which few others got, and I was able to fulfill my promise to make a difference in the war.

When the landing team took control of the Predator, Alan and I swapped out with a new crew. Before I drove home, I stopped by the office to draft an after action report. The paperwork after a shot took a couple of hours to complete. While I worked, some of my squadron mates stopped in to talk about the mission. It made a long day a bit more exhausting.

When we shot, part of our mission commander checklist was to call the chaplain. He was present following the after action report to serve as a counselor, if necessary. I passed him in the ops cell on my way out. I didn't think I needed to talk with him. I'd seen this stuff before. I did point him toward Alan, just in case.

It was after dark when I pulled into traffic and headed back toward the lights of Las Vegas. My daily metamorphosis on Interstate 215 from combat aviator to normal civilian started after I cleared the gate.

Each day was the same. Wake up, complete the morning routine, and start the long, forty-five-minute drive to work. En route, I changed my mental state to that of someone capable of killing another human being without thought, hesitation, or remorse. The return trip home was worse. I had to remove myself from the war. The easiest days were the ones when nothing happened.

The days drenched in blood remained difficult. How many convoys did I have to watch get hit by Improvised Explosive Devices (IEDs)? I once watched helplessly as Taliban fighters executed suspected spies because the rules of engagement didn't let us defend them.

But that didn't make it easier when the face of your enemy was staring back at you in high-definition. No other pilots got to see the target like we did. Most fighter pilots dropped only a couple of times on a deployment, some not at all. When they did hit a target, they had weeks or months remaining in theater to come to terms with their actions.

Fighter pilots also rarely saw the whole engagement. They just got the call and put bombs on target. The closest they got to the fight was strafing runs and the occasional flash from the bomb or missile as it passed their windscreen. Their proximity to death and violence stirred their blood, but the images in their targeting pods were tiny and fuzzy compared to our high-def pods, keeping them remote to the effects on the ground. Our targeting pods not only showed us everything, but also lingered over the carnage, searing the images into our brains. Our experience was far different from that of the fighters.

I was almost home when it hit me. Sitting at a traffic light, I was overtaken by the idea that I'd taken a life. It wasn't the first one, but this one stuck with me because of the intimacy of it. My other shots were in defense of troops under fire. That made sense to me, and they were nameless fighters, targets with guns aiming at my brothers-in-arms.

But this one was different.

The engagement was never a "him or me" scenario. There was no way the Facilitator could harm me. I had all the power. He also wasn't shooting at American troops at the time. He was on the phone with his wife. I knew his name. I'd followed his every move for more than a month.

One of the biggest misconceptions surrounding the RPA community is that the aircraft allows us some distance from the killing, since we're thousands of miles away. The opposite is true. We are too close. We know too much, and when it is time to shoot, we can zoom in until our target fills the screen. Because we are not face-to-face and our lives are not in danger, we can't tell ourselves it was either us or them. It was never us, and they had no chance. There was coldness to the way we killed, but it never lacked humanity: At the end of the day, the pilots and sensor operators took the images home.

The gravity of what I'd done overtook my emotions. My mind and body struggled to cope. I had just taken the one thing from two men that I could never return, no matter how hard I tried. I had ended their existence. Worse, I had removed one of God's creatures from His world.

What greater sin could I have committed?

I looked around at the cars stopped at the light. Most of the civilians had no idea what I'd done. They fiddled with their phones, listened to the radio, and impatiently waited for the light to turn green. The snarled commute was at the forefront of their minds, but my mind was back on the target.

I couldn't breathe. I couldn't think.

What had I done?

None of them had any idea they were mere feet from a killer, a man with fresh blood on his hands.

Only the sound of the engines revving as the light changed brought me back to reality. Traffic inched forward. I knew I had to get past this shock quickly. When I got home, I called a buddy from the squadron. He invited me over and I drove to his condo. I didn't want to sit at home alone.

When I got there, he already had a drink ready for me. We'd bagged a big target that would set enemy operations back. It was big news for the 17th and the Predator community in general. We were quickly making our mark as an effective counterterrorism tool.

But my mind was still fixed on the last image of the Facilitator. My shock wasn't unique. I was sure it wore on other pilots, but we didn't talk about it.

Savoring a cigar and a freshly mixed martini, I took a seat outside on his balcony. The lights of Las Vegas made it impossible to see any stars. We talked about the mission for a while. It felt better to tell the story. When my buddy brought out a new round, I made a toast to the man I killed.

I raised my glass.

We both drank to the death of an enemy.

This mission was complete, but I still had a job to do.

CHAPTER 9

Never Alone

The Predator Operations Center-N compound seemed deserted when I pushed through the security turnstile at the front gate to start my night shift.

I was working vampire hours. It was the time when the crazies went to Walmart and the party on the Las Vegas Strip kicked into high gear. I left the house around ten o'clock at night and I was in the seat by midnight. The day shift relieved me at eight the next morning.

I walked past the triple-wide trailer where we had office space and headed for the POC building. The trailers always made me laugh. We were located next to the building where the Air Force managed its massive "Red Flag" training exercises and across the road from the aggressor squadrons that flew against our fighter squadrons. Both were beautiful new facilities.

We got trailers and no money for upgrades. The RPA squadrons all worked out of trailers. It was a common theme at Nellis Air Force Base. Predators were the redheaded stepchildren of the base despite the media attention making us sound like we were the cover models.

The only brick-and-mortar building in the RPA compound was the operations center. The 15th and the 17th shared it. A single hallway separated the two squadrons and their independent ops cells. I walked through the steel door of the 15th's ops cell. A sign hung by the door read, "Welcome to the CENTCOM AOR." We were eight thousand miles from the Middle East. Yet the squadron wanted its crews to remember that inside the building, they were deployed to the US Central Command's area of responsibility.

The fastest way to get to my squadron, the 17th, was to cut through the 15th's operations center. But the shortcut was a matter of contention between the crews. The 15th held a grudge because they were not cleared to enter our operations center, but we could use their ops cell as a hallway.

We didn't do it to annoy them. We did it to avoid the only bathroom in the building. It always reeked. I went the long way, seeing no reason to antagonize them. The hall between the squadrons smelled like raw sewage as I walked toward the door to the 17th's ops cell. Apparently, the men's bathroom was backed up again. It wouldn't be fixed until the morning, if we were lucky.

I opened the door to the 17th's ops cell and was taken aback. This wasn't the sleepy room I expected. It was abuzz with activity. Mongo looked tense behind the MCC's massive desk. More tense than normal. He didn't shoot me his gap-toothed grin when I came into the ops cell. I looked at the screens on the wall to see what was going on with our birds. Both aircraft were on the ground. The weather map showed that an intense band of thunderstorms was pushing through southern Afghanistan. I couldn't tell why Mongo was so spun up.

"What's going on?" I asked.

"We just lost a SEAL team," Mongo said. "They'll update you in the briefing."

That got my attention. Any joke I had prepared died on my tongue.

His secure phone rang and he rushed to answer it. Mongo was MCC for the shift. He provided updated information on our missions and oversaw all of the 17th's flights. He spelled us for latrine breaks during our shifts and worked with the JOC when our LNO wasn't tied into the mission. He was the conductor of the orchestra.

I gathered up my paperwork for the flight and went into the mass briefing room to get our mission. Whatever happened would be mine to deal with once I was in the box. The air in the room was tight. No one joked. Everyone knew something bad had happened. The intelligence officer stood first. This was rare, as the outgoing MCC usually started the brief, but Mongo was still at the desk, tied to the secure phones.

"A SEAL team was overrun in the Kunar Province," the intelligence officer said. "The customer has cut us loose to support."

The customer—the JOC—was good about that. Tier-one targets were important. But supporting Americans trumped everything.

Four SEAL Team Five members were overrun on a surveillance and reconnaissance mission. The team had been sent into the Pech District of Afghanistan's Kunar Province ahead of a Marine operation to secure the area in advance of the Afghan parliamentary elections. The SEALs were identifying safe houses used by Ahmad Shah, a Taliban leader in the area. Once the houses were identified, SEALs and Marines would capture or kill him.

The team set up on the slopes of a mountain named Sawtalo Sar, twenty miles west of Asadabad. They were compromised by local goat herders and ambushed by Shah's fighters. After the SEALs were ambushed, a Taliban rocket-propelled grenade shot down a CH-47 with the quick reaction force coming to help. Eight SEALs and eight Army aviators were killed in the crash.

"Your mission," he said. "Find the survivors."

I raised my hand.

"What about CSAR?"

Combat Search and Rescue, or CSAR, were usually the first guys on scene. A quick reaction force usually went ahead of them. I wanted to get the lay of the land as we rushed to help. Kunar was almost five hours from our base in Kandahar. A fighter from Bagram could get there in thirty minutes.

The intelligence officer had anticipated the question.

"The QRF was shot down," he said. "Weather will tell you the rest."

The slide on the overhead projector changed to a map of Afghanistan overlaid with a massive red blob. Red was bad.

"A line of thunderstorms is pushing through the theater right now," the weather officer said. "Nothing is flying out of Bagram."

The radar picture showed a line of storms stretching southeast across our other major base in Kandahar. There was nothing in theater that could launch into that maelstrom. I still didn't understand our role. The Predator was an electric aircraft. Its avionics were not sealed against the weather. We avoided light rain for fear of shorting out the delicate circuitry and possibly killing the aircraft. Thunderstorms were a guaranteed kill.

"So where do we come in?" I asked.

"You're going to find a hole in the weather and find them," the intelligence officer said.

I started to object when Mongo walked in.

"You'll launch regardless," he said. "You'll be launching on a Chariot Directs. The Combined Air and Space Operations Center [CAOC] bought the aircraft."

We needed aircraft to break through a storm system without risking the lives of the pilot and crew. Finding SEAL Team Five was the goal and we were expendable.

Mongo patted me affectionately on the shoulder.

"You're the first one in for us."

"Great," I said.

There was nothing else I could say.

The 15th launched two lines as I did my preflight checks in the box. I watched Pacman's yellow icon and Roulette's red icon wind a path north as I passed Kandahar. Each icon twitched from side to side as if caught in an epileptic seizure.

I put the planes' HUD video feeds on my side monitors so I could see what they saw. A mass of boiling dark-gray clouds filled both screens. The feed flicked between day TV and IR cameras in a vain attempt to find a hole in the weather. IR could burn through haze to see a clear picture, but it sometimes missed ice. Day TV was less reliable but could show a downdraft that would toss the aircraft about and eventually tear it apart.

I was a few minutes behind Roulette and Pacman, so their feeds gave me a preview of what I faced. Both crews struggled to find a hole. I watched the monitors as the pilots wound through the clouds looking for a clear line. Roulette found a hole first. I heard him over the radio tell the controllers that he was going to try to make it through.

As he turned to fly through it, the clouds quickly closed around the Predator. Without the benefit of weather radar, the Predator had no chance. The pilot was lost. The HUD rolled as he tried to find a way out of the clouds. After a few minutes of nothing but gray clouds, he started to head back the way he'd come. It was the only airspace he knew.

The clouds had started to thin when a bright flash erupted on the monitor. The screen turned to static. "Loss of Clock, Loss of Data" flashed across the blank screen. The satellite link to the aircraft was severed after the lightning strike. After the shift, we reviewed the video. It was so good that the camera captured the light of a lightning flash a couple of frames before the current fried the aircraft.

Roulette was gone.

I watched the yellow icon work its way around the new cell. Pacman followed Roulette on a nearly identical course. She avoided the cell that had doomed Roulette and worked her way to the thinnest part of the line of storms. The thin line either meant a break in the clouds or the radar wasn't powerful enough to see through a thick area.

Pacman shot the gap and started toward the thinning clouds when the Predator's nose pitched up. The horizon bar was pinned against the top of the HUD. A couple of bursts of static flashed across the screen before the dreaded "Loss of Clock, Loss of Data" message appeared. The whole incident took about seven seconds.

I had seen this before. When a Predator was flying near a storm, ice built up on the aircraft. You couldn't see it. It just showed up. An attentive crew would do frequent weather sweeps to detect the lift-killing substance. Ice must have built up on Pacman's "angle of attack probe," which measured the aircraft's deck angle. If the nose rose too high, then the computer thought the aircraft was about to stall and would adjust pitch and power to correct it. When Pacman dipped into the cloud, ice forced the probe up, indicating a stall. The autopilot slammed the nose down, breaking the ice loose. The aircraft realized it was diving at full power and the autopilot pulled the nose up. The sudden g-force snapped the tail off and the aircraft disappeared.

Two down, one to go.

It was my turn.

I didn't have a better answer than the other two pilots. But their failed attempts gave me a chance to see what didn't work. Before diving into the clouds, I took a second to plan my route. I would be no good to the SEALs on the ground if I crashed.

The storm that took Roulette fizzled out almost as quickly as it had built. I aimed in that direction hoping that the collapsed storm would leave a void through which I could pass. The path took me about sixty miles west of where Roulette and Pacman had met their fates. The bigger cells were pushing east. A small gap showed on the weather loop. I called the Marine Air Traffic Control, which oversaw the airspace, and told them I was going to descend.

"Roger," the Marine said. "You're the only thing flying. The country is yours."

I brought up the nose camera on my HUD. The Predator had a small forward-facing camera built into the fuselage. We rarely used it to fly. The targeting pod had a better camera, but I needed the targeting pod to clear turns and find open air. Two cameras were better than one.

"Katie, I need you to scan for me," I said. "I'm going to find a hole to fly through. I need you to clear my turns and help me find a seam."

"Yes, sir," she said.

Katie was one of several female sensor operators in the squadron. She was the sensor operator when the Predator was shot down over Baghdad. I hadn't flown with her much, since I mostly got the new guys in my role as chief pilot. It was comforting to have her level of experience in the cockpit with me as we tried to shoot through the storms.

I pointed at my weather display on a side monitor.

"I'm going to aim at these gaps," I said. "Spend most of your time ahead of us."

We worked our way into a bank of clouds. A large storm cell billowed out of the deck in front of me and bubbled skyward. We couldn't go over it. We could only go around it.

"Scan left," I said.

Despite the high stress level, no one raised his or her voice. I couldn't hear any tension in Katie's voice. Knowing the stakes on the ground, we weren't afraid to push the aircraft. I leaned forward as if doing so would make the picture any clearer. Katie rotated the pod to the left. All we could see was a solid wall of cloud.

"Anything to the right?"

The pod swung about. The sky was a little clearer in that direction. I could just make out some sunlight poking through. I pushed the control stick to the right and swung around to match where the targeting pod was pointing. The aircraft started a lazy turn and rolled out to match the targeting pod's heading. The clear air lasted about a minute before the clouds closed in around us.

"Scan left."

I felt like a broken record. We zigzagged between cloud banks for a few minutes, jumping between patches of clear air. If we went left, we headed across the line of storms. Right put us parallel to them. We worked our way down the line until finally a hole in the clouds opened. Two towering cumulus clouds framed clear sky. It looked remarkably like the one Roulette saw.

I checked the satellite feed. It showed nothing on the other side of the weather line. It also showed us nearing the mountains, where turbulence and stalled thunderstorms awaited us. It was now or never.

I turned the aircraft to point down the hole. Katie and I watched as the cumulus clouds passed us by. I knew it was a trick of the camera. The clouds were still in front but outside the nose camera's thirty-degree field of view. I began to let out a breath I didn't know I was holding, until a wisp of cloud popped back into view.

"Uh-oh," I said.

I initiated a ten-degree turn away from the cloud.

"What?" Katie said.

"Scan left," I ordered.

I was still calm on the outside. Inside, I started to sweat. The pod moved left. The picture showed a cumulus cloud about to overrun the aircraft. If it enveloped us, a third aircraft was lost. My best bet at survival was to turn right and run from it.

"Scan right," I said as I turned the Predator.

I wanted to see where we were going. Katie didn't ask questions. She was tracking the same threat. The pod slewed right. Another wall of cloud rose right where we were turning. One cell had stagnated while the other kept moving, closing the trap. I turned back toward the hole and decided to take my chances shooting the gap.

Tendrils of clouds reached out on both sides, attempting to claw the bird out of the sky. The hole collapsed until only a tiny pinhole not much larger than the aircraft remained. I aimed the cross hairs at the center of the hole and waited. The cloud closed in, blocking the remaining light. Then the screen went dark gray as we penetrated the cloud itself. I counted three seconds, expecting to see the dreaded "Loss of Clock, Loss of Data" warning.

I was barely at three in my countdown when the aircraft burst from the cloud into bright sunlight. We were finally clear of the weather and surprisingly close to the target area in Kunar. I took a deep breath and looked at the tracker above the HUD to get my bearings.

No one spoke. There was no reason to congratulate us, because the most important part of the mission was still unfinished.

I breathed a sigh of relief as I typed in chat.

> WF_81> *through wx, proceeding to coords.* [We're through the weather, proceeding to coordinates.]

The mission commander came back right away.

> 17RS_MCC> *c.*

Katie plugged in the target coordinates. The pod fidgeted while she typed; then it locked onto a gray nothingness.

"Is that ice on the pod?" I asked.

Katie worked her controls. The camera was in IR mode and suffering from thermal crossover. The outside air temperature matched the terrain's temperature. We weren't going to see a person in this mess.

"Okay," I said. "Zoom out and look for a hot spot."

Immediately, a bright spot materialized in one corner of the HUD. Katie centered the picture and zoomed back in. The QRF's CH-47 wreckage came into view. The helicopter had fallen into a wooded area and exploded. The engines and fuel tanks still burned brightly. The broken rotors and downed trees glowed in the light from the fire. There could be no survivors.

"MC, we're on the wreckage," I said. "You got a vector?"

"Head up the ridgeline at the top of your screen," the intelligence officer said. "Follow it for about five miles. That should be the area of their last known location. You are looking for up to four individuals."

The intelligence officer didn't have to say "moving with discipline." It was understood. The Taliban would scramble over the rocks in a disorderly fashion. SEALs would make coordinated movements, always covering one another. We had no issues telling friend from foe in these circumstances.

Katie scanned the ridgeline in silence. She was still battling the thermal crossover. Katie drew a box pattern around the Chinook as she examined every gully, crevasse, and outcropping. For all we knew, the team was still on the move.

I fidgeted in my seat and leaned in closer to the screen. If I were the team on the ground, I wouldn't want air cover to give up on me because of a little thermal crossover.

"You see anything?" I asked, just to break up the silence.

"Negative," Katie said.

I didn't speak much more than that for fear of losing my focus. We wanted to find these guys. God only knew under what conditions they found themselves. I wanted to get them to safety. Were they wounded? Dead? We had no communications with them or their leadership. We didn't know it at the time, but their leadership was in the Chinook that we'd just seen burning on the mountainside.

For the next hour and a half, we combed over every inch of the ridgeline and valley. Nothing moved. Even the Taliban seemed to be taking a breather. Katie was slowly scanning every rock and tree when she started to talk with the intelligence officer about movies they'd watched that month. I didn't even register the names since I was too absorbed in watching the screen for any movement. The conversation between them was less about the content and more to keep their minds engaged. It was difficult to stay sharp when every rock and tree looked the same. There were supposed to be more than two hundred Taliban crawling through these hills. Where the hell were they?

Then I heard it. A garbled transmission came across the radio. The voice was low, almost a whisper. I didn't hear the first part of the message, only the last part.

"[GARBLED] . . . Come in."

Whoever was on the radio was trying to raise someone.

I cocked my head and pressed the ear cup tighter to my head. The voice was on the radio, not the intercom. I checked the frequency. It was set to the CSAR emergency frequency. Our radios were terrible and couldn't talk with anyone more than five miles away, which meant air traffic control wouldn't get me even if they were on the frequency. I checked the clock. It was five past the hour, the standard check-in time. It had to be someone on an emergency radio.

The message came in garbled again. I could understand only "come in." But it was a man's voice, speaking at a whisper.

"Everybody shut up," I yelled into the mic. "I think I hear something."

Katie and the intel coordinator stopped talking. The tone in the GCS changed immediately. I thought I heard his call sign but couldn't confirm. I took a chance and keyed the mic.

"Calling Wildfire, say again."

Nothing.

"Calling Wildfire, say again."

Silence.

Either he didn't hear us or wouldn't respond without the code word.

"Calling Wildfire," I said. "Hold tight. We are triangulating your position. Friendlies are on the way. Friendlies are on the way."

It was terrible radio discipline that completely violated the CSAR standard communications. I didn't care, though. The SEAL needed to know we were there, assuming he could still hear us.

I dropped a marker on my tracker to indicate where I'd heard the radio call. I couldn't truly confirm I had heard SEAL Team Five, but I had to report it. No one else should have been on this frequency. No one else would be whispering. I calculated the coordinates and passed them to the Joint Personnel Recovery Center.

We strained to listen to the radio for the rest of our sortie, circling in the same spot in hopes of another transmission. We needed more contacts to triangulate his position. An hour later, my part in the mission ended. The relief crew came out, received our mission brief, and assumed control.

The ops cell didn't look excited at all when I walked in. There was a tension there that said, "We are still looking." I knew they would, too. SEAL Team Five was still out there. I left the ops cell and walked to my car. The sun was rising and I knew most of Las Vegas was shaking off their Saturday night hangover. I felt the same way, but for a different reason. I'd really wanted to find the SEAL team, but I'd failed.

As I drove back into town, I felt like the weight of the whole mission rested on my chest. It was worse than the stress of shooting. We were the only aircraft to make it to the site and we did our best to find them. There was little we could do, but I wouldn't let myself off the hook.

For the rest of the week I scoured news sites and hit up our intelligence officers for an update. The mission was unfinished in my mind. Finally, Army Rangers recovered Marcus Luttrell, the lone survivor from the four-man team. He was holed up in a village only a couple of miles from where we heard his transmission. A local Pashtun tribe had protected Luttrell from the Taliban until the Rangers found him.

We took pride in knowing we were the only aircraft able to make it to the area that day. The Predator's unique qualities were an asset in such a dangerous location. The Air Force would never put a human pilot in harm's way in those weather conditions given the threat from the Taliban, and even though we lost two Predators, my aircraft provided the first pictures of the crash site and possibly confirmed Luttrell's position through his radio transmission. Without that information, it would have taken a lot longer to launch the rescue operation.

I did get my closure on the mission when Luttrell visited the squadron while writing his book *Lone Survivor*. We had done well.

CHAPTER 10

Hunting Taliban

The scrub that covered the mountains in eastern Afghanistan filled my HUD.

We were tracking one of Osama bin Laden's suspected couriers. We were just watching tonight, trying to catalog his movements and establish his pattern of life. Our ultimate mission remained the same—find and eliminate Osama bin Laden. The courier could hold the key to that operation.

Our flight path took us close to Khost, a dreary place with crumbling Soviet-era concrete office buildings, garbage-strewn streets, and only a few paved roads. The province was one of the places where the hijackers who crashed into the World Trade Center and the Pentagon had trained.

As we flew, I practiced simulated Hellfire shots. We were told not to waste any mission time. If we found ourselves on a long flight across country, we had to practice by picking a spot in the landscape and simulating a shot. It wasn't much different from what I'd done with Wang when I'd first started flying two years earlier. In transit we picked a spot, like that old fortress near our old airfield, and went through the procedures leading up to a shot. We couldn't train on our off time because we were considered deployed, which was another way of saying that only combat operations were conducted.

Even soldiers in theater went to the shooting range regularly.

Not us.

We just didn't have time. Most shifts I'd fly eight hours and then spend another four hours doing collateral duties. So to make up for the lack of training, pilots in the 17th practiced Hellfire shots on every flight. The 15th's crews didn't. They were barely keeping up with the mission with many of their target areas surrounding their bases.

The RPA community was expanding faster than the Air Force could train pilots. Aircraft like F-16s generated hundreds of hours of flight training at home before deploying to combat. A young wingman would spend at least six months in learning mode before being considered for deployment. Then the whole squadron would begin spin-up training ending in a Red Flag exercise at Nellis Air Force Base, where they flew in a large force practicing the exact missions they would execute overseas.

Predator squadrons didn't have that luxury.

Over the years, training had been trimmed. Pilots graduated barely qualified for combat, a stark contrast to the full program I had completed nearly two years before. The ever-increasing need for crews in combat justified these cuts. A crew's first flight with their permanent squadron was in combat over a live target with live weapons. Spin-up happened on the fly, literally.

The 15th's operations expanded to six combat air patrols

covering both Afghanistan and Iraq. The 15th's commander canceled leave requests and turned life in the squadron into a grind. It didn't surprise me that the 15th's pilots didn't want to learn new techniques. Most of the guys looked like zombies, with dark circles under their eyes and pallid skin. Exhaustion sucked the life out of the crews and made them sloppy. I could understand the fatigue. I couldn't understand the sloppiness.

I was the chief pilot for the 15th and 17th at Nellis. Until the squadrons got a certified weapons officer who graduated from the Air Force Weapons School, the job of fixing our tactics and procedures fell on my shoulders.

We'd made some mistakes lately and it cost us. Several of our shots in Afghanistan had gone astray. One of the worst was when the 57th's deputy group commander made a hard turn only seconds from impact. Fighter pilots often rolled aggressively after a shot. Their pods were designed to keep up, but not the Predator's pod. The motion pulled the laser to the side and the missile detonated harmlessly fifty yards off target.

These practice shots slightly slowed our transits, but nothing was worse than a crew missing a shot. We couldn't afford to miss, and taking a few minutes from the JOC's target time was fine if it was used to practice.

We still had more than an hour to go before we got on target. I was preparing to make another practice run when Mongo came over the radio. He had left the squadron two weeks before to work as an LNO at the JOC.

"Hey, Squirrel."

"Hey, Mongo," I said. "Long time no see. How goes it?"

"Lovin' the cookies, man."

I smiled.

We all stayed at the same hotel near the JOC compound. One of the perks was a large tray of cookies laid out in the hotel lobby each night. They went with a dinner buffet the hotel provided guests. A lot of guys gained weight on those trips.

"What'cha got, man?" I asked.

"A FOB"—forward operating base—"just got hit near you," Mongo said. "They're taking casualties. Got POO coords when you're ready."

POO, or point of origin, was calculated after a mortar or rocket attack. Counterfire radars helped calculate POO sites based on the round's ballistic arc. The radars didn't add much to the defense of the bases, though. Usually, the one or two shots lobbed over the walls detonated before the base PA system even announced the attack. Soldiers joked that if you heard the "Giant Voice," then you were safe.

The Taliban loved mortars and rockets. A small team could terrorize a base daily, even hourly, with attacks. The mortar rounds and rockets didn't have to kill American soldiers. Each attack stopped or slowed operations.

The Taliban often fired rockets on a timer. Some timers were constructed from ice separating two metal plates. As the ice block melted in the summer heat, the plates came together and closed the circuit to fire the rocket. Mortars needed a team. Usually, three or four guys would set up the tube and lob a few rounds before retreating back to a village.

Alan, my sensor operator, and I looked at each other. No one had ever called us for close air support. The attack must have been bad if we got the call.

"What about our target?"

Mongo was ready. He'd probably asked the same question.

"Al says this is the priority."

If Al—one of the JOC directors—said it, we did it.

The POO coordinates were directly underneath me. I put the plane into a turn while Alan trained the targeting pod on the coordinates. The ridge was one of a couple of fingers extending into the Afghan valley near Khost. The Army set up Forward Operating Base Salerno to monitor the major border crossing between Afghanistan and Pakistan.

"Scan up the ridgeline," I said.

Alan had already shifted his cross hairs up the slope of the mountain.

It took him about thirty seconds to reach the POO site. It looked like a flat rock that jutted out from the ridge like a shelf for a vase. To my surprise, the three-man Taliban mortar crew was still on the shelf. A bright flash erupted from the tube.

"They just fired again," Alan said.

My jaw dropped. We rarely saw a crew shoot.

"Mongo," I said. "We've got eyes on a mortar crew."

"Copy," he said.

There were three fighters dressed in long shirts and baggy pants with scarves covering their heads. We could clearly see the black mortar tube and the plate set up on the shelf. After the last round, the mortar crew started packing up. One fighter shouldered the tube and the other grabbed the base plate. The third took the extra rounds. The trio of fighters headed east up a narrow goat path.

"Hey, Mongo," I said. "Crew's on the move."

"Follow them."

I checked FalconView, a new moving map program developed at Georgia Tech that tracked every friendly unit in Afghanistan. Even in this terrain, the Taliban fighters could make it to a safe haven in no time.

"Mongo, these guys are making a run for it."

"Copy."

I maneuvered the plane to keep the Taliban soldiers in sight without flying directly over the top of them. I hoped they were deaf after firing several mortar rounds, because the mountain slopes had to be funneling our engine noise right to them. The radio in my headset crackled again.

"Hey, Squirrel."

It was the mission commander at Nellis this time.

"Go ahead."

"I've got Roulette and Pacman coming to you."

The 15th had two aircraft in the area.

"How am I going to get their eyes on the target?"

We couldn't share video feeds with them, so it was going to be hard to coordinate. The MCC had a solution.

"I've sent our standby crews out to commandeer the aircraft," he said. "Comm has diverted the feeds."

The communication, or "comm," techs could patch a connection to the 17th ops cell, allowing all our aircraft access to one another's feeds.

I watched the fighters walk down a footpath that ran along the base of a valley. The men were relaxed, unaware of our presence. The other two Predators arrived thirty minutes later. I gave them a quick talk-on to the target, using their video feeds to direct them. The trio of fighters was about to get away.

Why did we have three aircraft trailing these guys? Why were we diverted from hunting the courier for this? This seemed like a mission for the 15th, and I wasn't sure why we were no longer following Bin Laden's suspected couriers.

Mongo chimed in before I could ask.

"All crews, spin up missiles."

I'd spun up my missiles when we first acquired the target. There was no reason for us to support the base otherwise. Mongo passed instructions for Roulette, flown by Skid and Pikachu, to strike first. Looking at FalconView, I saw they were flying at a lower altitude.

They could shoot and then move to the side to make way for the next highest aircraft to shoot. As a practice, we don't drop weapons through altitudes occupied by an aircraft on the improbable chance that we might accidentally hit one. The guys on top had to wait.

Skid was our default weapons officer because of his F-16 background. He would have been our first "official" weapons officer had the Air Force allowed Predator pilots to attend the weapons school.

Pikachu was a young, blond airman, barely five feet with heels. Her size and energy reminded everyone of the small, ball-shaped yellow Pokémon monster. The name stuck. She was now seven months pregnant, so this mission was one of her last before she went on maternity leave. Her belly was so distended that she could barely reach the controls, and I had to smile when I'd see her waddle around the squadron. There was really no other aircraft where she could still be at the controls, but I was glad she was on the controls today. She had a deft touch and a keen eye. We used to joke that if the fighters killing themselves in Afghanistan had any idea they were getting shwacked by a pregnant woman, they would fight smarter.

I listened to Skid line up his shot. The valley walls were close in. The steep slopes made any shot from the side impossible. From the HUD, I watched Skid thread the missile into the valley. The Hellfire hit just behind the trio, knocking down the fighter carrying the mortar base plate.

"Splash," Skid called out on the intercom.

The two surviving fighters dashed into a thicket of trees on either side of the trail. I watched the squirter to the south disappear in the foliage. On the side monitor, Skid's feed showed his cross hairs following the man running to the north.

"Follow the squirter to the south," I told Alan.

I turned the Predator and set her in a lazy orbit so we could watch the trees. For thirty minutes we circled. The trees were collected in clumps rather than as a forest. Finally, we saw him scamper out of the underbrush. Alan's cross hairs tracked over to him, placing him at the center of my HUD. His partner came out at about the same time.

"Squirters on the move," Pikachu said in the intercom.

"Follow them," Mongo said.

They met over the body of the third man. One fighter picked up the mortar plate and tube. The other picked up the fallen fighter in a half-assed fireman's carry. They slowly walked east down their original path.

"We've got a second group of pax," someone said over the radio.

We could see another group of fighters on the path. The squirters stopped as they approached. The new fighters shouldered the mortar tube and base plate. The squirters carried their dead comrade.

"Skid," Mongo chimed in. "Continue pursuit. Cleared to engage second group."

The JOC let their fangs out tonight, I thought. Our pursuit was highly unusual. I stayed silent, letting Skid coordinate his strike on the intercom net. I was top cover while he finished the fight. Over the radio, I heard the "Rifle" call and listened to Skid count down to impact.

"Three, two, one . . ."

The Hellfire landed in the middle of the fighters. A white-hot plume blotted out the HUD video. As the explosion dissipated, I saw several survivors dart in different directions like roaches caught in a light. Two more fighters went down.

All three Predators began to circle again, tracking different groups of squirters. Like before, the fighters hid in the brush for at least half an hour before picking up their wounded and continuing to hurry down the trail.

"Targets have stopped at a shack," someone said.

"Copy," Mongo acknowledged.

I could see on my HUD the small shack nestled in an elbow of rocks. The single door and window cast a pale finger of light across the path. Several fighters carrying rifles emerged from the door. They seemed agitated, their hands moving as fast as their mouths. I saw one point up in the air like they were talking about the strikes.

The fighters in the shack had undoubtedly heard the Hellfire shots. The echoes would have rolled like thunder up the valley. I wondered if they were angry that the fighters had stopped at the shack, but it didn't really matter. Being armed, they were now legitimate targets.

The Taliban had shown great resourcefulness in figuring out our rules of engagement. They stayed close to women and children and tried to move with civilians when possible. Some wore women's clothing to avoid detection. They knew we'd honor the rules of civility and used them against us to maintain the advantage.

But I could clearly see the fighters from the shack holding AK-47s. One of the men got in a HiLux truck and drove it back to where Skid had fired the second Hellfire missile.

"Follow the truck," Mongo said.

Roulette, flown by Skid, was out of Hellfire missiles. The Predator carried only two. Pacman, the other Predator, was up next. I still orbited above. I'd be the last to shoot because I was flying higher than both Skid and Pacman.

In my HUD, I watched the fighters load the dead into the back of the truck. They were most likely taking them to get buried. Islam required burial before the sunrise of the day after death. There wasn't enough room for all the fighters in the truck, so several ran behind it.

"Pacman, you are cleared in," Mongo said. "Primary target is the truck."

The truck inched along the path, jostling in the dried ruts of the track. The path finally widened into a road barely the width of the truck itself.

"Pacman copies," I heard over the radio.

On the FalconView display, Roulette maneuvered higher into the mountains to clear the line of fire. Pacman then rolled in to set up the shot. The first Hellfire landed in front of the truck. The blast sent chunks of rocks and debris into the engine and tipped the truck onto its side.

A pair of fighters stumbled from the wreckage as the second missile landed.

It hit the fighters running behind the truck. They had fallen far enough behind that they were no longer in our field of view. It was unlikely that they had even seen the result of the first shot before they were hit.

Alan kept the cross hairs on the damaged truck. Bodies—likely some that were dead before the strike—littered the scene. We had no idea how many fighters were in the cab. As we tried to get a clearer picture, Skid came over the radio.

"Roulette is bingo."

An aircraft was "bingo" when it had enough fuel to fly home

and land with only one approach. Additional approaches might result in a flameout.

"Copy, Roulette," Mongo said. "You are cleared off target."

Pacman and I were left to finish the fight. Only my Predator had weapons remaining, a single Hellfire. An MQ-9 Reaper was in route. It was bigger than the Predator and had a larger payload. Unlike the Predator, the Reaper carried four Hellfire missiles and two GBU-12 laser-guided bombs.

"Pacman, stay on the truck," Mongo said. "Wildfire, stay on the walkers."

"Copy," we said in unison. We were Wildfire.

Alan shifted the cross hairs back to the group hit by the second missile. We circled the area, adjusting our camera to monitor the road and clearing. Three bodies were strewn around the crater, contorted in death. The bodies were already cooling in the mountain air, making them difficult to see with the infrared camera. Nearby, two bodies lay side by side off to the edge of the road. Our cross hairs froze on the pair.

"When was the last time you saw two dead bodies lie straight like that?" Alan said.

"And side by side?" I said. "Mongo, Squirrel."

"Go ahead," the MCC said.

"I think I got two targets playing dead," I said. "Center screen."

Mongo was silent as he studied our feed. The analysts probably did too.

"Stay on them for now."

Pacman cut in before I could respond.

"Truck's on the move."

A couple of fighters with the truck were well enough to tip it back upright. The Hellfire hadn't done enough damage to disable it. The truck raced down the widening road faster than before, ignoring the jarring ruts. I tracked their progress on the side monitor while we remained fixed on the two playing dead.

I had to give it to our "dead bodies." They were disciplined. They held their position for a long time, waiting. I was sure they couldn't hear us after the concussion of the missile. Most likely, their ears had been blown out. I looked at my fuel gauge. We still had hours on station. I was willing to wait them out.

"Wildfire, could you please scan up the road?" Mongo said a few minutes later. "Confirm there are no other survivors there."

"Mongo," I said. "What about these two?"

"They have been assessed as KIA."

"Mongo, all indications are that they are playing dead," I said. "Let me take care of this and move on to the next target."

Mongo passed the request to Al.

"Negative," he said finally. "Move up to the truck hit."

"Copy," I said.

They were right in a way. These guys didn't appear to be armed. But I didn't want them to think they had outsmarted me by playing dead.

Alan moved the cross hairs up to where the truck had been. We scanned the crater around and followed the skid marks to where the truck had tipped over. There were no signs of any fighters or movement.

"Nothing here," I reported.

"Okay," Mongo replied. "Go back to the first strike and check on it."

Something told me they didn't really believe the two Taliban were KIA either. Alan shifted the targeting pod back to the elbow in the road. The three Taliban remained lying as before.

The two hot spots on the side were gone.

I was livid.

"I knew it," I said to Alan. "We had those guys."

We scanned the nearby tree line and searched the area for several hundred meters, but I knew in my gut they were gone.

Lucky bastards.

I checked Pacman's feed on the monitor. The truck pulled into a small village and stopped at a large compound. High walls separated the multifloor house from the other much poorer one-story huts. From the HUD, it looked like a cheesy Hollywood action flick where an insanely wealthy villain controlled a small town. The truck pulled right inside the compound. Fighters filtered through the gate behind the vehicle. All were armed. A lone figure walked out and climbed into the bed of the truck. We could see him gesturing. It looked like a pep talk.

The men around him lifted their weapons in the air. Some fired skyward.

"Reaper's in the target area," Mongo said.

There was no chance I was going to shoot now. The Reaper was more accurate.

"Squirrel," Mongo said. "I need you to orbit to the south. Be prepared to conduct BDA post-strike."

"Copy," I said.

We kept our cross hairs centered on the scene as we orbited nearby. From the top of the screen, we saw the GBU-12 bomb whistle into the compound. It landed in the bed of the truck.

It took a few seconds for the camera to adjust after the fireball died. When we finally got a clear picture, the truck was gone, replaced by a massive crater. Bodies and debris scattered in a pattern radiating outward like a compass rose. One of the compound's walls fell backward. The house itself seemed relatively unscathed.

We watched for a few minutes. Nothing stirred. Mongo finally ended the mission.

"Guys, need you to proceed to your assigned targets," he said. "Pacman, prepare to return control to the 15th."

As I turned the Predator toward my target, I couldn't stop thinking about the two fighters playing possum. We took a little heat off one of our bases for a while. But there was something strange about the mission. I still didn't understand why Al had pulled us off our planned mission to chase a random group of fighters.

I got my answer a few days later. News agencies reported that a local Taliban warlord and more than 130 of his men were killed in an air strike. When news broke about the strike, I followed up with our intelligence staff to get some answers. The intelligence officers had known the warlord was in the area and used the fighters to lead us to him.

Attacks on Forward Operating Base Salerno slackened significantly after the strike, for a while at least.

CHAPTER 11

Steel Curtain

The Marine Air Traffic Control message popped into my chat room just as I was flying over Al Anbar Province in western Iraq.

DASC> DR31, new coords. State ETA when able.

I was Dagger Three One, or DR31 in chat. My target was a low-level facilitator somewhere in Haditha, but the Marines needed help. They had new coordinates for me and wanted to know how long it would take me to arrive.

I was flying a mission for the 3rd Special Operations Squadron as a favor. Air Force Special Operations Command had officially entered the RPA field and tapped me to help train their initial cadre. The new squadron was still part of the 15th for the time being.

Once the unit was sufficiently manned, the 3rd and the 15th would split and become two autonomous squadrons.

Until then, we had to lend a hand. My job as chief pilot was to train the squadron's new instructor corps. When not training, I chose to fly missions as often as possible to maintain my skills. It added to my credibility in the eyes of the students. Plus, I joined the RPA community to fly missions. After two years at Nellis, I was finding myself pulled into more duties that kept me from getting stick time. So when I got the chance to fly, I took it.

Most of our missions were in support of a specific Army unit. We needed permission to leave the unit to help another. But a fundamental shift in Army tactics occurred over the summer. Leadership decided that minimizing casualties was more important than offensive operations against al Qaeda. In the risk-averse atmosphere of Iraq, Army commanders recognized the potential of the Predator and how it could maximize their advantage on the battlefield by providing up-to-the-minute intelligence on a target. But they needed control of the aircraft. The Air Force wouldn't give it up. So Army units began to assign operation names to simple missions so they could get air support.

Too often we orbited trees or empty buildings while the Army companies planned operations elsewhere. To admit they had no targets for the day meant they would lose their asset. We were never released for TICs for the same reason. Cutting us loose would lead someone in Baghdad to realize we weren't busy enough.

The Marine controllers, on the other hand, didn't hesitate to pull us off a target if troops were under fire. They owned all the airspace below ten thousand feet in Al Anbar Province. When operating in that area, the Army wanted us to stay high and under their control. We tried to get low and out of their control when we could. That way we might get pulled off target for something interesting.

I plugged the coordinates from the Marine controller into FalconView. A new target icon appeared over Al Qaim, a small Iraqi village near the Syrian border. I sent an update via chat.

DR31> En Route, ETA 30 mikes.

Al Qaim was only thirty minutes from our current target in Ramadi. I turned the aircraft to the west and pushed up the power. The Predator was still slow, but we could shave a few minutes off the transit time if I could eek out a couple more knots.

DASC> C, contact BRUISER 21 for further guidance.

As summer ended in 2005, the situation in Al Anbar Province had become the center of the war in Iraq. Syria, like Iran, was actively supporting the insurgency. They weren't sending troops, but they were allowing thousands of foreign fighters to cross the porous border. Young, idealistic, militant men from throughout the region flocked to Iraq to fight.

Al Qaim was a hotbed of terrorist activity. To call the fighters in the region insurgents would be a great disservice to insurgents everywhere. Terrorists had taken over the city. They raped, tortured, and murdered the local Sunni residents, the very residents who had supported their presence only days before.

When I got close to Al Qaim, I contacted Bruiser Two One (BR21). He was in the tactical operations center in Fallujah. At this distance, all our conversations with the JTAC would be through the chat rooms.

DR31> BR21, checking in.

BR21> C, post when you get eyes on coords, say when ready AO Update.

The AO Update was a briefing on the local area of operations (AO) the JTAC was working.

We were still about fifteen minutes from the target area. The FalconView map showed a bright red target where the main east-west highway bisected the Euphrates River. A road paralleled the highway on the opposite bank and marked the border of the town.

DR31> Ready update.

I saw no reason to wait.

BR21> We have a convoy under fire, taking heavy casualties. No air threat, no artillery. Expect small arms and RPGs. Friendlies at coords only. You are third UAV on site.

We were the third aircraft to arrive. Last in the fight meant we were not in charge. I dialed over to our Predator radio frequency to check in with the other aircraft on scene. The private frequency allowed us to coordinate without gumming up the radio traffic for the other aircraft.

Dragon Four Two was on the radio.

"Looks like a seven-ton got hit. It's burning."

A seven-ton truck was a large flatbed troop carrier with up-armored sides to protect troops sitting in the rear. It was part of a convoy ferrying troops back to Al Asad Air Base as American forces prepared to launch Operation Steel Curtain. The Marines were in the process of surrounding Al Qaim. Civilians were encouraged to evacuate while the Marines attempted to restore order. Anyone left in the town was a target.

I pushed up the power a little more. The small airplane didn't have much left to give. I dropped the nose a bit more, trading altitude for a couple more knots of airspeed.

"Dragon, Dagger coming in from the east, seven thousand."

I was at seven thousand feet, give or take.

"Copy, Dagger, we are at 5K, and Mace is working at 6K."

Dragon and Mace were the two other crews flying for the 3rd Special Operations Squadron. They were flying at five thousand and six thousand feet, respectively.

"I'll stay at 7K," I said.

"Dagger, take south bank. Help Mace find the incoming fire."

"Copy."

Brett, my sensor operator, was on one of his first missions. He came to the program from Air Force Special Operations Command, where he had flown as an enlisted crewman. I couldn't remember the aircraft. I hadn't flown with him yet, and we'd been called to help before we could really get to know each other. But I was confident he was ready if we had to shoot. I didn't subscribe to having a shot list like the 17th did. If you passed the training and the check ride, I considered you ready to perform when called upon.

We were about ten miles away. A smoke plume from the burning seven-ton armored truck cast a nasty blotch on our screen. The auto-contrast in the sensor ball tried to compensate but managed to only suppress most of the image as it filtered out the worst of the illumination.

Brett adjusted the picture, using the sensor's manual controls. Looking at the burning wreck in the HUD was like looking into the sun. At eight miles, the flare from the fire reflected off something inside the ball, sending ghosts fleeting about the picture. Brett tried to balance toward the bright spot, but the detail bled out of the remainder of the picture.

"Zoom in on the riverbank," I said.

The camera might work better if it focused on another area. The camera could zoom in only so far. The minimum setting was called ultra narrow. The next setting cut the picture in half digitally and expanded it on the screen. It wasn't a real zoom. It just made a part of the picture larger. We still couldn't see much, but I hoped the resolution would improve once we got closer.

"Dagger on target," I transmitted.

I backed it up in the chat room.

BR21> c.

As we got closer, the picture cleared up and we could make out some of the details. Rocket-propelled grenades had hit the front quarter of the truck, destroying the engine and igniting the fuel. Another barrage of RPGs had battered the thick armored plating around the bed, killing fourteen soldiers.

The convoy was stopped on the road and we could see soldiers recovering the bodies. Two HMMWVs blocked the bridge while the others set up a security perimeter near the burning truck. Their turrets were trained down the bridge. The other seven-ton trucks moved to a safe distance down the road, their troops spilling out to support.

Across the river, twenty or so terrorists crouched, firing RPGs and spraying the Americans with a steady stream of AK-47 rounds and PKM machine-gun fire. The American soldiers were pinned down.

I was excited because we were in a position to make a difference. We couldn't help the dead, but we could help the guys still struggling to survive down below. My Hellfire missiles were ready. I started to develop my shot solution. I assumed the two other Predators on scene had done the same.

MC80> TGT in sight. Request clearance to engage.

Mace Eight Zero beat me to the punch.

BR21> C. STBY ROE.

Bruiser Two One was still working clearance and told Mace Eight Zero to wait for the rules of engagement. While we waited, the terrorists across the river stopped firing and, as if signaled, retreated back into the town.

The sensor ball rolled and Brett put the cross hairs on a group of terrorists as they picked their way through labyrinthine alleys. The terrorists avoided the deserted main streets, sticking to the narrow passageways between the flat-roofed single-story buildings.

The irregular track of the alley made it difficult to see the enemy as we orbited.

Mace and I pressed in closer to keep an eye on them. From time to time, I saw Mace shoot through my screen. I flinched and peeked at my side monitor. It showed me where and how high Dragon and Mace were flying. Mace was still a thousand feet below me, but because of the magnification, it looked like he was in my lap.

The terrorists formed a single-file line as they ran through the alleys.

"Dagger, Mace," I said over the radio. "You got the leader. I'll take the tail."

"Copy," Mace said.

I recognized the voice. There were only a handful of female pilots in Predator at the time. She was a very experienced special operator and likely the sharpest of the three of us flying today. She had flown gunships before joining the Predator. The AC-130 was a converted cargo plane armed with Gatling guns and an M102 howitzer. The gunships flew only at night, providing air support mostly to special operations forces. They could loiter over a target longer than a jet fighter, and the aircraft's immense firepower would be devastating at close range. She brought with her a quiet confidence that I admired.

"Watch for them to split," I said to Brett.

Mace and I bracketed the fighters. At each turn, we were ready to split off, but they stayed together. When we finally got cleared to shoot, we planned to block them in with two shots—one on the leader and one on the tail—and wait for friendlies to kill or capture them. We'd developed a groove anticipating their route when a message popped up in the chat room.

> BR21> DN/DR/MC—contact KL36 flight on [frequency].

The communication card indicated that KL was Klyde, two Marine Corps Cobra attack helicopters. They looked like dragonflies, with a large canopy and fuselage and two tiny wings with rockets. A machine gun sat below the nose. The helicopters had been used by the Army in Vietnam but had been replaced by the Apache. The Marine Corps version, known as a Super Cobra, resembled its Vietnam-era cousin with upgraded weapons and avionics.

We all switched radio frequencies.

"Klyde, Dragon Four Two." Dragon maintained his role as lead.

"Dragon," the lead helicopter responded. "Klyde up."

Dragon passed the most current coordinates for the retreating terrorists.

"Confirm eyes on?"

"Negative, buildings are ruining line of sight."

"Okay," Dragon said. "We'll let you know if they break into the open. I've got two assets about to engage."

"Negative," Klyde said. "We get the shots."

His voice left no room for discussion. These were his boys. He was going to get payback. Normally, the Cobras worked in tandem with a spotter. The spotter was usually a light helicopter with a bulb-shaped sensor pod mounted over the rotor. The spotter could hide behind trees, exposing only the sensor. The Cobras would pop up to launch a missile and then drop back down while the spotter guided the weapon to the target. This was an old Cold War tactic for countering Soviet armor.

It didn't work so well in Iraq.

Neither the Cobras nor the spotter could see the targets. They also weren't about to fly close enough to get eyes on. RPGs could take them out of the sky. The Cobras had to keep their distance.

"Any chance you can buddy lase for us?" Klyde asked.

Theoretically, we could lase any weapon. Weapons didn't care who fired a laser, only that it contained the right codes.

The issue had come up a few weeks earlier. I had just finished my three and a half hours in the seat and was on break before starting a mission commander shift. Limited manning meant we all took shifts in the box. It was only fair. Crews sat in the seat for up to eight hours a day. The MCC would give them breaks, let them eat and hit the latrine.

When I'd left to fly, a Predator and a Reaper found a camp where a source reported that a regional warlord was meeting with a high-level facilitator. The meeting was to exchange weapons and to coordinate a strike against one of our bases in Kunar. Our job was to find the meeting location and eliminate the warlord.

Two tents sprouted like an odd triangle out of the dirt. A truck was parked just off the road to the north of the camp. Box, one of our senior pilots, stood behind the MCC desk when I got back to the ops cell. He alternated between looking at the plasmas and talking on the phone.

"What's going on, Box?" I asked.

"Upstairs is trying to decide what to do."

Upstairs was our code for the JOC. It was a double entendre of sorts, referencing both their actual location on the fifth floor of their building and the fact that they were our bosses.

"Oh?" I said.

"They want to hit both tents, but they are too far apart for one bomb to hit."

I could see he was frustrated.

"Can't we hit one at a time?" I asked.

Box shook his head.

"They want simultaneous hits."

Both targets were very important. A single hit would wake or warn the other man and he'd run. Hitting a running target in the mountains and trees was difficult. All our engagements were single shots. Even my two missiles against the Facilitator had been a first.

A T-37 over Virginia at sunset.

T-37s in formation over Mississippi.

A flying selfie.

Photographs on this page courtesy of Lt. Col. T. Mark McCurley

An Air Force crew prepares to launch a Predator.

U.S. Air Force photograph by Tech. Sgt. Kevin J. Gruenwald

An MQ-1 Predator at Kandahar Air Base, Afghanistan, taxis out for a mission in support of Operation Enduring Freedom. U.S. Air Force photograph by Maj. David Kurle

An MQ-1 Predator basks in a desert sunset at Balad Air Base, Iraq, ready for nighttime operations. U.S. Air Force photograph by Master Sgt. Jonathan Doti

A fully armed MQ-9 Reaper taxis down an Afghanistan runway.

U.S. Air Force photograph by Staff Sgt. Brian Ferguson

Airmen preflight
an MQ-1 Predator
at Ali Air Base,
Iraq.

U.S. Air Force photograph
by Airman 1st Class
Jonathan Snyder

An MQ-1 Predator takes off from Creech Air Force Base, Nevada, for a training mission.

U.S. Air Force photograph by Senior Airman Larry E. Reid Jr.

Airmen assigned to the 432nd Aircraft Maintenance Squadron assemble an MQ-1 Predator at Creech Air Force Base, Nevada.

U.S. Air Force photograph by Senior Airman Larry E. Reid Jr.

An MQ-1 Predator armed with AGM-114 Hellfire missiles flies a combat mission over southern Afghanistan.

U.S. Air Force photograph by Lt. Col. Leslie Pratt

An MQ-9 Reaper on display at Holloman Air Force Base, New Mexico.

U.S. Air Force photograph by Airman 1st Class Aaron Montoya

A sandstorm at Al Taqaddum Air Base, Iraq.

A VMU-1 pilot launches an RQ-2 Pioneer using a remote control box.

The Officer's Club, Bada Bing!, at Al Taqaddum Air Base, Iraq, in 2006. The club occupied the top floor of an abandoned air traffic control tower.

Photographs on this page courtesy of Lt. Col. T. Mark McCurley

A tail gunner over Lake Habbaniyah, Iraq.

A ScanEagle UAV being prepared for launch at Al Asad Air Base, Iraq.

A ScanEagle UAV returning from a mission at Al Asad Air Base, Iraq.

Launch and Recovery Ground Control Station at Balad Air Base, Iraq.

Photographs on this page courtesy of Lt. Col. T. Mark McCurley

The 60th Expeditionary Reconnaissance Squadron commander's office.

A Predator awaits its next mission under a sunshade at Camp Lemonnier, Djibouti.

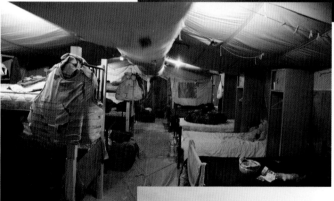

Visitors' quarters at Kandahar Air Base, Afghanistan.

A UH-60 Blackhawk flies past the Predator compound at Kandahar Air Base, Afghanistan.

Photographs on this page courtesy of Lt. Col. T. Mark McCurley

An MQ-1 performs a simulated Hellfire-missile shot at the Nellis Air Show in 2005. This was the first time a Predator had performed at any air show.

An MQ-1 Predator waits its turn to fly in a Hardened Aircraft Shelter (HAS) at Balad Air Base, Iraq.

An MQ-1 and an MQ-9 prepare for missions at Camp Lemonnier, Djibouti.

Box looked disgusted.

"I'm going to hit the head," he said.

What he didn't say was that he wanted a break to think about the situation. Maybe I had the benefit of seeing the problem cold, but the solution seemed so obvious. I followed him into the hall and stopped short of the men's bathroom.

"Box," I called. "Buddy lase."

He looked back at me like I had a third arm growing out of my forehead. He shook his head and disappeared into the bathroom. I waited in the ops cell until he returned. He had one question for me.

"Why?"

I looked up at the plasmas.

"We train to buddy lase for other strikers. This is no different. The targets are close together. Bombs have different PRF codes." The pulse repetition frequency, or PRF, codes were an identification mechanism embedded in a laser beam that a weapon, if programmed for the code, would home in on. "Drop on one target and the other bomb will still have the energy to reach the second."

Box looked at the screen.

"And the Pred lases it in."

"Built-in support," I said.

Box looked skeptical. We had never used two RPAs together for a strike. It had always been a Predator doing the lase for a manned fighter hauling the bombs for us.

"And the crews already know how to do it," I added.

"All right," he said after a moment of consideration. "Thanks, Squirrel."

I stuck around to watch. Box passed the new plan to the Reaper pilot. He would be the one to drop both bombs.

A few moments later, the bombs sailed into the picture. One HUD video blossomed with an incredible explosion. The GBU-12's detonation was so much stronger than the smaller "cat fart" of the Hellfire.

The second bomb did not detonate. The weapon streaked into the other HUD video and ended its flight with a puff of dust. The bomb was a dud. A ground team later confirmed that the weapon actually hit the warlord, killing him instantly. Even though the weapon failed to operate properly, we considered the attack a success, since the weapon still accomplished its mission. The "buddy lase" worked flawlessly.

A few weeks later, I wasn't sure if we could lase the Cobra's weapons.

The squadron's new weapons officer said the Hellfire could not be lased from a separate source. But that wasn't entirely true, since the missiles didn't activate their IR sensors until after they launched. At that point, it didn't matter who fired the laser.

Mace Eight Zero figured this out before I did.

"Mace copies, stand by for coords."

She spent the next minute outlining what she could do for the Cobras. I listened intently, ready to help if called. Our biggest challenge was Al Qaim's position on the Syrian border.

Syria was hardly neutral, but we could not fly into their airspace, so that limited the angles we could use. The Syrians placed several SA-6 antiaircraft missile batteries near the border town on the off chance we would stray into their territory.

The terrorists were closer to the center of town. We could fly directly overhead in a tight circle and stay away from the Syrian missile batteries. I listened to Mace brief the helicopter to fire on the coordinates she passed to them. The Hellfire missile had several launch modes. Most of the time, we used a direct strike mode where the missile sped straight to the target. The missile could also dive to the ground and skim the earth on a flat, low trajectory to hit targets under cover. This was ideal for hitting the caves in Tora Bora.

The first two modes were useless in this case because of the buildings. The alleyways were too narrow. We could use only the "high mode" that guided the missile to drop vertically down on a target. Dragon was ready and started passing the Cobras coordinates. I had the video feeds of the other two aircraft piped to my side monitors. My targeting pod was firmly fixed on the last guy in the gaggle. The fighters continued to run in a single-file line.

BR21> ROE and CDE complete. You are cleared hot.

"Klyde Three Six, Rifle."

I watched Mace's feed and counted down from thirty seconds. The Cobra's Hellfire missile left the rail and started to climb. As it nosed over, it locked onto the Predator's laser spot in the alley. The missile hit dead center. As the dust and smoke cleared, I could make out two twisted bodies in the dirt. The concussive force funneling down the alley stunned the survivors. They stopped running for a moment, shook their heads clear, and then took off again in a line.

Why didn't they scatter? There were enough doors around to duck into and hole up. But they continued in a line like lemmings.

"Two KIA, squirters on the move again," Mace said.

"Copy," Klyde said.

BR21> ROE and CDE remain good. Cleared hot.

A second missile fired from the Cobra. This one hit at the feet of the first runner, killing him instantly. The surviving runners stopped like before to recover their bearings and then continued in a line.

"You've got to be kidding me," I said.

Brett shook his head.

"You can't make this stuff up," he said.

Bruiser gave us an open clearance to keep engaging the runners until he called us off. He agreed to keep running the CDE—collateral damage estimates—along the route. The Cobras shot six more missiles. The Predators successfully lased each one. After each strike, the survivors shook off the shock of the strike and kept running in single file down the alleys.

"Mace, Klyde."

"Go," Mace said.

"We're Winchester missiles, still have twenty mike mike available."

The choppers were out of missiles but still had the 20mm Gatling gun available. This could be useful, but stray rounds and ricochets in the alley would create a collateral damage nightmare. The heavy rounds would penetrate the cinder-block construction of the average building in the region far more efficiently than the frag from a Hellfire.

Dragon passed the news to the JTAC.

BR21> Mace, you are up.

"Copy," Mace said. "We'll take it from here."

She transmitted the message so the choppers would hear.

With the Cobras heading back to base, Mace and Dragon rolled in. At our height, we didn't need to buddy lase for each other. We could line up a shot and lead the runners so they ran right into the frag cloud. Mace and Dragon took turns firing at the line of terrorists. The pair fired their complement of two missiles each, with strike after strike thinning out the number of terrorists in line.

I rolled in last.

"You ready?" I said to Brett.

He nodded. We'd gone over the shot while we watched Dragon and Mace work. The few remaining terrorists continued in line on my monitor. I still couldn't figure out why they stayed in the open.

I pointed my nose down the alley and started my final run. The targeting pod's cross hairs overlapped the lead runner as if they were physically attached to his shirt. Once the missile left the rail, there wasn't anything else to do.

The missile sped straight and true toward that lead runner. He ducked around a bend in the alley, a bend that resembled the zigzag of a lightning bolt. Brett smoothly adjusted his aim to meet the runner as he spilled out the other side. The runner grew large in the picture as we drew close. The clock ticked down.

The explosion happened right on cue, killing the last of the runners. We watched for a few minutes, but no one got up. If there were survivors, they must have finally wised up. I didn't expect it, though. They were too close to the blast to have survived.

Something deep inside me, perhaps that bit of humanity that hated war, felt sorry for the anonymous men running afraid and very much aware that they were in the final moments of their lives. I figured they came from some foreign nation, most likely Syria, where they were brainwashed that killing Americans was somehow holy.

It was ironic, really.

We had no business being here, either. Iraq kept its oil. Saddam Hussein for all his bluster was really just a regional joke. No one took him seriously, except his own people. Yet all we accomplished was to enable sectarian violence and create a magnet for all the wannabe terrorists in the Middle East to come and get their jihad on.

At least they were here now instead of attacking America. I took comfort in knowing that if we had to fight, it was in someone else's backyard. But this was a turkey shoot. There was no humanity in it at all. I took no joy in it, nor could I mourn the loss. The whole incident was by its nature mortifyingly absurd, but it did prove that the buddy lase on running targets was effective. The Predator was becoming even more lethal, but I wouldn't understand the true extent until a few months later in Iraq.

It was also after Operation Steel Curtain that interrogators started hearing the term "White Devils." The insurgency and al Qaeda both agreed that their greatest fear was not soldiers. They feared the Predator, the silent enemy whose presence was known to them only after their buddies blew up.

CHAPTER 12

Keeping Up with the Joneses

Colonel Michael McKinney sat at the head of the long conference table, his squadron commanders arrayed on each side. A "Commander's Comments" slide was displayed on the screen across the room.

As commander of the 57th Operations Group at Nellis Air Force Base, he held weekly staff meetings for all his commanders and senior officers. As the group's chief of standards and evaluation, or chief pilot, I was invited to the briefing to consult on training or certification issues. For the most part, the meetings were boring. Commanders complained about manning levels as their squadrons expanded missions. I complained about eroding flight standards in the face of such an aggressive expansion. McKinney did his best to balance the needs of the Air Force with the needs of his men. It really was no more interesting than a staff meeting at any corporation in America.

I was seated along the wall taking notes when McKinney brought up the "Commander's Comments" slide, usually the last slide in the brief. It was his time to talk about any issues he had or to give us guidance. It was part pep talk and part issuing his instructions.

"The Marine Corps gave me a call yesterday," he said.

My heart stopped. I knew where this was going.

"Seems they need a Predator crew," McKinney said. "Apparently, they want them for an operation they are planning."

"When do they deploy?" asked Chainsaw, the 3rd Special Operations Squadron commander. His squadron was now separate from the 15th and operating in both Afghanistan and Iraq.

"Right away," McKinney said. "The Marines understand we will have some pre-deployment training requirements. Poll your people for volunteers."

Then McKinney turned and looked right at me, an inquisitive eyebrow raised. There was no doubt what he meant. He said nothing. He didn't have to.

A few days earlier, I'd approached McKinney about the Air Force's changes to the promotion system. Increasing combat requirements on the ground in Iraq meant longer tours for the Army. By the end of the war, Army units were spending fifteen months overseas. They needed more troops to lower their deployment rates.

In response, the Air Force and Navy started downsizing to free space for the Army to grow. Officers from both services could transfer to the Army, but few did, leaving the services no choice but to start letting officers go. The easiest way to do that was through promotions. Either move up or move out. They changed the rules to make it harder to move up. In order to make rank, everyone needed a combat deployment since 2001.

The change caught a lot of officers by surprise. Most fighter units had never rotated overseas, leaving hundreds of pilots vulnerable. Likewise, those in the training command had no opportunities to deploy. It also affected nearly every officer in Predator. We had only a small cadre of pilots and sensor operators deploying to theater to launch and land the aircraft. Predator pilots never took off or landed the aircraft from the United States. We took over control in midflight. There was no need to deploy us to theater or to expose us to the typical dangers of combat. It was cheaper to keep us at our home base.

I was due later that year to meet my lieutenant colonel's promotion board. I had met all the other standards for promotions. I didn't want a technicality to be the reason I didn't make rank. One thing was always drilled into me—my record met the board, not me. If my personnel record didn't exceed all the requirements, then I would not be selected to make rank. I needed a combat deployment.

I had two goals leaving the Air Force Academy. I wanted to make lieutenant colonel and command a flying squadron in combat. My best chance was command of one of the detachments sent to launch and recover the aircraft. But first I needed to make rank, so I had gone to see McKinney.

When I explained my desire to deploy, he nodded and said he would see what he could do. It was a professional brush-off. He normally didn't get involved in the deployment manning, even for the commands. So when he told us about the Marine Corps request, I had no choice. I volunteered immediately because I had asked for a deployment.

If I went, not only would I get combat credit, but also a line pilot in the squadrons wouldn't be forced to go. I wasn't on the regular flying schedule, since I worked bigger operations issues at the group. My job entailed qualifying and evaluating the new instructors and pilots in every squadron. When I was not flying, my role was to establish a standard from which the squadrons operated. In aviation, flight standards worked hand in hand with the safety office to enhance the skills of the crews and limit the potential for crew-caused accidents. The job tended to limit my flying significantly, a drawback of senior leadership. Since I didn't fly much, my departure would not adversely affect the schedule.

A month later, I was on a plane to Iraq. During a layover at Ramstein in Germany, the Marines informed us we were no longer going to augment an operation as Colonel McKinney had led me to believe. I was still headed to Al Anbar in western Iraq, though, to assess the theater's unmanned aerial vehicle capabilities, especially the video we shot through our targeting pods. The feeds had left a significant impression with national and military leadership. Prior to late 2005, Predators were assigned to support Army units. Most lines flew over Baghdad, Mosul, Basra, and Nassiriya. It took an Act of Congress to get chopped, or released to support the Marines. We passed the test during Operation Steel Curtain and they asked for us in the Second Battle of Fallujah.

As the Marines pushed through the tight alleys and dead-end streets a second time, a sniper hit a unit passing through the intersection. The platoon ended up pinned down and called for air support. At first, Marine F-18s responded. But the sniper was in a third-floor window, so the fighters begged off because their weapons would cause extensive collateral damage. Rules of engagement were changing and we couldn't just drop bombs in the city anymore. A Predator flying nearby took the call. The crew, whose names I never got, threaded a Hellfire right through the window. Fire from the sniper stopped instantly. It was an impossible shot, and from that point on, the Predators were legend among the Marines.

Being able to keep a constant, high-definition eye on a target helped when fighting from house to house. The Marines wanted to make sure it was a capability for all its units now.

We landed in Baghdad and then rode in Army Black Hawks to Al Anbar. We flew low over the city, skimming the rooftops. The blockhouses flashed past in a brown blur. Occasionally, a vacant lot where a house had once stood would slide into view.

I was based in a palace at Camp Fallujah just south of Fallujah City and adjacent to the Abu Ghraib prison. Though attached to the 2nd Marine Expeditionary Force staff, I mostly traveled throughout Al Anbar working with RPA units in the province. I needed to see what kind of capabilities they had before I could offer ways to improve things.

One of my first trips took me to Al Taqaddum Air Base. TQ, as the air base was known, sat on the shores of Lake Habbaniyah, southwest of the Fallujah-Ramadi area. It was a minor air hub used to resupply the Marine units in the area. C-17s and C-130s stopped through at regular intervals ferrying men and equipment.

The airfield was an Iraqi bomber base prior to the war. Old IL-28 Beagle medium bombers littered the end of the runway like ghosts of the Cold War. Their World War II designs upgraded with jet engines hadn't greatly improved their performance. They were ancient even by Cold War standards. The lake itself was beautifully blue, so much so that Saddam Hussein built a resort for the Baath Party a couple of miles down the road from the base.

When I arrived, the Marines put me up in an abandoned Roland SAM battery. There was no sign of the tracked missile system or its parts. It had probably been destroyed years before. The Alamo, as the Marines dubbed it, was a two-story compound that wrapped around a courtyard where the SAM vehicle would be parked.

My room was an abandoned toolshed. Someone had ripped the shelves out long ago, leaving only jagged holes where the bolts had been. A dirty mattress sat on an upended metal-frame bed. The mattress rested on the head and footboards, leaving it much higher than normal. Maybe that was because of the rats. Marines had hung a plywood panel to serve as a door. It didn't latch but swung freely in the winter wind, banging irregularly as eddies flowed through the Alamo. I propped my bag against the door to keep the night air out.

This was my first trip to Iraq. For most of the war, I watched from a GCS thousands of miles away. But now, I was actually in harm's way. I was on the ground and vulnerable to attack. It thrilled me.

But this world was a different place from the string of hotels I'd visited on prior deployments. I realized how easy I'd had it before coming to Iraq. But I also had a greater appreciation for what the guys on the ground were experiencing. We saw them only on missions, but after a few days on the ground I understood nothing was easy in theater.

Basic necessities were different here. At night, all exterior lights were turned off and the area became impenetrable black. The stars overhead offered no illumination as you struggled, eyes wide, to navigate through the blacker-than-black maze of Conex dormitories. My only light was a small clip-on LED flashlight that offered a small red glow.

I spent the majority of my time with the Marine squadron flying the RQ-2 Pioneer unmanned aerial vehicle. The Pioneer was about the length of an office desk. Its small two-stroke engine, better used on a lawn mower, was mounted in the rear between two tail fins. A small targeting pod not much larger than a grapefruit was stuck under the aircraft's chin.

The Marines either launched it from a catapult like on an

aircraft carrier, or it took off with the assistance of rockets that dropped off once it was airborne. The Marines required the flexibility since they didn't know if they would have roads or runways long enough to operate it while on the move.

With each launch, the Pioneer's engines would scream in protest as it labored into the sky, circled over the airfield a couple of times, and then headed off to its targets. The pilots controlled it with a GCS at the base.

The Marines wanted to use the Pioneer like the Predator but faced a challenge. Commanders always wanted to see and observe a target before a raid. The information was critical to minimizing casualties. To do so, the Pioneer had to fly so low the engine noise gave it away. To the enemy, nothing said run and hide like a flying lawn mower circling their house for an hour.

So the squadron came up with a better option.

The Pioneer flew convoy support and IED searches along the two main convoy roads through Fallujah and Ramadi, named Route Washington and Route Michigan. The roads were the most dangerous routes in theater.

The mission required no stealth. The small planes flew ahead of a convoy and watched for any danger on the road.

One morning, I went over to watch a mission. I stood in the operations office watching a crew fly a convoy security mission. A crew sat at a HMMWV-mounted control station, flying the aircraft. The truck containing the control station was backed up into a hole in the wall cut to fit its shape. On the monitors, Route Washington slipped by as a Pioneer searched for roadside bombs. Like most of our missions, it was boring and took monk-like patience and dedication to stay focused.

As I watched the feed, I talked to a young lieutenant who soon started digging around in a desk for something. Lean and tall, with the stereotypical high-and-tight haircut, he finally fished out a DVD with "Greatest Hits" scrawled on it in black Sharpie.

"Sir," the lieutenant said. "I've got a video to show you."

The lieutenant knew why I was in the squadron. "Greatest Hits" was a common title for flying squadrons' videos. Normally, the videos showed a series of important shots the unit had taken. I smiled inwardly. Apparently, the name stuck for nonshooting squadrons as well.

He guided me into the ops cell. He slipped the disc into a laptop on a table nearby and brought up a video on one of the computer monitors mounted on the wall.

"This one, we're proud of," he said.

The video flickered on and showed footage of a typical road scan. A paved road filled the screen as the targeting pod flitted about searching for telltale signs of IEDs. As it passed across a four-way intersection, the cross hairs stopped on a car parked at one corner, its hood up.

"When was this?" I asked.

"About two months ago," he said. "We scan the roads outside town to find the guys arming IEDs."

When no convoys required support, the Pioneers flew over the outskirts of Fallujah looking for car bombs. Bomb making required skill and a light touch. The slightest mishandling could kill the bomb maker and level several houses. For safety, the insurgents built car bombs and then sent the driver out to the edge of town to arm it by connecting the bomb to a car battery. If it detonated, only the suicide bomber died.

On the video, the crew called the QRF after it spotted the car with the hood up and sent them to check it out. The Pioneer continued to orbit the vehicle just in case something happened before the QRF wound its way through the city. After a couple of loops, the sensor operator noticed a head pop out of the driver's window. The image wasn't very good, but it looked as if the person looked right at them.

"What's he doing?" I asked.

"At this point, we didn't know," the lieutenant said.

A man slowly emerged from the car and walked out to the center of the intersection. He threw his hands up in the air and turned to face the aircraft. He shifted his position, shuffling his feet to turn to continue facing the Pioneer as it flew in its orbit.

Voices on the video discussed what they were watching in real time.

"I think he's surrendering," someone on the Pioneer's crew said.

"You've got to be kidding me," another crew member said.

"At this point the pilot called the watch officer," the lieutenant told me.

"Who was that?"

"I was on shift," the lieutenant said.

On the video, I heard the Pioneer call the lieutenant.

"What do you want us to do?" the Pioneer said.

"Stay on him," I heard the lieutenant say on the video.

Soon, I could see HMMWVs coming down the highway toward the car. The man never wavered. He always faced the aircraft with his arms raised. The Marines parked outside of the suspected blast radius, dismounted, and slowly walked up to the man.

I leaned in toward the screen, waiting for the slightest movement that would indicate that the man was activating a detonator. More Marines walked into the blast radius. My heart raced. I was ready for the Marines to kill the Iraqi as he went for a weapon or detonator. With each step, the Marines moved slowly forward, as if sensing the fear I felt. The danger was palpable. The man kept his hands up, frozen in place.

The first Marine reached the Iraqi with an interpreter in tow. The other Marines waited and watched. The Marine and interpreter chatted with the man, who gesticulated wildly as he explained his case.

Another Marine wandered over to the car to examine it. The Marine looked inside, then glanced under the hood.

Over the radio, we heard the QRF report.

"All clear."

Then the video ended.

"So what happened?" I asked. They didn't touch anything. No one opened the trunk, where explosives could have been hidden.

"The man's car actually broke down," the lieutenant said. "Few Iraqis actually own cars. They are expensive status symbols. The man didn't want his car destroyed by an air strike and decided to surrender to keep it safe. We helped him out by calling for a tow."

I nodded, finally understanding.

"You are probably the first RPAs to capture a prisoner."

"Exactly," the lieutenant said. "It could've been the first time someone surrendered to a plane, ever."

I wasn't so sure about that, but it was possible.

"Anything else?"

"Just videos of raids and stuff. That was our big thing to show."

"Okay," I said.

It was a nice mission for the history books, but what impressed me was how the Marines were using the Pioneer's negatives for positives. The Iraqis knew the buzz of the Pioneer meant the Americans were watching. And the Marines used it as a deterrent. I was impressed.

"Hey, you should talk to the Shadow guys," the lieutenant said. "They do some neat stuff too."

"Who?"

About a mile down the flight line was an Army Shadow platoon. These guys were regular Army and were sent to Al Anbar to support Marine forces during the worst of the fighting for Fallujah. The platoon itself was split between Al Taqaddum and their main post at Forward Operating Base Ramadi.

The Shadow platoon flew the newer RQ-7 Shadow. Similar in size and shape, the Shadow was essentially an upgraded Pioneer. Despite the newer feel, it remained as limited in function as the Pioneer due to its engine noise. The Army used the aircraft the same way the Marines used the Pioneer, but in Ramadi it was used for base security.

I hopped a flight to Ramadi before heading back to Camp Fallujah. I wore a Gore-Tex jacket to ward off the cold night wind at altitude. The Marines laughed at me when I got onboard the CH-47 Chinook until we reached altitude. The chopper pilots discovered that the open side doors, essential for the protective gun mounts, acted like a wind anchor slowing the aircraft. The crews lowered the back ramp a crack to give incoming air an escape route. That resulted in subfreezing temperatures in the cabin. I shivered in the web seating while the Marines around me turned blue.

Silly Marines, I thought. Adapt and overcome.

The looks on their faces said the irony had not escaped them, either.

As we got close, I could see the city and the river. The base sat inside a bend in the Euphrates. From the air, I saw how the city of Ramadi wrapped around the north and east sides of the base. Farmland stretched out to the south and west. The river provided a natural barrier to direct assault, making the south and west the most vulnerable areas.

The air was thick with white dust as I climbed out of the helicopter. The winter shamals were blowing out of the west again, kicking up dirt and contaminants.

An Army staff sergeant picked me up at the ramp. Nearing his fifties, he was slightly overweight and carried a saltiness that came with having done his job for decades. He was a National Guard soldier from Pennsylvania, as was the entire Army brigade combat team in Ramadi.

"Morning, sir," he said over the noise of his HMMWV. "Welcome to FOB Ramadi."

I bounced along in the right seat as the HMMWV drove along the rutted streets.

"The FOB is a bit busy these days," he said. "Activity has picked up lately and we are seeing more attacks than usual. Occasionally, you will hear angry bumblebees go by. When you do, go stand behind a wall."

Angry bumblebees piqued my interest.

"Say again."

"Insurgents get froggy from time to time and unload a magazine at the base," the staff sergeant said. "They usually do it from a safe distance where we can't see it. The rounds lose a lot of energy at these distances. Once they start tumbling, all you will hear is a hum like a big bumblebee."

"Dangerous?"

I hadn't experienced this phenomenon. I'd been shot at before. Usually, the accompanying sound was a *crack* caused by the supersonic shock wave of the round's passage. The "bumblebee" was a new one for me.

"It'll poke a hole in ya," he said. "A lucky hit could still kill ya. Cinder block and sandbags are usually enough to protect you."

"Got it."

I dropped my bags in borrowed quarters. The soldiers who normally lived there were away on leave. My stay was meant to be just for the day and then I had a night departure back to Al Taqaddum. The guys would never know I was there.

After dropping my bags, I drove over to the Shadow Flight. As I got close to the unit's area, I saw they had stacked several Sea-Land shipping containers, on top of which they affixed their transmitters. It was completely nonstandard from what we saw in Predator. The bottom container housed their control station, where they flew the sorties. Next to it was another Sea-Land container used as office space.

Seasonal rains made the parking area a bog. Huge puddles littered the roads and parking lots. I pulled up to a palm tree, hoping for a patch of dry land. An Army captain greeted me as I shut off the HMMWV. He was a young kid, probably wearing freshly minted rank.

"Welcome to the Shadow platoon," he said.

We shook hands.

He filled me in on the unit's mission while we walked across wooden pallets to get to his office. The filthy pallets provided the only solid footing in a lake of mud. Though interested in his brief, I was more intrigued by the mud. Both the water and the mud had a slick sheen, giving it a tie-dyed effect in the sunlight.

"What's with the colors?"

The captain looked disgustedly down at the mud as he walked.

"Diesel fuel."

"Pardon?" I said.

"When we took the base, the troops poured diesel fuel on the ground to control the dust. Now, when it rains, the diesel leaches out of the soil."

I nodded. Diesel was lighter than water and would float to the surface of the puddle.

The office was cramped with mismatched chairs and a desk made of plywood. Shelves built into the wall were crammed with gear, radio chargers, and manuals. On one wall was a map of the local area. On the other wall was a map of the base.

The captain explained that pilots and sensor operators at Al Taqaddum simply launched and landed the aircraft. Without the benefit of satellite control, they could fly the aircraft only within line-of-sight limits. The main force at Ramadi flew the mission portion.

It was a representative of what we did at Nellis. They used LOS for the mission, where we used satellite. Other than that, it was the same concept of operations.

"We don't fly raid support anymore."

"What do you do now?"

"Most of the attacks against the base tend to come from the city," he said. "They don't assault the front gate anymore. Usually, they just lob mortars at us."

"That must be frustrating," I said.

The captain shrugged.

"The insurgents are pretty predictable," he said. "They have twelve POOs that they launch from."

"Okay," I said, looking at the map.

"The plane is too loud to be used to support a raid until after the action starts," the captain said. "By then it's a bit of a waste. Their noise can be used in other ways."

On the map of the area, the captain started pointing to the POO sites.

"We fly each sortie the same," he said. "The aircraft goes to the POO coordinates and watches. The insurgents are predictable enough to go to that site first. They drive up in a HiLux and park in the middle of the intersection. The other cars steer clear of them. An insurgent will get out and walk around for a minute as if listening. If they don't hear us, they attack."

"And if they do hear you?" I asked.

"They move on to the next POO," the captain said. "They'll do the same routine at each location throughout the day."

"Has it been effective?" I asked.

"Mostly," the captain said. "We've been in position for most of the teams. But sometimes one will get through. Not often, though."

"So you use the airplane as an area denial weapon, like the Marines in Fallujah?"

The captain considered that for a moment and said, "Yeah, I guess so."

I judged the mission a success and an ingenious way of turning the aircraft's faults into gains. This kind of forward thinking is what won wars, in my opinion. The RPA community, from the Pioneers and Shadows to the Predators and Reapers, was forging a new kind of air war. From using the buzz of the engine as a deterrent to the use of the buddy lase, it felt like the RPA community was quickly becoming a fixture in the American method of war. It was unlikely American forces would ever go into harm's way again without an RPA.

That night, I traveled back to TQ by convoy after my flight was grounded because of weather. We ended up driving Route Washington around Lake Habbaniyah, past rows of Iraqi mansions, the Baath resort, and Al Taqaddum, before finally reaching the main gate.

It was my first time outside the wire on the ground in Iraq, since I did most of my traveling by helicopter. I was riding "bitch," or in the seat behind the driver of the command HMMWV. In every patch of high grass, I imagined RPG teams popping up and firing. My goggles fogged over as I sweated in the heat of anticipation. I wondered if this was the same emotion these guys felt each and every time they left the base. How often did those targets just pop up in front of them? I was nervous on that trip. I'd hate to feel like that every day for a year.

But the ride, while nerve-racking, finally gave me a sense of just how bad Iraq was. Route Washington was a microcosm of the insanity.

The route wound through decrepit slums and farmhouses near the base in Ramadi and then joined a beautifully maintained six-lane highway that flashed past massive mansions of the Baath elite. The Sunni minority built a tragically wide income gap that kept the ruling party wealthy while average Iraqis lived in squalor. I wasn't sure our attempts to establish a free-market-based society would work. Too much hatred existed between the Sunnis and Shia to let any real peace exist.

When we finally reached the gate near Fallujah, I was exhausted. I walked like a zombie back to my room and collapsed on my cot. I needed to remember those emotions the next time I supported troops on the ground.

I spent sixty days in Iraq working on my assessment. My last stop before leaving Iraq was Al Asad Air Base. I had to speak with Bruiser, the JTAC who controlled Operation Steel Curtain. I wanted to debrief him on our actions there. I also wanted to get the perspective of the guys controlling the fight from the air.

The second largest airbase in Iraq, Al Asad was the main hub for Al Anbar Province. It had an indoor pool, a massive Base Exchange (think military Walmart), and several American fast-food chains. It was a stark contrast to Fallujah and the diesel-soaked dirt of Ramadi.

I met Bruiser in the basement of an old office building that served as staff offices. Naked bulbs provided a little light as we talked around a folding white plastic picnic table. The lights dimmed and dust sprinkled down on us as artillery nearby sent rounds downrange against mortar teams.

Mark was a Marine major who looked far older than me. He could easily have been younger, but the weight of some burden clearly aged him beyond his actual years. He slumped in his seat like he was huddling in on himself.

We slowly went over all the actions at Al Qaim. I had some briefing slides showing what we'd done on target. Mark nodded along, but his eyes were haunted.

"I killed over sixteen hundred people in that fight," he said. "But they were all bad guys."

He said "bad guys" as if seeking absolution for his actions, confirmation that he had done the right thing. He may not have pulled the trigger himself, but he felt the responsibility anyway. Every time he mentioned an engagement, he repeated his bad-guy mantra to himself.

Toward the end of the brief, I mentioned what I'd done. When he learned that I flew Predators, his eyes lit up.

"Really," he exclaimed. "I owe you a beer, man."

"How so?"

"You guys kick ass," he said, alive again. "Predator killed at least fourteen hundred in Steel Curtain."

The number shocked me, and I had him confirm it. I didn't think we had shot so many.

For the rest of my stay, word spread around base. Random guys constantly offered me beer, even if it was nonalcoholic. It was a fame I had neither expected nor knew how to handle. I ended up waving off the praise and saying things like, "It's our job to keep your guys alive."

The Marines always smiled when I said that. I felt lame. But I was pleased at how the Predator had become their number one choice for air cover. It wouldn't last, I knew. But for now, Predator got to bask in its fifteen minutes of fame.

Before leaving the base, we ran by the ScanEagle detachment to see what a smaller aircraft could do. The Marines didn't have enough Pioneers to cover the whole province, so they brought in the little ScanEagle.

The squadron occupied an abandoned MiG-21 revetment at the far end of the airfield. The concrete barrier supported three aircraft in individual compartments. The squadron, after removing the MiGs, had installed small Conex quarters. One section housed the living areas, the middle section contained their ops cell, and the opposite end held their dining and rec room.

Above the bunker, the crusty, old lieutenant colonel, nearing his twenty-eighth year in the Corps, had built a cabin out of two-by-fours and plywood he scraped together from around the base, complete with porch and hammock.

"It's the only retirement home I could afford," the squadron commander said, kicking back on his twenty-square-foot covered porch.

If the Pioneer was a medium-size unmanned aerial vehicle, then the ScanEagle was borderline small. Dainty, it had no landing gear at all. The crews launched the aircraft from a catapult and recovered it by snaring a cable with hooks mounted on its wingtips.

The ScanEagles normally patrolled the areas from Al Qaim to Haditha. The day I visited, the aircraft was locked onto a decrepit old bridge. It bore signs of damage to the supports and structures. The patchy road surface looked like a mess of potholes and debris. Tracks diverted down through the dry wadi to bypass it, telling me the bridge was unsafe for cars.

"That bridge is kinda far off the beaten path," I mentioned to the operator. The tracker display indicated it was miles from any normal traffic.

"Insurgency is using it," the contract pilot said.

I didn't see anyone around the bridge.

"All right, I'll bite. How?"

"Some idiot downloaded instructions on how to blow up a bridge," the pilot said. "The insurgency has been practicing on this one every night for months."

"Practicing?"

Bridge demolition explained the damage.

"They're not very good at it," he said with a smile.

"So I see."

Evening came early that time of year, and with it chilly air. Long shadows cast darkness across the revetments as we ate a half-way decent meal. The food wasn't as bad as I thought it would be. The ice cream was better. I thought it odd that few Marines were eating chow.

After dinner I asked one of the Marines where the head was.

"Outside the compound, next to the dorms."

I smiled. "Thanks." I turned to take care of business.

The Marine called out, "I'd be careful if I was you."

I stopped. "Excuse me?"

The Marine nodded at the nearby fence line. "Insurgents snuck up on the base a couple weeks back," the Marine said. "They fired a rocket at the compound after dark and shredded the john."

"Seriously?"

The Marine pointed at a building about one hundred yards away. It was the flight line access checkpoint.

"The Nigerian guards that man it insist on shining their spotlight in our direction to see into approaching cars. At night, we are the only building visible from outside the wire."

"What happened with the rocket?"

"It hit next to the john. It's got shrapnel in it still. The concussion knocked everyone out of their beds."

"Really?" I said with some skepticism.

"The guys haven't eaten dinner for weeks because they don't want to use it after dark."

I pondered that as I walked into the blue plastic port-a-john. I'd never complain about the port-a-johns or the backed-up bathroom at the Predator compound at Nellis again. At least there, we didn't have to worry about RPGs.

My deployment had changed my perspective on the war in ways both expected and unexpected. For one thing, I'd never forget that in Iraq, even going to the head is dangerous.

CHAPTER 13

23 Seconds

"One minute."

The targeting pod's cross hairs were locked on a white pickup parked under a row of palm trees outside a small white house in Hibhib. The truck was nondescript in every way. There were no markings, dents, paint details, or anything else to set it apart from the other trucks in the Baquba area. We recognized it only because we had tracked it for the past 480 hours, give or take.

The truck wasn't the target. The man who had just left the house and climbed into the passenger seat was the priority. He was Abu Musab al-Zarqawi, the declared leader of al Qaeda in Iraq.

Al-Zarqawi was a Jordanian who set up militant cells in Iraq prior to the 2003 invasion. He then joined the insurgency during the occupation. For his efforts, al-Zarqawi was given the title "Emir of al Qaeda in the Country of Two Rivers." He was accused of abducting and executing Nicholas Berg in May 2004 and beheading Owen Eugene Armstrong, another American working in Iraq, two years later. Al-Zarqawi had a hand in more than seven hundred killings in Iraq, mostly from bombings like that of the UN building in Baghdad in 2003.

And by 2006, he was priority number one in Iraq.

Back from my deployment, I resumed my duties as the group's chief pilot. I spent most of my time helping train pilots for the new squadrons forming in the wake of our success, training new students at the 11th, and flying missions. The number of squadrons had expanded from three when I joined the RPA community three years before to five stateside and a couple more in theater.

More pilots were learning to fly the Predator and Reaper than any other aircraft in the Air Force. The RPA community was slowly climbing out of the basement of the Air Force fleet and taking its place near the top. Unlike when I joined, pilots in the training pipeline wanted to be part of the RPA community because this aircraft was fighting the war on all fronts.

"Thirty seconds, laser on."

The pilot's voice crackled through the intercom speaker. I stood behind the 15th Reconnaissance Squadron's mission commander, watching the event go down. The flight and the crew belonged to the 3rd Special Operations Squadron.

The Task Force in Iraq assigned to the mission to eliminate al Qaeda cells wasn't looking to capture al-Zarqawi. They wanted him eliminated.

The Predator angled into range, unheard over the surrounding urban noise. Traffic was sparse on this street. There was little chance of collateral damage. A strike now would likely hurt only al-Zarqawi and his spiritual adviser, Sheikh Abd al-Rahman.

Standing in the ops center, I'd invested too much time in tracking him not to be there when we got him. The other crews around me likely thought the same. I was sure other pilots were in the ops center watching me when I'd gotten the Facilitator the year before. The big missions always drew an audience.

Few aircraft had their missions transmitted live around the world like Predator did. Pred porn permeated every office that could access the video feeds. In a way, the world was watching.

But I had mixed feelings about killing off al-Zarqawi.

On the one hand, he was a symbolic leader of the movement. Eliminating him sent a message to al Qaeda and its supporters throughout the world that they could not win. On the other hand, the war was already over if al-Zarqawi was the best and brightest al Qaeda had to offer. We'd watched him so much that I thought he was more bluster than anything else. There was video showing him unable to work an AK-47 and mishandling a stolen SAW machine gun. It always made us laugh. An AK was designed so an idiot or a child could operate it. What did that say about him?

Trailing al-Zarqawi had become our primary mission as tensions in Al Anbar wound down. Fighting still raged in the Sunni Triangle, but it had subsided to a level where the Marines could transfer control of the Predators back to the Army. Al-Zarqawi had been busy while coalition forces focused on Al Anbar.

The year before, al-Zarqawi had declared war on the Shia in Iraq. He'd used suicide bombers to attack coalition forces and Shia militias. He'd also developed a series of terrorist training camps within the city limits of several towns. Locals were afraid to turn him in because of threats of violence. His cells operated openly, making car bombs and setting up IEDs.

What he worried about was the "White Devil." We were a

silent killer whose mere mention brought fear into their ranks. They suspended operations when they knew we were in the area.

Pushed out of Fallujah, al-Zarqawi set up shop near Baquba. There he directed the rebuilding of an organization we had torn apart during the battle. When we started the hunt, intelligence could only point to an area and tell us he was in there somewhere. It was the best their sources could give them. So we sent our aircraft there on the chance we'd get a whiff of his activity. It turned into a slow, methodical hunt like the one for Bin Laden in Afghanistan.

The Task Force's efforts to capture al-Zarqawi kicked into high gear in February 2006 when interrogators began building a picture of what al-Zarqawi's organization looked like. They started small, with captured operatives, and held them at a compound on the base. Abu Ghraib was for the common insurgent. If you got sent to "the compound," you had something the Task Force wanted. The interrogators had a reputation for getting every drop of information.

My first assignment in the Air Force was as an interrogator. In fact, I was one of the last Air Force interrogators before headquarters transferred the function to the Army in 1995. I supported our early operations in Somalia, Rwanda, and Haiti. I even won the CIA's Exceptional Human Intelligence Collector Award in late 1994 for my work supporting Haiti. Contacts my team cultivated revealed an assassination attempt against former president Jimmy Carter. Ever since, I appreciated what the interrogators could bring to the fight and I vowed to use the information to track down al-Zarqawi and the leaders of al Qaeda in Iraq.

When they got a tip that al Qaeda fighters were operating near Al Kazariya, we flew to the village and started to scan the area, looking for any trace of movement. It was my turn to fly for the 3rd

Special Operations Squadron and I could see a road suspected of trafficking weapons in my HUD. It ran northeast from Baghdad, through Baquba on its way to the Iranian border. It was late, and the road was devoid of cars and trucks.

We suspected Iran was supplying al Qaeda in Iraq and the insurgency with guns and explosives. The Iranians had no real interest in the Iraqis. Their support was an attack on the United States. I watched too many Iranian helicopters fly from bases deep in Iranian territory to drop supplies for the insurgency in marshy eastern Iraq to be convinced otherwise.

I even tried to shoot one down once, but the three-star general running the air war called me off.

My sensor operator scanned the road as we got to the outskirts of Al Kazariya. I rotated between the squadrons so much that I had no idea with whom I was flying. Most flights I got a name and a little small talk. I was a guest at the squadrons now, not a member. I missed being one of the boys, so I enjoyed the time I got on the stick even if it was doing pattern-of-life missions.

The intercom connected to the tactical operations center remained quiet. The 3rd Special Operations Squadron was now directly tied to the Task Force, just like the 17th was linked to their JOC. We could talk directly to the collection managers, JTACs, and commanders.

Nothing stood out as we scanned the road and village. There were no indications of a possible IED. No one walked around the streets. This was the start of the hunt, and the Task Force threw out a wide net, looking for anyone we could follow up the chain.

Moving to the cluster of houses, we searched for any movement. The blocks were small, maybe three to four houses per street. We could see most of the village and keep an eye on the main road all at the same time. We were running the targeting pod parallel to the main road, and houses zipped through the HUD in a blur. We were in the process of shifting to another sector for a fresh search when we saw the flash.

"Whoa, what's that?" I said.

The sensor instinctively stopped the ball in place.

"What?"

"You didn't see that?" I asked.

"See what?"

He looked confused. I pointed to my HUD in the direction of the flash.

"Move back that way, slowly. I saw something flash. A hot spot."

It could have been anything. Cooking fire, guy taking a piss or a smoke break. But I still wanted to check. The sensor panned the ball back slowly and paused to give us both a chance to truly see the picture. After about three blocks, we saw another flash in the extreme corner of the HUD.

"Up there," I said.

The cross hairs shifted up and to the right and stopped on a house with a walled-in backyard. The yard was large enough to hold a crude obstacle course. Fighters ran around the obstacles. Others were shooting AK-47s. The whole area looked like a cheesy 1970s James Bond flick.

We sat for a moment, surprised at the audacity of building a training facility within a block and a half of a major road. Apparently, security wasn't a concern for these guys.

I called the Predator LNO. He wasn't there. He hadn't checked off for a relief break or even to change out with another LNO. *Bad timing,* I thought as I posted my query in chat.

DN31> Hostile Act on-screen, request permission to engage.

We were there. We were armed. A single Hellfire could have taken out the whole complex.

TF145TOC> STBY.

We were told to stand by. I felt a little deflated as I spun up the missiles. I didn't expect to shoot, but I got ready just in case. We were still a new asset for this supported unit and they had so far been reluctant to use us as a strike asset.

TF145TOC> need you to stand off 5nm.

Standing off five nautical miles meant we would not be shooting.

DN31> c.

We were being positioned for overwatch duty. The Task Force had a lot of tools at their disposal, most of which were more suited to a mission like this than we were.

DN31> orbiting to the SE.
TF145TOC> c.

From that vantage, I could monitor the street entrance to the house and see the entire training compound. I watched one figure jump over a barricade, fire half a dozen rounds from the hip, and attempt to smash a dummy with his rifle butt. His motions were so spastic that an American would have downed him before he'd even scaled the barricade. I sort of felt sorry for the guy. He was full of spirit and machismo but had no inherent physical talent. Lucky for him he would be captured soon.

Just as he finished with the dummy, I saw clumps of dirt explode around the trainees. One insurgent collapsed immediately.

"Oh shit," my sensor operator blurted out.

"Watch for squirters," I said.

The sensor refocused and started actively scanning the perimeter. Rotor blades from a pair of Apache attack helicopters flashed through the HUD. Judging by the size of the divots, these were 20mm rounds hitting the compound.

"Runners to the south," the sensor called out.

One of the trainees or maybe an instructor smartly ran around the corner of the building and joined up with a couple of other armed insurgents. They huddled low against the wall. These guys looked more competent, more experienced. They assumed the helicopters would lose sight of them, but they must have missed the lesson at terrorist school about the White Devils.

DN31> Squirters south side.

Another helicopter flashed through our HUD. Moments later, a second burst hit. Unlike the first pass, which strafed the length of the compound, this burst concentrated on the men hiding against the wall. The 20mm rounds cut their silhouettes into the wall before they collapsed in the dust. The attack choppers made a couple more passes before pulling off target.

We hadn't been released from the target, so we continued to watch. Occasionally, the flash of a rotor could be seen in the HUD.

The helicopters were orbiting the compound, searching for any movement.

I wonder what they are waiting for, I thought. Then a Black Hawk dashed over the target and hovered in the street. Thick black lines dropped from both sides. Fast ropes.

In seconds, a special operations team descended and spread out. There was no return fire. The team blew open the gate of the compound and flooded inside. A small convoy of HMMWVs rolled up and a couple of bodies were loaded into the back.

We'd found one of al-Zarqawi's camps. It was like fitting a piece in the puzzle, but we were a long way from finishing it. Over time, information from the survivors of this raid and others led the Task Force to capture some of the facilitators and leaders. The Task Force kept working until a team of interrogators got one of al-Zarqawi's associates to betray him.

Sheikh Abd al-Rahman became our target.

The first night, a crew found Sheikh Abd al-Rahman and then promptly lost him as the driver weaved through rush-hour traffic. The second night, we reacquired the truck, and the crew managed to stay on him. The truck was a white HiLux with a crew cab. It was well maintained but not flashy. It could be anyone's car; it just happened to be a more reliable vehicle. The truck blended in well with the traffic in and around Baquba.

We were required to have a long standoff from the target. This limited our chance of being detected. But it also degraded the optics so that facial recognition was impossible. The Task Force had to rely on other sources to verify that we were in fact following al-Rahman. So while they worked out that problem, we remained locked on the little white pickup. By day, we trailed discreetly behind him as he made his rounds. By night, we watched his home. We documented anyone who came and went and analyzed if it was al-Zarqawi or just a courier.

It was early morning when I got my first chance to track al-Rahman. The truck was still parked at the safe house when he climbed into the cab with his driver. I shut off the autopilot and made a slight turn to the right to make sure I had control.

I checked the tracker map above the HUD and put the Predator in a lazy orbit off to the side of the road so I could watch him drive in either direction. The engine started and the driver slid into the traffic moving up and down the road. The sensor operator kept the truck in the middle of the HUD as I turned the Predator so we could follow. All around him, taxis with orange-and-white panels rode nearby. Trucks lumbered along the road, passing carts pulled by donkeys. A white vehicle in Iraq blended in with the environment like a rabbit in a snowstorm. I pressed my finger against the target truck on the HUD screen. I figured I couldn't miss him if I was touching him.

He drove for a few miles before turning onto a dirt road. I had no idea where he was going. Though we'd been able to do so with other targets, it was too early to figure out his complete pattern of life. And he was more erratic than the others. He didn't keep a schedule like the Facilitator or the Captain.

He was good.

I let the Predator fly past for a few miles before circling back. We never lost sight of him and I wanted to make sure we didn't overfly the car. When that happened, we would momentarily exceed the gimbal limit inside the targeting pod, sending it careering toward the horizon.

We had to avoid that mistake.

I checked my imagery overlays. Intel used a photo of an area frequented by al-Zarqawi. On it were drawn colored lines to indicate his probable destinations. Each color represented a different path, or the level of frequency used. I wanted to see if al-Rahman was going on an established route.

I had no idea where he was going, but I kept him in sight for my whole shift. We never lost him as he drove between villages, meeting with facilitators. When I heard the two knocks on the GCS, I was relieved. I didn't realize how tense I had become.

Sheikh Abd al-Rahman's truck was on the highway when the new pilot showed up. In normal conditions, we would brief the incoming crew and swap seats. When chasing the spiritual adviser, we had the autopilot off, which meant we had to keep our hands on the controls while swapping seats.

"Ready?" I said.

The new pilot nodded. He squeezed himself into the narrow space between the pilot's couch and the rack of computers. He then reached over my shoulder and took control of the stick. He had to figure out what I was doing with the aircraft and match the pressures on the spring-loaded controls. Once he was good to go, I ducked under his arm and out of the seat. He slid around and sat down.

I took out the keyboard and set it on the table between the sensor operator and the new pilot. I sent a note to the TOC in chat.

DN31> new crew in seat.
TF145TOC> c.

Eventually, we determined that al-Zarqawi traveled often with al-Rahman, and through that we established al-Zarqawi's pattern of life with a high level of confidence. After two weeks, we could identify where on the route he was based with a mere glance at the HUD picture just as we had with the Captain. We had seen the same buildings enough times to nearly memorize his every move. We knew exactly where he was for the 480 hours leading up to the night of June 6, when the Task Force finally gave the nod to the Predators to strike.

I was watching the mission with the other pilots in the squadron. This was our chance to show the special operations community what we could do.

"Lasing," the sensor operator said.

I returned my focus to the wall-mounted plasma screen. The truck grew large in the image. I expected "LRD Lase Des" to flash on the HUD picture to indicate the laser was firing. The letters were a shortened note signifying the Laser Range Designator was firing and marking the target. In the cockpit, "laser firing" should have been flashing as well.

Nothing showed.

Inside the cockpit, the sensor operator had forgotten to arm the laser. Maybe the pilot had forgotten to tell him. Both should have gotten it right. This was not a good start.

"Laser's not armed," the pilot said.

The sensor replied calmly.

"Arming."

They were both calm, professional. They had time to get it right.

Then the picture disappeared. No graphics or image showed. Only a uniform gray remained.

"Oh no," someone behind me said.

They had given the crew clearance as al-Zarqawi emerged from Sheikh al-Rahman's house. Their goal had been to hit the truck just before the two pulled out of the driveway, but then the screen went dark.

"What the hell happened?" the MCC roared.

I put my hand over my face. I knew what he had done.

The sensor operator had NUC'd his targeting pod. Prior to any shot, sensors typically wanted to calibrate the targeting pod to ensure the best picture possible. The nonuniformity correction, or NUC, accomplished this task in under half a minute.

Computers managed the inner workings of the Predator, like most modern aircraft, and the computers worked only if the software was valid. The factory issued frequent software updates as we identified glitches or requested improvements. The most recent change had left a bug in the system that we were learning to work around. A function was added to activate the keyboard space bar as a "hot key" that when hit would repeat the previous command. So if a sensor armed the laser as his last command, then hitting the space bar would arm it again.

Simple, really. And it worked only on the sensor's console. The pilots didn't have the capability.

As they lined up the shot on al-Zarqawi, the sensor operator had inadvertently brushed against the space bar as he reached to arm the laser. NUC was the last command in the system, and the space bar had sent the system into a twenty-three-second calibration that could not be reversed. The misstep wasn't the factory's fault. It was clearly a sloppy hand motion by the sensor operator. It was avoidable.

The twenty-three seconds passed before the house emerged from the gray screen as if from a fog. The truck and al-Zarqawi were gone.

The ops cell fell completely silent. I didn't have to say anything.

Everyone knew instinctively that the targeting pod had been NUC'd. Privately, everyone metaphorically wiped their brows in relief that they weren't the guys in the seat.

The military world had just watched that crew screw up the biggest shot of the Iraq War.

Fortunately, another Predator followed the truck as it continued its rounds and we didn't lose him. But we lost our chance to do the strike.

The next day, June 7, the Task Force authorized another strike. They kicked the Predator far enough from the target that the crew could barely see the building. This time, F-16s from Balad dropped GPS-guided bombs on the house.

The community felt an enormous amount of frustration in the wake of the failed air strike. We had worked so hard to track al-Zarqawi, only to be denied the endgame following the self-induced glitch. The missed opportunity was a simple error. There was no incompetence involved, no unprofessionalism. Just a simple mistake that was as statistically probable as a bad missile or a mechanical breakdown in the laser. But it happened on one of the biggest missions in the community's history, with what felt like the whole world watching.

We'd made important shots and mistakes before, but this one was a huge setback. The Task Force scaled back Predator strikes after the failed mission. They claimed that they needed our persistent imagery more than our strike capability. But we all knew the real reason. Despite all the strides we'd made, we were back to proving ourselves again.

The RPA community had to eliminate those annoying statistical anomalies if we wanted to be given the privilege of taking the next critical shot.

CHAPTER 14

Camp Cupcake

It was four in the morning local time and the sky was still dark. I could see the lights of Al Udeid Air Base sparkling around me. There were no blackout conditions this far from the fighting.

The base was the forward headquarters of Air Forces Central, which oversees all American forces in the Middle East. The air base, west of Doha, Qatar, was also home to the Air Force's head-quarters in charge of the air war over Iraq and Afghanistan.

We milled about the parking ramp while maintenance unloaded the cargo bins from the C-17. The heat and humidity in January was enough to give me pause as I emerged from the dry aircraft interior. All the passengers, officer and enlisted alike, unloaded the baggage from the bins and lined them up on the tarmac to pass through Qatari customs and then through the Patriot Gate.

Named in the wake of September 11, 2001, the Patriot Gate was really just a plywood holding area where checked passengers waited for final boarding on the way to Iraq, to Afghanistan, or back home. Troops from years past had scribbled messages and their names on the plywood. The gate became a living memorial to those who had passed through.

I wasn't passing through or leaving. I'd worked out a deal to spend a year in Qatar working reconnaissance issues on the Air Force staff. I needed to leave Nellis Air Force Base if I wanted to get promoted and take command of a squadron. The one deployment to Iraq wasn't enough and I needed staff time. To get the year, I had to string together three consecutive four-month tours, which was the Air Force standard deployment length at the time. I had to fly halfway across the world and work in an office to accomplish what the Air Force required of me as a professional.

Gringo, a fellow Predator pilot, met me outside the terminal. He was another 17th alum. I was his relief, there to assume his duties so he could rotate home. We threw my bags into the back of his truck and drove toward the barracks area.

"We're in Ops Town now," he said. "This is where all the flying missions are done."

I vaguely remember seeing the buildings as we flew past in the darkness. Most of the squadrons were dark. A Green Beans Coffee shop already had a line out the door. The patrons were a mix of new arrivals and aircrew coming in for their morning briefs. Gringo steered the pickup onto what looked like a road to nowhere snaking off into the darkness.

"Ops Town was the original base when we moved in," he said. "Most of the buildings are relatively new, but a few, like the pax terminal, were here when we arrived. Since then, the base has really expanded."

We approached a heavily armed gate. The metal bars remained locked in place as we drove up. On either side were two-story towers fashioned in an Arabic theme. Qatari flags atop the towers flapped in the light breeze. Gringo swerved onto a side road and passed the checkpoint.

"That's the Qatari Air Force. We don't go in there."

"What do they fly?" I asked.

"Beats me," Gringo said. "Haven't seen them fly anything."

A bright spot on the horizon grew larger as we approached. At first I thought it was the coming dawn. But as we got closer, it turned into a massive camp. The Coalition Village, or C-Town, was the living area on the base for the Americans and other Western allies. C-Town boasted thousands of dorms built in triple-wide and triple-long prefab buildings. At the center of the area was a large open-air tent (just the top, no sides) that looked like one of Bettie Page's lost bras.

The Bra, as someone cleverly named it, was the center of social life for Al Udeid. The USO performed shows there. A gym, bar, movie theater, coffeehouse, Olympic-size pool, Base Exchange (BX), and small bevy of fast-food joints surrounded the Bra. It was a pretty nice setup as far as deployments went. Better than my toolshed in Fallujah.

Gringo dropped me off at our room, a cramped, paneled space dominated by a bunk bed and two metal cabinets. Gringo and I shared the space for a couple of days until he left for home. I got it all to myself after that. Standing in the middle of the room, I considered myself lucky. The younger guys had to sleep two or three to a room in the same space.

I took a couple of days to get settled in. The military required numerous briefings to set the tone for each assignment. But the longer I was there, the more I sensed something was off about the base. I said as much to Gringo over a beer before he left for good. Gringo eyed me for a second. Then he nodded at a kid across the Bra.

"See him?"

The kid was in the Army, judging by his uniform. He hobbled awkwardly on crutches across the crushed white rock. His lower right leg was in a cast.

"Yeah."

"The Army," Gringo said, "sends their wounded here to recuperate."

"I thought they went to Germany," I said.

"Those are the ones not coming back. That kid will be back in the fight in a couple weeks. So the Army sent him here for rest so he could return quicker."

"Oh," I said.

Gringo smiled.

"Those guys call this place Camp Cupcake."

"I can see why," I agreed.

"Everything is easy here," Gringo said. "At least that's the impression."

My job wasn't easy. I was in Qatar to manage fourteen reconnaissance platforms in CENTCOM's area. It was my job to make sure they were doing the correct missions in both theaters as well as a new hot spot developing in Yemen. I didn't really meddle in the daily operations. Mostly, I pushed paper since the platforms were fairly self-sufficient. There always seemed to be some crisis I had to solve to keep the planes flying.

By the spring, I'd been at Al Udeid for four months. You really couldn't see any seasonal change in the environment, since nothing grew on the base. The crushed white rock remained just as dead as before. The first I noticed the change in seasons was when the mornings became foggy.

I normally walked the mile from my dorm to my office. Walking was exercise. Working sixteen-hour days had taken its toll in only two months. I shed workouts from my schedule in favor of a few hours of restless sleep. I gained weight and it didn't make me feel good. I missed flying. There was an inherent healthiness to performing tasks with my hands and seeing their outcomes.

Staff work was not a natural talent of mine. It was boring. I didn't take well to the strictures of paperwork and the staff processes that went with it. And all of this would be for nothing if I didn't get promoted.

The Air Force promotion board released its list in the spring while I was at Al Udeid.

Every officer in my year group was on edge in the weeks leading up to its release. The Air Force held three promotion boards. The first two boards didn't count, in my mind, as around 1 percent of the officers made rank through them. The third and last board was where most of us would learn if we made it.

I shared an office with Muggles, who'd gotten his call sign from the Harry Potter books. We had been academy classmates, which placed us on the same promotion board. I hadn't known Muggles personally at school, nor had our paths crossed once commissioned as officers. After fifteen years, Muggles was nearly unrecognizable. He was my height and a little heavier. While my hair was graying on the sides, his had receded significantly.

We became fast friends instantly. We drank beers at the Bra

and ate dinner together, when we could fit it into our sixteen-hour days. The night before the list was made public, we decided to stick around the office and see if the Al Udeid leadership saw the list early. Typically, the Air Force released the list to the command staffs. The Wing and Group commanders would then notify the affected members the night before the official release. Usually, they called only the guys who didn't make rank. They were given the usual platitudes and told not to come in the next day so they wouldn't have to be around the celebrants.

We both thought we'd made the cut. But there was something about being evaluated, graded against others, that put us on edge. With nothing to do but wait, we sat in the conference room anticipating the news. We didn't talk. There was nothing to say while we sweated over our fates. At the time, I was one of two officers from the RPA community on track to command. Mike was the other. If we both got promoted, we'd be the first RPA pilots to take command. Fighter pilots looking for command time sponged up most of the slots.

I have no idea how long we sat there, sipping water and waiting. The other staff members were long gone when my boss popped his head in and saw us. Usually, he wore a broad smile. This time he frowned.

"What are you guys waiting for?"

"Waiting on the promotion news, sir," I said.

He looked at Muggles and then me.

"Has anyone called you guys?"

"No, sir."

He nodded.

"Then you made the list. Get out of here."

Sure enough, the list was published the next day. I marveled at my name. I did the math and determined that I would pin on lieutenant colonel in January. Mike was far enough up the list that he would probably make rank in December. I let out a sigh of relief. I was still on track to get command, a goal I'd wanted since I'd joined the Air Force. But first I had to survive a year on staff pushing paper.

It did not go well for me. The Army constantly complained about the lack of air support and blamed the reconnaissance community for the Army's planning failures. I did the best I could to meet every requirement. I put more effort into biting my tongue. I simply could not blanket the sky with stars.

By mid-May, my frustrations came to a head. After four months I had grown weary of hearing Predators being blamed for everyone's mistakes, especially the Army's. During a biweekly videoconference with units in Iraq and Afghanistan, one of the collection managers briefed us on a soldier who had been separated from his unit and died in a flash flood. The collection manager, an Army captain, blamed Predator for the whole incident. I checked my mission logs. No Predators were tasked to support the unit.

I couldn't hold my tongue as the captain heaped the blame on the RPA community. I keyed the mic.

"Hang on a second."

I rifled through the papers on my desk and found the log.

"Captain," I began. "I don't appreciate you blaming the Predator for your failures. I cannot understand how, when my asset is so abused, that you refuse to follow doctrine in its employment. You treat them like a tank. This model failed in 1942 and continues to fail today. It is the principle reason you are losing this war."

The Air Force J-2 officer at CENTCOM started laughing on the screen. I couldn't tell if he was laughing at me or with me. The

Army and Marine officers in the room were less amused. I pressed on anyway. I'd already started the rant. The damage was done. I might as well finish it.

"I appreciate the fact that you consider the Predator invaluable. What I can't understand is why you cancel operations if one is not available. When I was a ground pounder, I was trained to develop a plan based on worst-case and best-case scenarios. We also made a plan based on what we actually expected to get. Seems to me you only make one plan that hinges on Predator support or nothing at all.

"As for your troop, I am truly sorry he died. But I ask you one question: Where was his leadership? Where was his squad leader? He should have had eyes on all his guys while on foot patrol. Where was his platoon leader? His company commander? No, Captain, that young man did not die because a Predator was assigned to a unit eighty miles away."

Fortunately for the captain, time for the video teleconference (VTC) ran out and cut off the forum. He never got to respond, and I had no idea how he had received my criticism. It was harsh, but the Predator community wasn't to blame. I watched the screen for a moment, my sails slowly deflating. On the one hand, I felt a total rush from the experience. My pulse raced in my throat. In just a few minutes I had released pent-up frustrations resulting from watching the Army lay blame on us in public forums.

The captain represented all that was wrong with how the Army employed air power at the tactical level. I just didn't get why they didn't understand that. I walked away feeling vindicated. Sure, I metaphorically fell on my sword by addressing the issue in such a manner. The general officers wouldn't let that outburst go without repercussion.

I found out a couple of days later that my deployment was cut short. I was going home at the end of the month. None of my leadership would admit that my rant was the reason. It didn't matter really.

The denial of my orders at Al Udeid forced me to find an assignment. There is a funny rule in the Air Force. If an officer is assigned to one post for too long, he or she is moved to a new location. I had been in Las Vegas for nearly four and a half years when I returned early from Qatar.

It was a year beyond the Air Force's comfort zone.

I'd worked out the one-year assignment to Al Udeid to reset my clock at Nellis Air Force Base. I wanted to stay in the RPA community. Cutting short my orders nullified that deal, so I called the Air Force Personnel Center and asked what was available. I couldn't pull g's anymore, so nothing fast. I had a lingering neck and back injury that was quite painful and didn't let me sleep at night. After a few queries, they told me going to a combat aircraft squadron was impossible.

"You've been out of those aircraft for too long."

There also weren't staff jobs available. At the time, manning was so short in the combat units that the Air Force simply wouldn't release me for a desk job. I had to go to a flying billet.

"Is there a T-1 available?"

I was referencing the Hawker T-1A Jayhawk, a trainer derived from the Beech model 400 business jet.

The assignment was a long shot—I had never flown the plane before. The tanker and transport community had the lock on that squadron and the benefits were too good, but I could get three aircraft-type ratings for my pilot license and valuable business-jet time if I could land the job. If my career were to stall at this point, those qualifications would help me land an airline job.

"Air Combat Command has a slot that doesn't always get filled," he said.

"I'll take it."

I was reassigned to Randolph Air Force Base in San Antonio as an instructor teaching new T-1 instructors in the 99th Flying Training Squadron. The 99th was one of the original Tuskegee Airmen squadrons and the only one still active. They were the famous Red Tails.

After four years in a GCS, it felt good to be back in an airborne cockpit.

On my first flight, I took in as much of the scenery as I could. Randolph Air Force Base had always been at the top of my list of places to serve. Built in the 1930s, most of the original hangars, homes, and buildings remained. Two massive runways bracketed the base. A single main road ran up from the main gate. As I climbed into the blue sky on a warm fall afternoon, the base roads looked like a lollipop clutched between a child's dirty fingers.

After my two-hour flight, I walked up to the squadron proper and moved through the swinging glass door that led to our duty desk. I felt good. All the stress of the staff time was gone. If my rant forced me to finish my career as an instructor, I was happy because there was still no better feeling than flying. I'd accomplished most of my goals. I'd flown in combat and did my part during the war.

The commander stood there looking grim while I turned in my post-mission paperwork.

"Squirrel, we've got to talk," he said.

He didn't sound too happy.

"Yes, sir," I said.

I had an idea what was coming. One of the guys back at Creech had warned me. The commander sat on the edge of his desk.

"I've got to pull you from training."

I said nothing. He handed me a letter.

"The secretary of the Air Force is sending you back to Creech."

The Joint Staff had announced an "all-in" surge in Iraq to help General David Petraeus finally suppress the insurgency. I had hoped to be safe in training.

In the Air Force culture, no one could remove an airman from a formal training course once it had begun. Each course billet was tied to money predesignated for that training. An early departure meant the money was wasted.

"Is there anything we can do?" I finally asked.

"I'm sorry, Squirrel. We got trumped."

The four-star general in charge of Air Education and Training Command was told to shut up and color when he cried foul.

I moved out of my house I'd owned for thirty days and headed back to Las Vegas.

I checked in to the new Wing Operations Center (WOC) at Creech Air Force Base a few weeks later. The base had grown massively in the little less than a year I'd been gone. We had gone from borrowing space at Nellis Air Force Base to owning the whole base in Indian Springs. A new wing headquarters was under construction near the hangar in which I worked. For now, I was in a closet attached to the construction area. The WOC had just enough room for four desks, associated computers, and a few plasmas on the walls above.

We were a mini ops cell, only our mission was greater than ever. As a WOC director, I'd be doing the old mission commander job but on a grander scale. Gone were the days when only one squadron had flown the conventional lines. Now we had three Predator, two Reaper, and one British squadron operating in theater, and more were on the way.

"This is your job," Knobber said.

Knobber was an old F-117 pilot who transferred to Creech for a sunset tour, his last tour in the military. He had the sharp, aggressive personality typical of fighter pilots and perfect for this type of job.

"Love the broom closet," I said.

"It's only temporary."

"How many WOC directors are there?" I asked.

"Three. You, me, and Alley Cat."

I had expected as much. The three of us were really assigned here as a deployed position, which meant little time off.

"So what do we do?"

Knobber sighed.

"We are the oversight for anything flying. When nothing is going on, we are building the programs that run the WOC."

"Seriously? Can I at least fly?"

Knobber laughed. He patted me on the shoulder.

"Good luck with that."

The job was better than staff work, since I was still involved with the missions. It wasn't perfect, though. I was now one of the graybeards in Predator. The community had grown so fast that many of the positive changes Mike and I had worked toward had fallen into misuse. Professionalism slipped as fatigue wore down the crews. My goal was to try to bring back to the community some of the professionalism Mike and I had struggled to instill. But I was only one person in a nonleadership job.

By early spring 2008, I had sunk into a routine of working

twelve-hour WOC shifts. For us, flying the line was tantamount to working in the salt mines. Crews were having trouble overcoming the constant drudgery of repetitive sorties, seeing the same targets, and watching American soldiers being killed and not being able to do anything to stop it. Worse, the rules of engagement kept changing so that no unit, especially Predator, could actually fight the enemy. Our own leadership was hamstringing us.

Winter weather in Iraq and Afghanistan tapered off and the fighters came out of hiding. The workload increased significantly, even if I could do little of it. Most of my shift was spent behind a raised desk. A bank of monitors allowed me to watch the feeds and chat rooms. As I had in my staff job, I mostly put out fires or answered questions. I did my best to keep the absurdity and bureaucracy from getting into the cockpit.

I was well into my shift when one of my Predators sent me a warning.

RE27> WOC, taking shot soon.

A rarity, I thought.

It wasn't necessary to tell me he was going to shoot. Only his supervisor needed to know, but some of the crews, in the stress of combat, felt compelled to tell everyone about it. I brought up their feed. A small house with a car in the front yard filled my screen. A couple of military-aged males, or MAMs as we were now calling unidentified personnel, were milling about the yard. They appeared to be deeply involved in a discussion.

"What's that in his hands?" the weather troop asked.

She was a young airman who had little experience dealing directly with operations beyond briefing crews on their way to fly. A bright spot blazed in his hand. Occasionally, the MAM would lift the hand to his mouth and the bright spot would flare.

"That's a cigarette," I said.

"Really?" she said. "That seems too bright."

"Compared to everything else, it is."

Smokers at night often looked as if they held a miniature sun in their hands.

Since there was nothing else going on, I monitored the conversation in the mission chat room. The collection managers were discussing the targets and what to do. They wanted to kill the guy leaning against the hood of the car. I started to go through the steps in my head. Collateral damage estimate was complete. Rules of engagement checklist was complete. The JTAC was working final clearance from the ground commander. I watched the string of data as it posted in the chat room.

The target finished his cigarette and ground it out with his foot. Then he got into the car and drove off. At first the car wound through a couple of streets before it turned onto a divided four-lane highway.

BY41> Shoot, Shoot, Shoot, Shoot now.

What was that all about? I thought. The JTAC wanted the Predator to shoot, but I didn't remember seeing a 9-Line or clearance to fire. I scrolled back through the chat room. Nothing. At least, there was no written record. The vehicle had long since moved out of the target area, making any previous clearances moot.

The whole situation stank.

RE27> In from the south, 1 min.

The Predator pilot was lining up the shot. But from what I saw, he clearly had no business doing so. Worse, this crew was not trained for a moving-target shot. There was no telling what would happen or who would be injured if the missile missed.

My mind flashed to 1994 and my friend Laura Piper. She was an air operations intelligence analyst stationed in Ramstein, Germany. She was riding in a helicopter with NATO dignitaries surveying northern Iraq during Operation Provide Comfort, the humanitarian mission to aid Kurdish refugees after the Gulf War.

A pair of F-15 Eagles were vectored in to investigate when the pair of Black Hawk helicopters squawked codes meant to identify themselves as friendly, but they were the wrong codes. The fighters were within a week of leaving for home and they had not shot at anything during their tour. Their fangs were through the floor as they buzzed the pair of helicopters and then shot them down. The fighter pilots never identified them as friendly despite the choppers' American markings. In their minds, they were only targets.

Their incompetence cost a lot of people their lives, and cost me a friend.

I never forgave the F-15 community for that shot. I never understood how they could misidentify a helicopter painted green instead of tan like an Iraqi helicopter. They acted unprofessionally and incompetently and then blamed AWACS for it.

In a way I harbor a bit of survivor's guilt. Laura and I interviewed for the same interrogator job early in our careers. We were neck and neck going into the final interview. I eventually won. As a consolation, she was offered a job in Europe. I often wonder whether I would have been on that helicopter had she won the interrogator job instead of me.

It felt like I was watching the same debacle unfold on-screen. I knew that I had to act.

> *WOC-D> RE27 ABORT ABORT ABORT.*
> *BY41> Say Reason.*
> *WOC-D> Invalid ROE, invalid clearance, shot is not legal.*

The pilot called me seconds later on my desk phone. He was mad and cursed me for calling off his shot.

"I'll be by after my shift," he said.

I looked forward to the conversation. I was growing tired of poor decisions. It's one thing to deal with non-aviators attempting to direct operations well outside their expertise. I could no longer tolerate bad decisions from the marginally trained pilots. I had seen the community start to break down and something needed to be done.

"What the hell was that?" the pilot spit at me in the WOC doorway.

I had never met the pilot before he came to the WOC. He was one of the faceless reserve pilots who spent little time on the line and flew only occasionally to keep their qualifications. It didn't help that I had been away from the squadrons for almost a year at this point. I no longer knew many of the faces.

"I saved your ass," I said calmly.

"Saved my ass?" he said. "You ruined my shot."

"No, I kept you out of jail."

He stared at me. I stared back.

"Everything was in order," he said. "The shot was legal."

I shook my head.

"No, it was not," I said in a flat tone.

I ticked off my fingers.

"First, there was no 9-Line passed. The important pieces of information used to pass a target were never issued by the JTAC or validated by you. Second, 'shoot, shoot, shoot, shoot now' does not qualify as a shot clearance. The chat logs clearly show you engaging without a legal clearance. Third, CDE was invalid once the vehicle moved. He was more than a mile away from the house before you rolled in. You had no way of knowing what lay between you and the target. The missile could have landed anywhere or hit anything. I don't think the JAG would take kindly to you putting a missile into an innocent's house."

The Judge Advocate General, the military lawyers, analyzed every shot to ensure that all the rules were met. The JAG would have charged the pilot had he shot and killed an innocent.

The pilot eyed me angrily for a long time.

"We'll have to agree to disagree," he finally said.

I shrugged.

"Fine, disagree all you want," I said. "Just remember that you get to sleep in your own bed tonight, not in jail, because of me. Agree or disagree, I don't care."

The pilot spun on his heel and walked out of the WOC without another word. I am sure he complained about me, but his squadron leadership never called to hear my side of the story. Their silence told me that they had looked at the chat logs and agreed with my assessment. I was not going to let anything slip. We'd become sloppy and I knew the only way I could truly effect change was getting command of a squadron.

I couldn't bring Laura back, but I'd like to think I saved a life on her behalf that night.

CHAPTER 15

Command

Colonel David Krumm, the 49th Wing commander, thrust his hand at me.

"You're now commanding the 60th."

The commander's executive officer had called to warn me that Krumm was en route to my office. I had no idea why he wanted to speak with me, or why he hadn't asked me to come to his office. Wing commanders don't drop by the squadrons to chat with a squadron's director of operations.

I was in charge of operations for a training squadron preparing the next generation of RPA crews for combat. It was a leadership job offered to me after my second tour at Creech and a brief stint helping Air Education and Training Command build their RPA pilot production program. I'd been there for two years when Krumm came into my office.

I shook his hand without any idea what to say. I managed a quiet "Thank you, sir." The response did not invoke the presence expected of a commander. I felt shock, joy, relief, and pride rolled into one powerful emotion that threatened to burst from my chest. Most of all, I felt surprise. I was sure that incident at Al Udeid had ended my dream.

As I took Krumm's hand, it dawned on me that I'd finally reached my goal—to command a squadron in combat. All my sacrifices seemed trivial once. I became the first commander of the newly activated 60th Expeditionary Reconnaissance Squadron and only the second officer from the RPA community to take command. Mike stood up the 33rd Special Operations Squadron at Cannon Air Force Base in 2009. He got the job about a year before I took command of the 60th.

"The 60th is brand-new and deploying to Djibouti," Krumm said. "An advon is already on the ground."

The advon, or advanced echelon team, erected the hangars, installed the equipment, and cleared the diplomatic and technical hurdles to fly the first mission.

They also cleared out a bunch of African asps.

"You'll be flying the MQ-1B Predator," Krumm said.

I had been flying the newer MQ-9 Reaper as an instructor at Holloman Air Force Base in New Mexico. The Reaper was taking over for the Predator as the older bird was phased out of the inventory. It was larger than its older sister—about the size of an A-10—and carried a larger payload. It had space for four Hellfire missiles and two five-hundred-pound bombs. I participated in the early operational testing of the prototype and had been with the program for some time. The Air Force had offered the squadron the right to name the aircraft, and I had submitted "Vulture," choosing the name according to the current Air Force convention of naming fighters after birds of prey, like the F-15 Eagle and F-16 Falcon.

"I'm afraid to ask," Box said after I submitted the name. "Why Vulture?"

I smiled.

"Because we orbit our victims so long they are just as likely to die of old age as be captured."

Box rolled his eyes and walked away. Eventually, the squadron voted on and won the name Raptor. It was cool and menacing. Visions of the dinosaur more than the bird ran through my head. But the name fit. Thirty days later, the Air Force revoked the name and gave it to the new F-22. The MQ-9 became the Reaper.

After flying Reapers for so long, I needed a short retraining program before going downrange. The MQ-1B was an improved version of the aircraft I had flown for so many years, with updated avionics, data links, and targeting pod. It didn't take me long to get used to the old girl.

During my downtime, I concentrated on developing my squadron policies. I knew standing up a new unit encompassed building squadron programs and commander's policies, without which the squadron would be like a rudderless ship in turbulent seas. I had to set the squadron on the right course as soon as I got to country.

I also learned we were being sent to Djibouti to assist the Joint Task Force in the hunt for al Qaeda in Yemen. Pentagon and intelligence officials deemed the group a direct threat to the United States. We were going to provide imagery and strike capability.

Colonel Kevin "Fumez" Huyck, the 49th Wing vice commander, invited me to his office just prior to my departure. He was a tall, lanky fighter pilot with a smile that gave him a boyish charm and incredible charisma. He also exuded a competence and leadership that commanded instant respect. He wanted to see me before I deployed. I'd looked to him as a mentor since serving under him the year before. I could tell he had something important to say, so I let him speak rather than waste time with pleasantries or the typical rear-end kissing some officers expected.

I didn't kiss ass and Fumez didn't seem the type who expected me to.

"Squirrel," he said. "You've got a challenge ahead of you."

His eyes told me he wasn't giving advice to a new commander. This was a warning. I waited in silence.

"There is a leadership problem in your squadron," he said. "I don't know what it is, but there are a lot of unhappy people in theater because of what's going on."

I nodded. It wasn't the sort of thing I wanted to hear. My mind raced to determine what could have broken down in such a short time. Was it an incompetent advon commander? Flight discipline? Maybe infighting between the operations and maintenance troops? Anything could be the problem.

My late arrival due to my training couldn't be helped.

"This will be your challenge in the next couple months."

He didn't elaborate. I pondered this on my flight to Djibouti. Fumez wasn't the type to spell out solutions. It was my job as commander to figure out the problem and develop the solution, otherwise, why was I a commander? I had a hunch that part of the problem was differences between what we taught at Holloman and how Creech flew missions.

At Holloman, we flew to the Air Force standard. Creech aviators, on the other hand, deployed with unapproved abbreviated checklists. The standard thirty-page checklist was condensed to a single sheet of paper known as the "cheater" checklist. The writing, small enough to strain the eyes, made it easy to miss steps. We'd lost two birds in one week because the pilots forgot to turn on the flight controls. They'd missed a step, a step clearly outlined in the approved checklist. I planned to purge the "cheater" checklists from the 60th. Mike told me they didn't save that much time and only ushered in disasters. I trusted his judgment, since I had not seen one.

That would be step one, but I had other ideas as I traveled from Holloman to Djibouti. We got delayed in Rota, Spain, for a couple of days by weather and maintenance issues. I used the time to get myself mentally ready for my opening days in command.

After three days of travel, the Boeing 767 charter plane carrying me and other airmen, soldiers, sailors, and Marines to Djibouti finally landed.

I stepped off the plane on the civilian side of the airport into a wall of humidity reminiscent of a Mississippi summer. The air was hot and stagnant, the wetness pressing against my chest like a heavy blanket. We'd originally been scheduled to arrive in the morning, but now it was late evening. I suddenly didn't want to know what daytime felt like.

Djibouti, on the tip of East Africa where the Gulf of Aden and the Red Sea meet, is a small desert country. Though it had once been vibrant with life, weather patterns had turned the land into sand and dust. Now only acacia trees and shrubs grew. The country has the distinction of being the hottest in the world, maintaining the highest average temperature year-round. But its location near Somalia and across the Red Sea from Yemen made it the perfect place to base forces needing access to East African nations.

I passed through customs and emerged into the main lobby. Mosaic tiles adorned the floor like fine marble. Arches provided a uniquely Arab flair to the otherwise moldy Old World French architecture. The Djiboutians were thin, resembling marathon runners more than anything else. After a cursory look at our myriad bags and Pelican cases, they welcomed us into the country.

Americans in civilian clothes waited for us outside the terminal with several small buses. More than twenty of us crammed into seats designed for significantly fewer. There was no standing room, as folding seats blocked the aisle. The buses had to skirt the boundary of the airfield, rolling past primitive shanties before reaching the front gate to the brightly lit Camp Lemonnier.

I hadn't expected near-peacetime security as we pushed through, one bus after another. Granted, security checked all our identities, but I wasn't comforted by their relaxed posture. The buses dropped us off at an ad hoc movie theater, where we signed in and were released to meet our units. A stench tainted the air, stale and wretched to the point I could taste it. I hoped that wasn't normal.

Jason, a major assigned as caretaker of the unit until my arrival, waited outside next to a white extended-cab pickup. It was a HiLux, much like the ones driven everywhere else in the Middle East. Jason was a longtime Predator aviator like me. He had served as a launch and recovery pilot on previous deployments until finally being named to the advon team for the 60th.

"Squirrel," he called out.

"Jason," I said, shaking his hand with strength I didn't feel I had. Three days of travel had worn me out.

"Welcome to Djibouti."

"Thanks," I said.

I doubt I was convincing.

A couple of maintenance troops tossed my gear into the back of the truck along with the bags of the maintainers who had traveled with me. We climbed into the truck and pulled out, giving way to a mass of other newcomers looking for their unit mates.

Jason gave a tour as he drove.

"We're in the main base right now," he said. "Navy owns the camp. Most of their offices, along with the HOA"—Horn of Africa—"staff, are in the old base with the French."

I looked over in the direction he pointed.

The French forces worked in old colonial buildings, which were not well maintained. Only the Officers' Club, really a social club for guys who outranked me, was well preserved. Large murals depicting French naval feats and heroes adorned the walls of the main room. The only paved roads were within the old French section.

Gravel crunched under the tires as Jason turned away from the main base. Paths not much wider than a single lane interconnected over the remainder of the sprawling base. They weren't exactly organized, snaking here and there and occasionally to wider avenues. Only walking provided any direct routes.

"That big building over there," Jason said, pointing at a brown prefab structure, "is the chow hall. They're supposed to build a larger one. Started a year ago, actually."

He laughed.

"The local contractors mixed the concrete with salt water," Jason said. "Foundation crumbled within a month."

"Nice," I said.

"You'll be lucky to see the new one before you leave," he said. "The Navy contracting isn't moving too fast."

"Navy runs the base?" I said.

"Yep," he said. "They operate the support staff. Word of warning, if you want something done, don't ask the Navy."

Massive generators the size of eighteen-wheelers passed to the right.

"Those are the base power supply. Everything is 220 volts here, including the rooms. We couldn't get hooked into the supply, so we are still geared to 115 volts in the squadron."

"Why not?" I asked.

"No power junctions near the compound," Jason said. "Djiboutians charge nearly fifteen hundred dollars a foot to cut the trench we need to connect. So we do it ourselves. The diesel contract is much cheaper."

I nodded.

Huge columns of black smoke belched from the several dozen generators, each column disappearing into the blackness. I wondered where it went and how often I had to breathe it.

Jason turned again, dropping down a runoff.

"That the gym?" I asked, pointing at another large brown pre-fab building. So far, the base was far nicer than any others to which I had deployed, even Al Udeid.

"Naw," Jason said. "That's 11 Degrees North. The bar."

"The bar?"

"It's a combined officer/enlisted club," he explained. "Don't worry, you'll see enough of this place. The girls will dress in their party outfits and heels just to feel like they're in the States."

The bar was named after Djibouti's geographic location. The country is located 11°30' north of the equator. I envisioned a lot of discipline problems coming from a bar with easy access to alcohol. A stateside mentality would only be a conflict in combat. Jason pointed away from the club.

"Housing's over there."

The land sloped downward toward the ocean. Barracks rooms built from Conex containers lay in orderly rows extending almost the length of the base. Each Conex had two rooms. Space was limited for the more than five thousand soldiers, sailors, airmen, Marines, and contractors based at the camp.

"This is us," he said.

He guided the truck around the corner and onto a long straightaway. A brightly lit compound slipped into view. Two massive towers with pointed transmitters perched on top jutted above the fence line. It looked like a ship with two masts sailing through the African desert.

"That's Disneyland."

"What?" I asked.

"Disneyland," Jason explained. "The camp folks see a walled-in compound with scaffolding and think of carnival rides. We look like an amusement park."

I guessed it fit. Only, our rides weren't nearly as exciting, and the cost of admission was too great. Besides, the mice were probably real here, as were the villains.

Jason parked next to a Conex just outside the compound.

"This is you," he said. "I've got a commander's billet for you, but I need to finish packing before you can move in. Until then, this will be you while we get you spun up."

I looked at the key fob and smiled. It read "F-117." The F-117 was the designation for the Air Force's retired stealth fighter. It was funny only because I was exhausted.

The air seemed worse down near the dorms as I climbed out of the truck.

"What's that smell?" I asked.

"Burn pits."

Jason pointed to the south.

"Djiboutian dump is just past the fence line. They burn every-thing after dark. You'll get used to it."

His expression told me I wouldn't.

"Go ahead and crash," Jason said. "Sleep as long as you need, no rush. Wander over when you are ready and ask for me."

He pointed at a white armored shack outside one of the gates that served as our entry control point.

I nodded.

"Thanks, Jason."

I dropped my gear in the corner of the room and collapsed on one of the two beds. I could unpack later. Sleep came quickly.

I awoke a few hours later. I could never sleep during the day no mat-ter how tired I was. My biological clock always knew the sun was up and kept me awake. I couldn't even use blackout curtains.

I showered and prepared for my first day in Africa.

Jason met me at the gate and ushered me into the compound. The 60th Expeditionary Reconnaissance Squadron was at the end of the flight line. The squadron lived and worked in ten tan tents that resembled small Quonset huts. Each of the tents sup-ported a part of the squadron—operations, maintenance, and secu-rity forces.

"We're the first tent," Jason said.

He walked me past several rows of diesel generators. These ran at a high, labored pitch, easily topping eighty decibels as they strug-gled to power the tents and hangars.

The first tent was split into two sections. Four desks occupied the front half, where the operations staff sat. One wall had large plasma screens hanging on it and a bank of computers mirroring the monitors in the GCS's outside. The other half of the tent contained a couch, an entertainment center, lockers, and a cot. The entertainment center had an Xbox and a DVD player.

A long tube made of the same material as the tent's skin ran the length of the ceiling. Small vents funneled cool air from the air-conditioning units outside. Black gunk coated the opaque material and collected in the Velcro-sealed duct flaps. At first I thought it was mold. Then I realized it was diesel waste. The units sat next to the generators, sucking in their exhaust and pumping it directly into the work spaces. I felt a headache coming on.

I stepped outside and saw the GCS set up near the ops tent.

"That's the box," Jason said. "It's a dual GCS."

It looked like the standard Conex container, but instead of one flight rack, it contained two. Jason walked me past the tent city and toward the two large hangars. One had its clamshell door held open by chains.

"What happened there?" I asked.

"We just had a big thunderstorm," Jason said. "Popped up without notice and damaged the mechanism. We can't lower it, so we tied it up to relieve the strain on the structure."

Inside, the hangar was filled with smaller metal containers designed to fit inside the cargo hold of aircraft.

"We put supply in there until we can fix it," he explained.

The ramp, constructed of AM-2 matting, spread out before us. AM-2 is an aluminum-based mat coated in a green rubberized paint designed as a nonslip surface. The ramp was large enough to support two large hangars for our eight Predators. Normally, only six were inside at a time. Another tent, called the sunshade, stood at the opposite end of the ramp. It had no doors and served as a prep station before the Predator launched.

"You launch from here?" I asked.

Jason shook his head.

"No, we're too close to housing for the camp's comfort. We launch from the parking ramp about a quarter mile that way."

He pointed toward the sea, then walked me out to the ramp. The maintenance team had set up a horseshoe enclosure made of shipping containers. Inside, a Predator waited, two missiles hanging from its rails.

"We'll be launching this one shortly," Jason said.

"What's with the revetment?"

Jason shrugged.

"That's to keep the locals from seeing us in the ramp."

"As if they don't see us take off?"

"Exactly," Jason said.

I spent the rest of the day moving into my quarters near the operations tent and getting settled.

The next day, Jason introduced me to the camp staff. The N-3 operations officer, who would be my principle support liaison, was our first stop.

Worm, a Navy helicopter pilot, was a short, fat, pig-nosed man whose mannerisms reminded me of the *Lethal Weapon* character Leo Getz. He was a lieutenant commander but acted like he was an admiral. We'd just finished shaking hands when Worm started in about the gate. I looked at Jason. He smirked. The ambassador wanted a gate to hide the Predators from the civilian ramp. Jason's boss, Stern, had initially led the advon. He'd demanded that Worm build a one-hundred-thousand-dollar sliding gate to block our ramp from the taxiway. Stern had left before I arrived but had left me with an angry Worm and this gate fiasco. I'd learn later that Stern had walked around the base demanding all kinds of support and had stepped on a lot of toes. He'd created my leadership problem.

I still remembered staff work and the ridiculous, petty battles it generated. My guess was that Worm wasn't going to build the gate on principle; logic didn't factor into his choice: It was his camp and his decision. But I didn't have time for this type of thing. We were given only sixty days to move the Predator, a technologically demanding system, to a new, unimproved location and set up full operations. Stern had had to step on toes to accomplish his objective.

"Forget the automation," I said. "The Seabees on base can fabricate something to meet the ambassador's intent, right?"

I could see Worm visibly relax, as he had expected an argument from me. I hoped the meeting would smooth some of the ruffled feathers I already sensed in the camp. I had a squadron to run, and this kind of pissing match only took me away from my mission.

I conducted an official assumption of command ceremony. It landed on Christmas Day 2010. We assembled on the AM-2 matting just outside one of the hangars. A Predator waited behind the small formation of airmen from the maintenance section.

Normally, a unit change of command called for a formal ceremony in front of the entire squadron. The ceremony served to graphically show the departure of the former commander and the arrival of the new commander. But a unit flying combat operations twenty-four hours a day didn't have the luxury. One of the crews was launching the next mission, and most of the maintenance section was on the ramp supporting. The security forces were manned just enough to guard the compound and couldn't be spared. Only the roving team stood with the maintenance troops as we assembled.

Jason said a couple of words of good-bye to the airmen who'd helped him stand up the 60th in Djibouti. Normally, as part of the ceremony, the outgoing commander passed the unit colors to the new commander as the symbolic changing of the guard. Our unit was so new, having been inactive since Vietnam, that we had no colors to pass. Instead, we simply saluted each other.

"I assume command," I said after I saluted.

I was now officially the first commander of the unit and turned to face my troops. Most of the troops were from Holloman. These were my guys whom I had worked with for the past couple of years. But Jon, my chief maintainer and one of the squadron's senior noncommissioned officers, told me the boys were unsure what to think about having a pilot as commander.

Jon and I had met on the flight over. He was also from Holloman Air Force Base. Jon had a lengthy career servicing fighter aircraft like the F-16 before transitioning over to the Predator. We talked at length about striking a balance in the squadron so all of its parts—operations, maintenance, security forces—felt like they were contributing to the fight. He helped me understand the need to assuage the maintainers' concerns by making sure they were an equal part of the team, not the guys who kept the pilot in the air so he could take the credit.

Air Force flying squadrons were separate units from their maintenance squadrons under normal circumstances. The pilots and the maintainers rarely got to know one another. This caused friction because the pilots had no idea what the maintainers did and vice versa. This led to problems because pilots rarely understood the work needed to keep an aircraft combat-ready and maintainers never experienced the rigor of flight and combat.

"It's my honor to stand here before you," I said. "I look at people with whom I have worked for years but have never gotten to know. I want you to know now that we are a family, all of us. The aircrew, the maintainers, and the security forces all belong to this great squadron. As we settle into our role here, understand that we have an important mission, one that is in the direct sight of the president. As such we need to ensure we are sharp at all times. We are not Creech. We don't cut corners. We don't use cheater checklists. We follow the tech orders to the letter. We do that and we will succeed, I have no doubt."

I later dropped by 11 Degrees North, the base social club, to celebrate. Tables and seats filled a basketball court–size area in front of a stage used by USO performers. Outside, there was more seating and an open space where an inflatable screen showed movies. A bar sat at one corner serving both the inside and outside patrons. I sat at the bar and drank a subpar French wine served in a plastic single-serving bottle. I wasn't antisocial. The squadron ran missions twenty-four hours a day. They had work to do. I didn't yet. I started in the morning. Besides, I was a commander now. I didn't have the luxury of friends, nor would I hang out with the guys. I had to get used to being alone out here.

As I sipped the wine, I savored the moment. I'd made command. But I still had a year to go and a mission to accomplish. I finished my drink and headed back to my quarters. After a quick shower, I flicked on my reading lamp to study the local procedures.

I would start flying soon.

CHAPTER 16

Losses

I keyed my mic.

"Chief, ready aircraft power."

"Power coming on," came the crew chief's response on the radio.

Outside, the crew chief opened a side panel and connected a ground power unit to the aircraft. Then, he flipped a switch to close the circuit.

I counted to ten before the HUD came to life. It flickered with static until finally the ramp and telemetry appeared. The Gulf of Aden spread out in front of us. The water was a brilliant sapphire blue, morning light glinting off the gentle two-foot swells. Acacia trees and scraggly bushes blocked my view of the muddy beach.

The maintainers stood off at a safe distance while the Predator woke up. The aircraft's main computer, the primary control module, sent out test signals to the Predator as it ran its internal checks. Power coursed through the aircraft, activating the various components.

"Power's on."

I ran through the checklist with my sensor, Han. He was a young airman just finishing his first deployment for the Air Force. His name came from the *Star Wars* character. It wasn't because of his swagger, but a play on the airman's name. Once he showed up at the squadron, there was no other choice.

This was one of my first flights as the squadron commander. I was finally flying after spending the first few weeks settling into the job and putting out the fires on base. In the cockpit, I was just another pilot, and all I had to worry about was the aircraft and the mission. I wanted to fly frequently because it was the only place I got a break from the pressures of command.

Han and I ran the checks to ensure that the aircraft was ready to crank. Some components needed to be on, others off. Starting with the wrong component could ruin a sensor or stall the engine.

Satisfied, I keyed my radio.

"Chief, ready to start engine."

"Copy."

A maintainer walked up to a panel on the side of the aircraft, pressed a couple of buttons, and waited. The aircraft rocked as the prop rotated once, twice, then caught. With a cough, the engine surged to life. I adjusted the prop lever to set the best RPM to warm up the oil.

Han keyed the mic.

"Chief, clear to activate the pod?"

We waited a moment for the chief to get back to us.

"Eyes are safe, clear to power up the ball."

The targeting pod's high-power laser had the potential to flash to life when activated. I'd never heard of it happening, but if it did, the laser would burn the eyes of anyone close to it. All of the maintainers moved out of the arc of the laser as Han worked on calibrating the pod.

I monitored the engine. This was the longest part of the starting sequence. We couldn't taxi until the engine warmed up. I was on guard as the Predator with tail number 193 hummed on the ramp. Gabby, as maintenance had named her, was a problem child.

Maintenance had a tradition, like pilots, of naming their aircraft. Our crew chiefs named each Predator after significant women in their lives. I asked about Gabby. Turns out she was named after the maintenance symbol GAB—ground abort. Apparently, Gabby didn't like to fly. I liked flying Audrey more. She was named for the great actress Audrey Hepburn and handled with similar elegance.

Most of our issues existed because the Predator wasn't sealed against the weather. Planes would fly a daylong sortie, then drop down into the moist air at the end of the mission. The supercooled instruments would condense the water in the air. Maintenance would refuel each aircraft and then launch it a couple of hours later. The water, still in the instrument bay, froze as the aircraft climbed to high altitude.

At twenty thousand feet, temperatures could plummet to thirty or forty below zero. In the cockpit, crews got false oil- or fuel-leak warnings. The pilots would bring the aircraft back to base only to reveal that the expanding ice had pushed a sensor out of calibration. We tried to explain the issue to the crews, to no avail. In the end, we had to land the aircraft, recalibrate the same instrument, and relaunch it.

It wasted valuable time. But we didn't have a choice. The mission crews were on the hook and could lose their wings if they ignored a warning.

I scanned the gauges and finished my checks. I loaded our flight plan, tested the flight controls, and prepared to taxi. The flight controls were the most important part of our preflight. If they didn't work, the plane wouldn't fly.

"Chief," I called. "Hands and feet clear, remove chocks, and make ready to taxi."

Maintainers pulled the safety pins that secured the landing gear and armed the missiles. One maintainer stood close to the targeting pod, hand resting on an emergency cutoff switch. If anything bad happened, he would shut down the aircraft.

Han and I let go of the controls so we didn't accidentally move the rudder or flaps. Nothing ruined a man's day like getting brained by a tailboard. The targeting pod remained fixed in place, staring at the maintainer while the others worked. The sensor on the ball was so sensitive that we could see the heat of his veins pulsing in his arms.

"That's a good ball," I said.

"It's one of the best ones we have," Han said.

The maintainers moved away from the aircraft.

"Sir, pins and chocks are removed, you are clear to taxi," the crew chief said over the radio.

The pins armed our missiles. The chocks blocked the wheels to prevent the aircraft from rolling off on its own.

"Thanks, Chief," I said, and released the brakes.

The aircraft waddled out to the runway. The steering was extremely sensitive, so the aircraft constantly wandered around the taxiway, pushed off course by light winds and the occasional bump. We had to fight the aircraft to keep it going straight.

"Tower, Bong Seven Zero ready for takeoff," I called.

A thick French and Arabic accent answered me.

"Bong Seven Zero, hold short."

The control tower wanted me to stay in my present position.

"Look left," I said.

Han shifted the targeting pod to the approach end of Runway Zero Nine. A couple of miles out, a DC-9 airliner appeared, lining up with the runway and starting its final approach.

"I take it airliners have priority here."

"Especially that one," Han said. "That's the eleven o'clock Ethiopian Airlines bird. The daily shipment of khat is onboard."

I raised my eyebrows.

"There is only one pastime around here," Han said. "Khat. And the only legal way to import it is via that aircraft."

Khat was a narcotic drug in leaf form. When chewed, it released addictive effects similar to those of many opiates. Side effects included brown-stained teeth and a general lethargy. Nothing could happen in the country until this shipment arrived. It was the only thing that made the afternoon heat tolerable to the Djiboutians.

The aircraft touched down and pulled off the other side of the airfield.

"Bong Seven Zero, winds are calm, you are cleared for takeoff."

"Bong, cleared for takeoff," I replied, and pushed the throttle forward.

The little airplane rolled down the runway. We traveled nearly five thousand feet down the runway before the wheels lifted off the tarmac. I almost aborted, thinking something was wrong. We needed half the distance to launch at Creech, and that was at a higher altitude. Finally, the Predator started to climb. Our only indication was the sudden absence of vibration in the HUD. The altitude slowly ticked upward and we passed the shoreline.

The humidity really killed our lift. Heat was a problem, but the humidity before and after the afternoon thunderstorms created conditions in which Predators had never flown. They were built in San Diego, flown in Las Vegas, and eventually deployed to Iraq and Afghanistan. All these places had one thing in common. They were dry. Admittedly, weather in Iraq and Afghanistan could inch up the humidity a bit, but never to this level.

Han tested the laser to ensure that it functioned properly, and then we headed out to sea. Our counterparts at Cannon Air Force Base checked into the chat room that they were ready to take control. Han swung the pod about to check on the aircraft. The pod swung to the undercarriage and verified that the landing gear had locked up into the fuselage.

Then it swung around toward the front. Below, the rusted hulk of a shipwreck passed by. Farther off, a bump on the horizon indicated a hill of some sort.

"That hill is in Somalia," Han said. "We're only about ten miles from there. The base is just south of Djibouti City. DJ is the only deep-water port in this part of Africa. All our aid to the interior comes through here."

Djibouti City spanned out onto a small pointed peninsula to the north. On the western side were the massive docks and cranes of the port. On the east side of the city were the beaches, hotels, and embassies. Han set the pod on the Gulf of Aden. We did all of our work across the water.

President Obama had refocused our efforts from the search for Osama bin Laden to Yemen and a new target, Anwar al-Awlaki.

It fell to the Predators to find him.

Anwar al-Awlaki was born in Las Cruces, New Mexico, in 1971. He lived in the United States until his family moved to Yemen when he was seven years old. He returned to the States in 1991 to attend Colorado State University and went on to earn his master's in education from San Diego State University and a PhD in human resources from George Washington University.

He portrayed himself as a moderate who did interviews for NPR, and he went to a breakfast at the Pentagon after the attacks on September 11, but the FBI started watching him after they discovered he was in contact with three of the hijackers.

Al-Awlaki left the United States in 2002 and moved to London, where he started preaching about the United States' war on Islam. Two years later he left London for Yemen, where he taught and preached in mosques in the southern part of the country. Al-Awlaki was arrested and sent to prison for eighteen months in 2006 on charges of kidnapping and taking part in an al Qaeda plot to kidnap a US military attaché. He was released in 2007 after his tribe intervened. But by then, al-Awlaki's fiery English sermons were inspiring terrorists in the United States and Britain.

In November 2009, Major Nidal Malik Hasan, an Army psychiatrist, killed thirteen people in a shooting rampage at Fort Hood. He had exchanged emails with al-Awlaki. After the attack, al-Awlaki praised Hasan.

"Nidal Hasan is a hero," he wrote in a widely publicized blog. "He is a man of conscience who could not bear living the contradiction of being a Muslim and serving in an army that is fighting against his own people."

Intelligence officials started to monitor al-Awlaki's communications, which showed the cleric's growing role in al Qaeda in the Arabian Peninsula. On Christmas Day 2009, a twenty-three-year-old Nigerian named Umar Farouk Abdulmutallab carried an underwear bomb onto a passenger jet headed for Detroit.

Al-Awlaki was his inspiration.

Abdulmutallab told interrogators that al-Awlaki helped plot

the attack. In the eyes of American officials, the American-born cleric was more than a skilled propagandist. He was a terrorist.

The Task Force started to track his network all around Yemen. To do it, we had to launch every sortie we could muster.

Maintenance had the biggest piece of this puzzle. The squadron's aircraft had come from Iraq and Afghanistan. All were old and worn down. We got the pigs that never seemed to fly right and hangar queens that the other bases could never keep repaired. I actually didn't hate the other squadrons for this. I would have done the same thing if ordered to give up an aircraft.

Once operations kicked off, maintenance worked twenty-four hours a day to get these aircraft in shape. And my crews got each aircraft airborne as fast as possible. We didn't get the payoff of flying the combat portion of the mission, but without my maintainers and crews, the Predators would never have made it into the skies over Yemen. I'd already worked the flashy part of the job. Now all my energies were focused on making sure the behind-the-scenes part got done so the pilots could do their part.

The mission became a grind. After a month in Djibouti, my internal clock was busted.

A tray of food sat untouched in front of me as I sat in the DFAC, or dining facility. By the looks of my meal, it was dinner. Like the rest of the squadron, I worked when there were things to be done. And it seemed there was always something to be done. It was impossible to keep a regular schedule.

As I sat there enjoying the quiet, not the food, Ziggy passed by my table. He was picking up a to-go order on his way back to the squadron.

"Sir," he said, greeting me near the door.

Ziggy was a lieutenant and a recent graduate of pilot training. On his first deployment, he had proven himself to be skilled despite his inexperience.

"How's the launch coming?" I asked.

He had a mission scheduled later that night.

"On time," he said. "Just getting something to eat before the chow hall closes."

I nodded.

"It's going to be a busy night."

"Oh?" I asked.

"Bong is RTB for an engine malfunction," Ziggy said.

I stared at him.

"Are you kidding?" I asked.

Ziggy looked at me and shrugged.

"The aircraft is too far out," he said. "The crew reported the same problems we've seen the past few days. Nothing significant."

"Yet they are coming home early," I said.

"They think it is worse," he said.

The previous few nights, the aircraft had exhibited mild erratic RPM and oil-pressure readings. Nothing pushed any limits or caused any problems. The crew chalked it up to turbulence and the engine's attempt to compensate. But something wasn't right with the engine.

I checked my watch. My crew day, as defined in Air Force regulations, was limited to twelve hours. I still had a few hours left, so I decided to land the aircraft.

"All right," I said. "Cover the launch; I'll recover Bong."

Walking back to the squadron, I wondered how much grief the Task Force would give me for yet another early return. I hoped maintenance could find something wrong with the bird. The last time, they had found zilch despite rebuilding the engine. Ziggy slipped into the cockpit nicknamed "Steelers." I took the other one, named "Pirates."

Stern, who'd led the advon, was from Pittsburgh and had selected the names. We programmed the names of our GCS units into Skynet, the computer program we used to track and schedule aircraft. It was named after the program from the *Terminator* movies, and when it went live, I was on duty at the WOC and got the pleasure of alerting my fellow pilots. "Skynet is active." The joke was never lost on me. Each GCS was assigned a set of frequencies. I happened to like the Steelers, since I was a fan of the team, and we were the Pirates. I let the names stand. Besides, I didn't want to deal with resetting Skynet.

It might have fought back.

Setting up the computer to see the airplane took only a couple of minutes. We pointed the receiver out to sea and waited. A grainy image materialized in the static. The receiver recognized the signal and rotated so it pointed right at the aircraft. The picture cleared instantly.

"What the hell are they doing on course?" my sensor said.

The 3rd Special Operations Squadron crew had flown the planned route back. With an engine malfunction, they should have flown straight back to base. The planned route added thirty minutes to the transit time as it detoured around airspace restrictions. We started the handover procedure and were just about to take control of the aircraft when the sensor noticed the altimeter.

"Sir, aircraft is descending," the sensor said.

Normally, the aircraft maintained altitude during the procedure, but this one didn't. I glanced at the engine readouts. Several of the indicators climbed into the red.

Red was bad.

The RPM dropped to zero as the engine froze. The plane was fifty miles away. I did a mental calculation. No way the Predator could glide back to land from that far out.

"We just lost an aircraft," I said.

Off the north coast of Djibouti, Tail 228 glided, but only for a few more minutes. There was nothing we could do to save it. There was nowhere to land except for a rocky beach. Our only chance was to ditch it in the water and hope to recover it before it sank. Theoretically, the Predator would float. Air in the fuel tanks could make the aircraft buoyant. On the other hand, the unsealed aircraft would take on a lot of water as well. The results were uncertain, especially since no one had attempted to ditch a Predator before.

The airplane remained perfectly level as the water rose to meet it. The little aircraft skipped across two waves before the third splashed over the nose. We watched the aircraft bob for a few seconds before the transmitters shorted out.

I switched the radio to the launch frequency.

"Chief, Pirates," I called on the radio.

"Go ahead, sir."

"Two Two Eight's down."

There was silence on the radio for a moment. The guys on the ramp were likely expressing themselves in a manner they didn't want me to witness.

"Copy, sir," he finally said.

I sent my sensor to find the Air Force safety officer on base. He had to officially start the Safety Investigation Board process. I was the only certified board president on base, but ethics didn't allow me to analyze the accident since my squadron was involved, so I collected all the maintenance and operator records required for a safety board and waited.

A rescue helicopter raced out to sea to recover the Predator. They searched for more than an hour looking for a gray object floating on dark water. They did manage to drop a raft and pararescue jumpers to secure the waterlogged aircraft once they found it. But aircraft 228 could wait no longer. The helicopter crew watched helplessly as it slipped beneath the waves as the swimmers reached it.

I left the GCS and headed straight to my desk. Instead of twelve hours, my day turned into nearly thirty-six as I spent my time answering questions from my headquarters, the Task Force, and the embassy. This was our first loss and suddenly every headquarters in the region wanted information.

A major from the Task Force was the most persistent. Every time I hung up the phone, it seemed like he was calling me for something else. I knew he was getting pressure from his chain of command, but I didn't have answers. I finally lost my patience.

"Major," I barked. "This is not your aircraft. I don't care what information you want or who is asking for it. I will pass it when I have time and not a moment sooner. Now I need to talk to my leadership."

With that, I hung up the phone.

Within a week, the Air Force Safety Center appointed an A-10 pilot as the formal Safety Investigation Board president. He called to coordinate with me.

"Squirrel," he said. "This is I.V."

"Nice to meet you," I said. I didn't know him. "I've got all your records collected."

"Good," he said. "Ship them to Creech. I'll be running the board from there."

"Okay, we'll get those out today."

I heard car noise over the phone.

"You driving right now?"

"Yeah, I am still en route," he said. "I will get there in a couple days and start looking things over. Confirm you didn't get the wreckage?"

"No wreckage."

"That's too bad," he said. "It's going to make it hard only looking at the logs."

The data loggers in the GCS acted like the aircraft's black box. We had two sets of logs from Creech and Djibouti that recorded the engine seizure. From them we could tell exactly what part had failed.

"When will you guys get out here?"

"Oh, we won't be coming out," he said.

My eyes narrowed.

"You probably should," I said. "You can get a better feel for the aircraft and our conditions if you see them firsthand."

"You are probably right, but we can do everything from Creech."

As I hung up the receiver, I made a mental note to closely track the progress of the investigation. I had a bad feeling about it, which was well founded in short order.

I.V. treated interviews with my maintenance chief as an opportunity to attack junior officers, and it had me on edge. I knew this would be a benchmark case for me. I never wanted an accident, but I also wanted to show the world that Holloman maintenance was as sharp as we claimed.

Maintenance discussed the problem with the engine installed on Tail 228 during one of the interviews. Over the phone line, the chief heard the factory representative say, "Nothing wrong with our engines. It's maintenance's fault."

I.V. jumped to his conclusion that it was our error.

"See, you guys did something wrong," he said to me when I talked to him about the incident later.

It felt like we were getting railroaded.

When the phone rang a few days later, I knew the news wasn't good. It was about two hours before I was to wake for my shift.

"Colonel McCurley," I said, wiping sleep from my eyes.

I still hadn't adjusted to the time even though I had been in Djibouti for nearly a month.

"Sir," Ziggy said. "We just lost another aircraft."

I groaned. I put on my uniform and hiked the mile to the compound.

"What happened?" I asked as I walked into the ops tent.

"We landed and I couldn't stop the aircraft," Ziggy said. "It went through the fence line next to the water."

"Okay."

Ziggy was sitting at the desk. He looked at the other crews collecting records.

"Is there anything I can do?"

"No," I said. "Sit this one out. It's better if you don't touch anything."

I didn't want any accusations of doctored records by the mishap crew. Seeing that the ops team had everything under control, I stepped outside and grabbed the first maintainer I could find.

"Is the senior at the crash site?"

"Yes, sir."

"Okay, I need a ride."

Moments later, I pulled up to the end of the runway. The airfield manager, a Navy lieutenant, was yelling and gesticulating wildly at a group of my troops. One of them was Jon.

Behind the maintainers, the Predator was embedded in a dirt berm about twenty yards past the flattened fence. The aircraft had passed between two reinforced poles, which sheared the wings off. A forklift drove into position to lift the stricken aircraft onto a flatbed trailer.

The lieutenant was cursing at Jon as I walked up.

"What's the situation?" I said to Jon, ignoring the lieutenant.

Jon turned his attention to me. The lieutenant reddened in the face.

"Sir, we're just about ready to lift the aircraft."

"Very well," I said. "Let me look at the scene first."

I turned to the lieutenant.

"Walk with me."

It wasn't an invitation. It was an order. I guided him out of earshot toward his truck.

"You're being a little rough on the guys, aren't you?"

"Sir," he said. "The airfield's been closed for an hour. An airliner had to divert. I am getting a lot of pressure to get this cleared up."

He had the gall to blast a senior sergeant in such an ungentlemanly manner and yet took the time to completely kiss my ass. He was pathetic.

"You know," I said, "we had a belly landing a couple months back."

One of our aircraft had a gear get stuck in the wheel well. The crew landed the Predator by skidding it down the runway on its belly.

"Yes, sir."

"It took these guys only twenty minutes to clear the runway."

"I don't know anything about that, sir."

"Weren't you here?" I asked.

"No, sir," the lieutenant said. "I was on my midtour leave."

"Ah," I said. "I see. You're holding things up. Why don't you wait right here and let the experts do their job."

I turned and walked back to Jon, leaving the lieutenant with no chance to respond. I sketched a diagram of the accident. Accident investigations normally did this, but time didn't allow a team to get here and look at the wreckage. I drew one out of courtesy since we needed to clear the runway quickly. I noticed that the Army and one of my security forces troops had formed a protective perimeter outside the fence line. A light wind blew across the aircraft and directly at my troop.

"Hey, Jon," I said.

"Yes, sir."

"Pull the airman back. I don't want him breathing any carbon fibers."

"Yes, sir." Jon sent the troop upwind of the aircraft.

The Predator's carbon-fiber body was highly carcinogenic if fractured into its individual fibers. I had no reason to believe there was any danger this long after the accident. Still, I didn't want to take any chances, either.

After finishing the sketch, I let Jon and the maintainers pick up the aircraft. The lieutenant seethed at his truck but did nothing. Our maintenance recovery team had the runway clear within fifteen minutes of my arrival on scene. They just needed me to remove the oafish obstacle.

I pulled Jon aside before I left the scene.

I told him, "I'm going to head back to the compound and see how collection is going there."

Jon eyed the lieutenant.

"What about him?"

"He should leave you alone," I said. "If not, call me. I'll set him straight and I won't be nice this time."

"You got it, sir."

As I drove back to the compound, I reviewed my first weeks in command. I now had two concurrent Safety Investigation Boards and I had to order a replacement aircraft to cover my losses. I also had to make sure we had the parts to keep the working Predators airborne. The job felt more like staff work than command.

I was back to putting out fires.

CHAPTER 17

A Fine Mess

Jon looked nervous as he stood in front of my desk with a pair of crew chiefs hiding slightly behind him.

"Sir, we've got a problem," he said.

I didn't need another jolt. Not today.

The Task Force had asked us to surge and I was scrambling to meet the demand. They had leads on important facilitators and needed the extra Predators to find them, and I couldn't tell them no. No one said no to the Task Force. But my yes answer had a large "but" attached to it. I could surge the squadron. But there would be a cost. I was down a couple of aircraft after our early losses and I was barely keeping the others airborne. I needed replacements, and one was supposed to have arrived today. If we surged, it would mean the squadron couldn't do other missions. We were all in to get al-Awlaki.

Jon's presence concerned me.

"What is it?" I asked.

"I think it's best if you see it," he said.

I stood to follow him out. Jon led me to the supply hangar. A group of maintainers were gathered near the entrance. To one side were the remains of Tail 126. After it had crashed into the berm, we'd packaged it up and planned to send it back to the States for analysis.

Inside the hangar, the men stood around the casket, the slang term for the massive Pelican case–style container that protected the Predators during transport. This was our new bird shipped from Kandahar Air Base by a C-130 Hercules transport. The lid was closed, but I could see that the latches had already been released.

"So what am I looking at?"

Jon signaled one of the troops. The airman used a small crane to lift the lid. I expected to see the gray skin of a new aircraft, but as the lid opened, only plastic and paper spilled out. The white Styrofoam bed molded to fit the contour of the Predator's fuselage was inside, but not the aircraft.

My first reaction was to laugh.

"You've got to be kidding me."

"Sir," Jon started.

I covered my mouth as I laughed at the absurdity, waving him off. Kandahar had shipped me an empty container.

Jon didn't know what to say. The look on his face suggested he thought I had finally lost my mind.

I hadn't. I had just realized I was reliving Yossarian's life.

Back in the ops cell, I checked Skynet to see where Tail 203 was located and then called NASA, the commander of the squadron at Kandahar.

"NASA," I said when he answered.

"Hey, Squirrel," he said. "How's it going?"

"Well," I said. "Thanks for sending us a new bird."

"No worries," he said. "I trust it got there okay."

"No, not quite."

"Come again?"

"We got the casket for Tail 203."

NASA was silent for a second. I could hear him tapping the keys on his computer.

"Two Oh Three is flying here right now," NASA said.

Skynet showed the aircraft active somewhere in Afghanistan.

"I know."

"Okay, let me look into it," he said and hung up.

NASA called me back and explained the error. The empty casket was accidentally stored with the full caskets. When the order came down from CENTCOM to ship 203 to us, the casket was pulled from storage and shipped. No one weighed it. A cargo plane flew an empty box two thousand miles for nothing. To make matters worse, the casket took at least two pallets' worth of space in a cargo hold. Someone else missed a needed cargo shipment because of our empty pallets.

The logistician in charge of shipping us the bird was fired immediately. But we were still short an aircraft at a time when the Task Force needed us. I still had a surge to sustain and not enough aircraft or parts to do it.

If the weather wasn't creating havoc for us, the lack of parts was. Some Air Force planner decided that it was cheaper to send our supplies on commercial air carriers rather than military transport.

The problem for us was that we were a good two to three weeks farther down the supply chain than the squadrons in Afghanistan. It simply took longer to get parts to us, so those snapshots rarely provided a clear picture of our needs. We were barely making ends meet when the civilian carrier lost our monthly supply shipment in Belgium. Then there were the inevitable delays through Djiboutian customs.

At least the hunt for al-Awlaki was going better. The Task Force was hot on the trail of a facilitator who could lead us to the American terrorist. They wanted three missions so they could keep at least one aircraft over the man at all times. I pulled Jon into my office. He looked exhausted but so far had kept the Predators airborne chasing al-Awlaki leads.

"We're going to cannibalize the remaining aircraft to keep the others flying," I told him.

It was a drastic move but the only way we could keep up. I ordered Jon and the maintainers to take apart the worst aircraft in the squadron to create parts for the remaining aircraft. We ended up tearing apart five of the squadron's seven aircraft.

While Jon took apart the aircraft, I called over to the Task Force. There was no way I could keep flying three missions. I needed to lower it to two. My reasoning was simple. Would the Task Force prefer more potentially unreliable CAPs or just the scheduled ones?

They went with the better odds.

My Holloman maintenance team had turned the squadron around in just under two months. Operations were running smoothly. The Task Force recognized the results and were willing to give us some leeway. It didn't hurt that I was willing to push as hard as they wanted. Accomplishing the mission was my main goal and cutting the third flight allowed me to do it.

One of the JOC deputies called after I briefed them on the changes.

"What can we do to help?"

"Nothing," I said.

"We can make some calls, see what we can break loose," the JOC deputy said. "We can even send a plane."

I appreciated the Task Force looking to help me out.

"Thanks," I said. "I have to work this through my channels."

"Okay," he said. "Let us know when things get right."

"You got it."

I expected the Task Force to bluster and go over my head to get that third CAP. But the team at Camp Lemonnier understood my situation and supported my efforts to keep flying.

Everything would be fine so long as nothing else broke.

I was at my desk in the ops cell when the odor of human feces and chemicals wafted into the tent. I didn't smell much at first, until Aaron, the security forces chief, opened the door. He looked pale and nauseated. A moment later, the incoming air hit me like a slap in the face.

"Oh my God, what is that?" I said.

"The shit truck just dumped in the road," he said.

Being so far from the main camp, the compound wasn't serviced with either power or plumbing. The power problem we figured out by employing our own generators, even if it was giving me a cough that wouldn't go away.

The plumbing was fixed by deploying a row of port-a-johns outside the fence. The wind blew the rather fragrant aroma across our tents.

A Djiboutian contract team had arrived to service our port-a-johns. They'd dutifully run the hoses from their tanker into the johns and started sucking. About midway through the process, the tanker had sprung a leak. Human waste dumped into the road outside our compound.

The effect was immediate.

I grabbed for a rag to cover my face. I'd take anything that could filter out that reek. Our senior sensor grabbed a bottle of air freshener she had bought at the Navy Exchange. She sprayed almost the entire contents of the can around the room. My eyes burned as the droplets hit my face.

It did no good.

"Oh my God, now it smells like shit and strawberries!" Aaron cried, leaving the ops tent.

I laughed through my rag. Security forces was one of my favorite sections in the squadron. I admired their dedication and professionalism. The guys worked hard, constantly standing guard over our aircraft and compound. They did it without question or request for special favors. The flight line gate was nothing more than a tent with no side panels. The guards, in full armor, stood alert with no air-conditioning in sweltering temperatures.

They never complained.

Air Force squadrons don't incorporate operations and security forces into one unit. Making sure my security forces troops felt part of the squadron was important. Aaron had never dealt with pilots before except to guard our aircraft or issue traffic tickets. He didn't know our culture. And the pilot world was apparently very different from that of the security forces. He didn't think that his career field had quite the sense of humor aviators did.

Since he worked in the ops cell overseeing the whole section, he got up to speed fast on pilot culture. But it was our naming convention that intrigued him the most. He liked the idea of tactical call signs and the camaraderie they brought. The security forces called one another by last name only.

One day, he asked us to give him a name.

I wasn't planning on doing a naming ceremony during my time in Djibouti. Most aviators deployed with a name from their home squadrons. That wasn't to say they couldn't be renamed following a strange incident in the field. After all, I considered renaming Ziggy "Punchline" or "Puncher" after he crashed Tail 126 through the fence.

But the ceremony was a chance to bring the squadron closer together and blow off a little steam. Operations were too intensive to take time at 11 Degrees North to celebrate properly. Instead, we decided to take a break at a coffee shop and conduct a modified naming ceremony for Aaron.

"So," I said after a short speech. "We thought long and hard, so to speak, about names for you."

Aaron looked on expectantly.

"We just couldn't agree on a nickname, so we came up with DEVA."

Aaron's reaction was one of confusion. He wasn't a prima donna as the name implied. He didn't see the connection.

"We wanted something that captures your job and your personality."

His expression became wary.

"We think DEVA fits."

"What the hell does it mean?" he asked.

"Donut-Eating Vigilance Accessory."

It was the best we could do. Security forces are part cops—they police Air Force bases back in the States—and part infantry because they protect the flight line both at home and overseas. It was the perfect way to accept the duality of the job. At first he was shocked until we told him what it meant; then he thought it was funny and embraced the identity.

Our spare aircraft finally arrived from Kandahar to replace the empty Tail 203 casket. This time, I watched as the maintenance team opened the case. It was Tail 249. Seeing that, I immediately notified maintenance that this would become our squadron aircraft.

Holloman, which provided the clear majority of our troops, was organized into the 49th Wing. It made sense to me that Tail 249 should represent our home unit.

Air Force squadrons around the world often assigned aircraft to individual aircraft commanders and crew chiefs. Our crew chiefs had their assigned aircraft, but our pilots did not. I decided Tail 249 would be the start of a new tradition. I chose to name her Kate and claim her as my aircraft. I let the guys pick which aircraft were considered "theirs." It wasn't more than a paper drill. But the younger guys had to appreciate receiving an honor normally reserved for senior guys in the unit.

Of course, Tail 249's cameras failed on its first takeoff. It was too late to abort, so I was forced to take her airborne with no ability to see. We flew for a couple of hours waiting for the sun to rise. Only then could we use the small nose camera to land the aircraft.

I hoped her record would improve from there.

After a few problem-free days, Worm, the Navy helicopter pilot in charge of base operations, called to end the streak. So far, I'd been able to avoid him.

"This is Worm," he said when I picked up the phone.

"Yes," I answered tonelessly.

I didn't offer him much courtesy at this point. He hated the Air Force. Since our first meeting over the gate, he had called to complain that our cookout sunshade erected to protect the grilling team from the sun had been up too long. The cookout was still in progress when he called. He also liked to ride by the compound to catch my maintainers with too much ordnance on the ramp or doing something else wrong. If anything was amiss, he'd cuss out the maintenance lieutenant.

It was Jon who complained to me.

I had confronted Worm about the harassment. He lounged behind his desk, refusing to stand in the presence of a superior rank.

"I know this is supposed to be a purple base, but it really will only be a Navy base while I'm here," he told me.

A purple base meant a joint base where all the services were equal. I was frustrated with him. He couldn't manage to do his job when I requested anything, but he had more than enough time to harass my troops. When I picked up the phone, I was ready to hear him complain about another perceived infraction. Instead, he was setting us up to fail.

"Admiral Mullen wants to visit your compound," Worm said.

Admiral Michael Mullen was chairman of the Joint Chiefs of Staff at the time. He was visiting the base but wasn't slated to visit my squadron. His change of plans couldn't have come at a worse time. We weren't ready to host anyone, let alone the big boss.

"When?"

"He's on the way there now."

The smugness in Worm's voice told me he knew I had always been on the agenda. Or at least he'd known about it for some time and waited until it was too late to prepare. I looked at the schedule on the whiteboard. My last two aircraft were already airborne. All that were left were my five cannibalized birds. One stood engineless in our sun shelter, running tests. It still couldn't adapt to the latest General Atomics software. The software load didn't mix well with our older aircraft, and nothing we did would make it work. It didn't matter much. The prop was broken anyway and none were left in supply.

The other aircraft were spread apart in our two hangars and on the metal AM-2 matting. We'd pulled the wings off one. The satellite and avionics panels were removed from all four, clearly showing the gaping holes where black boxes and critical instruments once had been. My squadron looked like a boneyard, not an operational unit.

Less than an hour later, a white Mazda minibus raced down the main taxiway. Two black SUVs followed close behind. The vehicles stopped at the end of our ramp and three men approached our guard shack.

Rear Admiral Brian Losey, the commander of US forces in the Horn of Africa, and Ambassador James Swan were escorting Mullen. I waved to the two security forces airmen standing guard to let the men inside our ramp. The rest of Mullen's entourage milled around near the van.

The visit was a standard meet and greet with the squadron. Mullen walked around my sections and passed command coins to every outstretched hand. I walked next to him. As we talked, I issued all the platitudes I had been trained to give.

Everything was wonderful. The base support was flawless. We had no complaints.

It was all garbage. He knew it and I knew it.

Mullen finally stopped at the sunshade and saw the rear end of our broken aircraft with its prop removed. He didn't look happy.

I felt claustrophobic even though we stood outside on the ramp. Mullen was inscrutable as I briefed him about our successes, leaving out any mention of the supply problems.

An old adage in the military was to never make a four-star general your action officer. That meant you didn't bypass the chain of command and air your dirty laundry to the big guys. They were the type to call other generals to get things fixed. After a call like that, things would roll back downhill to you. No general likes to be embarrassed by a colleague's call pointing out issues in his units.

I couldn't read Mullen. He had no expression to indicate how my briefing went. Finally, he stopped in front of my crew chiefs.

"What is your biggest challenge?" he asked.

Jim, one of my best crew chiefs, was on shift. He was a sharp kid. Young and energetic, he often performed miracles on the battered aircraft. But he didn't talk to a lot of flag officers, let alone the chairman of the Joint Chiefs. He looked at me as if the question was mine to answer.

I started.

"Sir, the—"

Mullen cut me off.

"Not you," he said sharply. "I want to hear from him."

He nodded toward the crew chief.

Jim looked at me. I nodded, dreading what would come next.

"Supply, sir."

He said it with a big, happy smile. He couldn't help it. He always smiled. Mullen's eyes returned to me, boring into my chest.

"Explain."

"Sir, we are at the end of a long and immature supply chain," I said. "It takes longer to get shipments here than Afghanistan. We've only just begun identifying issues and determin—"

Mullen's eyes bored into mine.

"I don't buy it," he said. "I worked logistics and I don't believe that."

He stopped short of calling me a liar. He offered me that grace in front of my troops. My heart sank. I had an ethical dilemma on my hands. Did I offer another platitude or did I explain the real problem? I decided to tell the whole truth.

"Sir," I said. "I'm down to my last two aircraft, both of which are airborne, because we can't get parts."

He eyed me.

"You've been reporting a ninety-four percent FMC rate," Mullen said.

FMC meant fully mission capable. The five carcasses around me said that number wasn't valid.

"Is there a disconnect?" Mullen said.

"No, sir," I said. "Normally, we do report that. But we happen to be at the end of a perfect storm where the supply chain has not caught up with us. What you see here has happened in the past couple days. It's not normal."

I decided to press my luck.

"The system of using commercial air to transport our supplies doesn't work out here," I said. "The pallets are frequently lost in transit. When they're not, they are stuck in the customs hangar across the flight line."

The ambassador looked at his feet.

"Simply put, sir," I continued, "I've gone as far as I can without something breaking free."

I paused and waited for Mullen's reaction. He studied me for a second and then turned to the ambassador.

"Can you look into that?"

"I can," the ambassador said. He wouldn't look at me.

A few days later, General Norton Allan Schwartz, the Air Force chief of staff, received an email about my supply problem. I knew because Mullen copied me on the email. By the end of the month, my maintainers had parts and we could get the Task Force the sorties they wanted.

We finally had enough Predators to hunt.

CHAPTER 18

East Africa Air Pirates

The twenty-foot fishing boat cut across the dark water.

The prow spit out white foam as it skipped along the three-foot swells. I could hear the high-pitched whine of the motor in my head as I watched it race at flank speed in the monitor.

The Predator watched from high above. Being faster, the pilot made lazy circles around the boat at a safe distance. The vessel's speed and the blackness of the night made it doubtful that the Somali crew could detect the Predator with its running lights off.

Inside the boat was a bomb maker. He floated between Yemen and Somalia as he worked with different nefarious groups. He wasn't a true believer, just a gun for hire. He went where the money was, and at that time jobs in the Horn of Africa were paying well. Al Shabaab was a jihadist group that would later become affiliated with al Qaeda as it shifted its operations from Ethiopia to Somalia. The bomb maker was headed south to join up with them.

The conditions were almost ideal as the boat raced toward Yemen. The night sky was clear and the wind was calm. The moon, only a sliver, offered little illumination. The boat continued on a beeline for Berbera. The coastal town was a hotbed for piracy in the Gulf of Aden. There, the target would be able to melt into the background and disappear. Pirates weren't necessarily his allies. They preferred the money he'd pay them for safe passage.

Over the horizon, the USS *New Orleans* waited. They too could see the Predator's feed on their monitors. Onboard, a SEAL team prepared to launch and snatch the bomber. The plan was for the target to simply disappear. The Task Force didn't enlighten me on why they wanted to roll him up. They didn't need to. They fed me, like all the other cogs in the machine, only the information I needed to perform my piece of the mission. My job was to get a Predator airborne so the Task Force could keep eyes on the target.

I was in the JOC operations center watching a Predator track the boat. This was one of our first big missions for the special operations task force based in Djibouti and I wanted to be there. My pilots had launched the Predator hours ago, and now pilots in Cannon Air Force Base were flying the mission. I knew how they felt, but I felt ownership over the aircraft. I wanted to be there while it performed the mission.

For an hour, the fishing boat didn't change course. We could see the crew moving around. The heat from their bodies was bright against the cooler boat and ocean. They were relaxed. The crew flying Bong—the Predator's call sign—connected to the secure net.

"Ten minutes."

In the operations center, a little icon on the map showed the

SEAL team's location. They were in two rigid inflatable boats (RIBs) just over the horizon. The RIBs carrying the operators split apart and came at the boat from both sides like a pair of pincers. With a soft bump, the three boats collided. I watched one operator near the gunwale reach out to steady the craft. One team headed for the helm, the other belowdecks. Within moments the operators emerged with several bodies bound with zip ties.

"All clear," the net crackled. "We got a jackpot."

The bomb maker had been captured.

The crewmen were positioned on their knees, hands folded over their heads, in the stern. The Predator watched for a bit longer as the SEALs wrapped up business. As the RIBs drove off toward the USS *New Orleans*, the Predator's camera shifted to the open ocean as it circled back to base.

I walked out of the operations center that night thinking there was so much more we could do with this aircraft. We had never had the opportunity to explore operations at sea in Iraq or Afghanistan. So far, most of our operations were against land targets. We had urban warfare and even remote mountainous tracking down cold. Yet no one had thought we could use the aircraft against maritime targets.

Pirates weren't the only problems. Smugglers used the waterways to avoid detection. We could track the rivers. Could we track on the open ocean? This war hunting al Qaeda as it spread back to the Arabian Peninsula and Africa would be the new proving ground. It was an opportunity for us to further expand our catalog of missions.

After the mission, it was up to my squadron to bring the Predator home. It was the least exciting part of the mission, but also the most nerve-racking. Not only did we have to land the temperamental aircraft, but also we had to do it at a commercial airport.

A few weeks after the bomb maker disappeared, I was flying Gordon home after a long mission tracking part of al-Awlaki's cell.

We orbited over the Gulf of Tadjoura, about twenty miles north of the airport. It was off the beaten path of other aircraft in the area and allowed us to swap control from the pilots at Cannon to my squadron in Djibouti. I had just taken control of the Predator when the air traffic controller at the airport came over the net.

"Gordon Four Zero, maintain position at one five thousand for departing traffic," the air traffic controller said.

"Gordon, maintain position, one five thousand," I said.

I was a little miffed at holding. Letting us descend and maneuver for landing would take us away from any aircraft departing, but it was their airport.

"Take a look at the airfield," I said.

The sensor shifted the pod. The city at nighttime glowed below. It took a couple of seconds to pick out the airfield from the glare and clutter. I could hear the air controller over the radio.

"Air France, you are cleared for takeoff, turn left heading three six zero, climb to two zero thousand and join flight planned route."

This was the weekly Air France A340 run from Djibouti to Paris via Jeddah, Saudi Arabia. Something about the clearance raised my hackles. A quick look at the tracker showed that the flight path would intersect where we orbited. The airliner with four hundred seats was cleared to a different altitude from ours, but it still had to climb. It would be close to our altitude when it passed our position.

"Whoa!" I said.

"What?" the sensor called out.

"Djibouti cleared the airliner right into us," I said. "Watch that plane."

In the HUD, the large A340 lumbered down the runway, lifted

off, and cleared the coastline. Then it turned and headed right for us. The Air France jet was to my south. I spun the aircraft around and headed west. I pushed the throttle up, hoping to gain some airspeed.

"Sir, he's still coming at us."

I shook my head. I told myself we would not be the first RPA to bring down an airliner. Try as I might, we couldn't generate the kind of speed we needed to get out of the way.

I pushed the nose down. The massive jet slid left a little in the HUD. As a rule of thumb, anything stationary when seen in flight would hit you. If it didn't move, it meant the aircraft was on a vector to collide with you. Anything moving was on a vector to pass you.

"Sir!" the sensor said.

In the HUD, the Air France jet's wings banked to turn right at us. They were still below us, but climbing.

"Gordon Four Zero, say position."

The call told me the controllers had noticed the conflict too.

"Sir, we are heading west to avoid traffic."

The Airbus's wings reversed direction to turn to my left. The pilots had heard me too.

"Gordon, maintain position."

I wasn't about to do that. Stopping would only keep us near the jet's flight path. I kept heading west. The Air France jet turned to the east. A few minutes later, we saw the Airbus pass by us in the darkness of the East African night. We missed each other by about a half mile. That is too close in aviation.

I exhaled for what felt like the first time in several minutes.

The squadron was finally in a groove. We were pursuing al-Awlaki and his network. My supply chain was back on track. Maintenance had the aircraft purring and the pilots were making huge saves. We were meeting the Task Force's surge.

The squadron was also coming together into one team. But I felt like we needed an identity. We needed something to bind us into a family, and after watching the sea-intercept mission, I had pirates on my mind.

The original squadron patch was a shooting star leaving Earth's orbit with six stars on either side of the patch. It was a play on the numbers six (stars) and zero (Earth and patch border). But it didn't resonate with me.

Our advance team replaced the star with a striking snake because a nest of asps was run out of the squadron area before construction of our ramp and tents could continue. They got a local company to modify the patch, but I didn't think the snake was distinctive enough. I wanted an identity that everyone recognized. I wanted something that spoke to our mission, our location, and events surrounding the deployment.

My mind drifted to the books I'd read about Vietnam and the Yankee Air Pirates. The term was used by North Vietnamese propaganda to refer to the United States Air Force. Of course, pilots took it as a badge of honor much like the Marine Corps adopted "Devil Dogs" when the Germans used it after fighting Marines during World War I. The same could be said for the "White Devils."

The pilots in Vietnam crafted a logo using a pirate flag with "Yankee Air Pirate" scrawled around the skull and crossbones. I wanted a history like that for the 60th. Instead of being Yankees, we were the East Africa Air Pirates. I didn't think the original Yankee Air Pirates would object, considering our prey.

I had shirts and patches made that resembled those of the Yankee Air Pirates. The new patch was a hit. The guys wore it with pride. But as the summer heat intensified, fooling around with patches wasn't enough to keep up the troops' morale. The heat topped one hundred degrees every day, with humidity that could wilt rock. The ramp temperatures were easily twenty degrees higher. To stand guard or work on aircraft in those conditions was brutal. I needed my troops happy, or at least not angry, to keep them at their peak performance.

I saw the perfect foil when a Marine aviation unit raised a Jolly Roger from an eight-foot piece of PVC pipe. The squadron, Marine Aerial Refueler Transport Squadron 352, flew KC-130 Hercules tankers. Their missions were aerial and ground refueling. Known as the Raiders, they were based in California.

The flag was lashed with parachute cord to a tent strut next to the wooden steps leading to the front door. To me, the flag was an affront, as there was only one "pirate" unit on base.

In the Air Force, a spirit mission pits one squadron against another in a prank war, which usually involves theft and ransom of important squadron property. Targets could be mascots like an animal or suit of armor or flags. Flying squadrons at Holloman nearly got into a fistfight when a Predator squadron stole the Reaper squadron's flag, took it out to White Sands, and shot pictures of it with the aircraft. They used the picture with no graphics to ransom the flag. Without the graphics, the Reaper squadron would never find the flag. The Reaper squadron paid the ransom of restocking the squadron's Heritage Room with several bottles of whiskey.

My goal was to meet the new neighbors. A spirit mission was more fun than a housewarming basket. Besides, we couldn't find a basket. It was time for our first antipiracy operation.

I walked into ops and spotted a young pilot, a lieutenant, sitting at the desk. Teflon was one of the pilots pulled straight from the Air

Force's pilot training program. Where his buddies got B-52s or F-16s, he got Predators. He was highly motivated and I often looked at him like I would a five-year-old, wondering where he got his energy. That kind of piss and vinegar had long since drained from my system.

"LT," I said.

"Yes, sir," he said, standing.

I pretended to examine a large map of Africa near the ops desk.

"That flag outside the compound."

"Yes, sir."

"I don't like it." I stared at a dot on the map. "It needs to come down."

"I'll see what I can do, sir."

I nodded and left the ops tent.

At shift change, Teflon grabbed Ponis, another lieutenant, and went over to the Raiders' tent. They fumbled with the flag for a while, unable to separate it from the pole. All I could do was shake my head in disappointment when they told me of their failure. The world's best Air Force had been defeated by darkness.

Lieutenants.

The next day, the pair went out while the light was still good. They got to the steps, climbed onto the railing, and started cutting the cord with a knife. A couple of Marine sergeants happened to pull up to the tent in a gator, a small golf cart–size utility vehicle. It was dinner hour. Everyone on base was on the way or returning to the chow hall.

"Hey, what are you guys doing?" one of the Marine sergeants said.

The lieutenants froze. Thinking fast, Teflon noticed that the flag was almost off the pole. The wind was brisk that day.

"The wind broke your flag," Teflon said. "We were just fixing it for you."

The sergeants relaxed.

"Oh, thanks, guys." They walked into the tent without another look back.

The LTs couldn't believe their luck. The Marines had actually bought the line. The pilots decided not to waste any time and chance being caught when the Marines figured out their mistake.

Teflon cut the last bit of cord and bounded down the steps and back into the safety of our compound. I flew the Jolly Roger from a tower for the next week. At fifty feet, the flag could be seen from nearly anywhere on the base. I expected the commander of the Raiders to call and ask me to return his flag, but he never called.

Finally, after a week, a Marine gunnery sergeant approached the compound and asked for the flag back. The guards checked the access list and apologized. The gunny wasn't on the list and couldn't enter our compound. A couple of days later, he returned with some friends. Again, he was turned away, but he didn't leave empty-handed. I sent a ransom note to their commander.

Teflon and Ponis drafted the note and printed it on fake parchment, as if it were a message from one ship's captain to another. In it, I declared that only the 60th could hold a pirate name. No other ruffians, scalawags, raiders, buccaneers, marauders, mercenaries, swashbucklers, bandits, brigands, and, of course, pirates could exist on the base. In order to secure the return of their standard—their flag—they had to host a joint cookout where the squadrons could mingle.

The next day, the Marines returned in force. This time, they didn't come empty-handed.

The gunny and his crew had nabbed a random Air Force officer and duct-taped him to a corpsman's bodyboard. It didn't matter that the airman wasn't from my squadron. The Marines presented him, trussed up, and asked for me. Abandoning a fellow airman goes against everything the Air Force believes. The gunny knew this.

His response was well played.

I wasn't on shift at the time, so Crash, my new director of operations, took the call. A C-17 pilot by trade, he was short and lean and wore glasses. He was the engine that drove the squadron. He never said something couldn't be done. Crash's enthusiasm matched his professional skill in the cockpit. He worked the twelve-hour shift opposite mine to ensure that we had senior leadership available no matter what happened.

Crash invited the gunny and his crew into the compound. We traded the flag for the airman and even offered them some refreshment. The whole time that gunny and Crash talked, the hapless airman remained strapped to the bodyboard. We never learned his name and he didn't stick around after Crash finally cut him loose.

The Raiders retreated back to their tents. They never attended any of our cookouts.

Soon after our spirit mission, Somali pirates took four more American hostages off the coast of Oman. The pirates seized the *Quest*, a fifty-eight-foot yacht owned by Scott and Jean Adam from California. Two other Americans—Phyllis Macay and Robert Riggle—were also onboard. The Adams had been sailing the world since 2004 with a yacht full of Bibles. They decided to cut the corner across the Red Sea to save some time and sailed right into the pirates' main operating area.

The USS *Enterprise* Strike Group was transiting from the Red Sea to its station in the Arabian Gulf at the same time. They responded immediately to the hijacking and surrounded the *Quest*.

At Camp Lemonnier, I watched the continuous news coverage on several big screens mounted above the tables in the chow hall. I didn't like watching Americans get attacked and I didn't like failing when it came to defending our citizens. It was the most important thing I did. My fangs were out. I anticipated the next step, so I finished my soda and headed over to the Task Force to speak with Frog.

Frog was a major from the 3rd Special Operations Squadron. He was the new LNO, between the Task Force and the squadrons. He looked harried when I arrived. He had been on station for nearly a month and the long hours had taken their toll on him already. He was the only Predator LNO, so he had to answer every question asked, no matter when it was asked. He had a room near the operations center where he could crash, but if the bags under his eyes were any indication, he didn't use the room much.

The room was buzzing. A live video of a dhow racing at flank speed was on one monitor. The hull's white paint was chipped and streams of rust ran down the sides. The camera wasn't a Predator. I wasn't familiar with the feed so I couldn't tell which aircraft was watching it.

"You guys watching the pirate thing?"

It was a redundant question. I could see he was deeply involved in it.

"Yes," Frog said. He was distracted trying to keep up with operations and talk with me.

"Is that the mother ship?"

"Yes," Frog said. "That's it."

A mother ship was usually a converted medium-size cargo ship. When hunting, they launched several smaller boats, fishing boats really, to attack ships off the coast. The boats carried a team sufficient to take a commercial cargo hauler. When a ship was sighted, the small boat would attack, seize the ship, and call for help. The mother ship raced to their location and took any hostages back to Somalia.

"First thing I'd do is take out that mother ship," I said.

Frog didn't even look up at the monitor.

"What ship?"

I glanced up at the monitor and the ship was gone. All that remained were a couple of waves radiating out in concentric circles. I didn't even see any debris. I had no idea what had happened to the dhow. One second, it was in the middle of the monitor. The next time I looked, all I saw was ocean. I didn't press the issue.

"I was going to suggest an air strike," I said. "Guess you beat me to it."

"Hmm," he grunted.

"Anything we can do?" I meant the 60th.

Frog looked at me. "The request is making its way through the channels," he said. "Can you give us coverage on the *Quest*?"

I considered that for a moment. "That will take a lot of aircraft," I said.

I knew the basic location based on maps shown on the cable news networks. If the news reports were accurate to even a basic nautical degree, my planes didn't have the legs to provide that kind of coverage.

"I would need—"

"More sorties than you can fly," Frog finished my thought. "I ran the numbers. You'll still have a gap flying at your max surge. We can't ask for more because we don't have enough GCSs to add CAPs."

I looked at the calculation sheet he handed me. His math was good. Only there was one variable he had left out.

"You can't sustain this for more than a day," I said. "Transit time is too long."

He nodded.

"We considered that. We just can't figure another way."

"What would augment us?" I asked.

"P-3?"

The P-3 was a nautical patrol plane made to hunt submarines. The plane had four props and a large boom that stuck out of the tail like a bee's stinger. It detected changes in the earth's magnetic field caused by submarines. It had pretty good legs, but I didn't think their station time was that long so far from home. We could manage our crews easily since they were home. The deployed P-3 crews would have to change their shift schedule every day to make the mission work. In effect, they would work a twenty-hour day, go into crew rest, and then launch again the next day four hours earlier than before. The human body couldn't safely handle that strain. Not in aviation.

I thought for a moment and then it hit me.

"There is one thing we did before."

"What?"

"Ever hear of heel-to-toe?"

Frog's forehead creased.

"No."

I grabbed the notepad from him and started drawing.

"Okay, I fly my normal complement of sorties. At this distance, you will get a couple hours on station with each."

I drew a line for each aircraft with hash marks to show the station times with enough overlap for a handover between aircraft.

"Flying like this gives us another six-hour gap, give or take, for the P-3. Agree?"

"I'm with you so far," Frog said.

"Okay," I said. "Add another CAP."

"We don't have the cockpit."

"You don't need it," I said. "Send the return birds home lost link."

Lost link meant no one would monitor or see the aircraft as it flew autonomously through international airspace back to Djibouti. It was the only time the aircraft ever flew without us in full control.

"We did it in the 17th in Afghanistan for some targets up in the northeast," I said. "We couldn't reach them from Kandahar and maintain constant stare. So we ran a program that tracked the aircraft and displayed the information to the mission commander. If something happened, then a crew would grab the plane and fix whatever happened."

"Sounds risky."

"It is, but its been done before," I said. "Look, you need to do something like this or get another airplane to augment. We can't kill the P-3 crews."

"Can you do it?" Frog asked.

I thought about it. The real answer was no, but the Task Force never accepted that answer.

"Yes, but there is a price," I said. "I am almost out of supplies. I can give you a couple days and then we are down, completely down. No sorties at all until we catch up."

Frog was silent for a few seconds as he thought about it.

"I'll have to check with the 3rd," he said. "We've never done anything like this."

I walked the mile back to the squadron. Had I done the right thing? Heel-to-toe was a technique that had worked in the past. It also carried with it great risk to the aircraft. There were no guarantees that a crew could get to a broken airplane to keep it from crashing. There would be no one to react to conflicting air traffic. No one wanted to be responsible for knocking down an airliner. The one saving grace was that the Predator flew well below most airliners. There wouldn't be much for the Predators to hit.

Crash saw me and came over.

"You're up late."

"Expecting a phone call," I said.

I knew the 3rd would be calling soon to put the plan in motion. There was no other course of action. When I got to my office, I checked my secure phone. I already had a missed call. It was from Air Forces Central Command (AFCENT), which oversaw all the Air Force's aircraft in the Middle East. I sighed and dialed their number. I hoped it was the daily call to coordinate something. They always called just after I left shift.

"Hey, Prozac," I said.

Prozac was a fellow Predator pilot assigned to the staff.

"You know what this call is about?"

"Yeah, hit me."

"CENTCOM is cutting the EXORD right now," he said.

An EXORD was an execution order, or an order to perform a mission. A PLANORD, or plan order, told you to plan a mission; a WARNORD, or warning order, alerted you that you were about to go; and the EXORD told you to go.

"You are to fly four CAPs until further notice to support the American sailboat."

"Got it," I said.

I outlined the limitations.

"Understood," Prozac said. "You're still getting the order."

"Copy."

Crash waited next to my desk. He had just arrived for his shift and caught the tail end of my conversation.

"AFCENT?" he asked as I hung up the phone.

"You're gonna love this."

The next day, we had all four CAPs up. When I wasn't in my ops tent, I was over with Frog watching the feed. The sailboat drifted with the current. We'd occasionally see a pirate on deck.

We kept up our constant stare for three days, but Jon came to see me on the third day. Our ability to sustain the four CAPs was deteriorating, he told me. I was worried that we'd lose the constant stare on the *Quest* in the next day or so.

At dinner, I tried to figure out a work-around, when I saw the news flash. I left my tray and headed straight to the JOC and Frog's station.

The pirates were in negotiations with the FBI when a pirate fired a rocket-propelled grenade at one of the destroyers patrolling nearby. The rocket missed. In the monitor, I watched as a Navy destroyer turned toward the small sailboat. Then I saw the "shots fired" notice in chat. SEALs in inflatable boats were headed toward the *Quest*. I watched as they scrambled from the RIBs onto the boat. Two pirates were killed and the other thirteen surrendered.

All four Americans—Phyllis Macay, Robert Riggle, and owners Jean and Scott Adam—were found below. They were severely wounded. Corpsmen tried to save them, but they were unsuccessful. Everything had gone pear-shaped.

I felt the failure in our bones. My whole body felt numb. It was the total lack of sensation that comes with the worst news ever. I knew on a visceral level that there was nothing we could have done to help or to prevent this action. But it went back to our core mission. We'd failed to protect Americans. I left the JOC and walked back to my compound. The weight of failure was much harder to bear than the stress of the mission. I longed to worry about supplies and keeping the Predators airborne again.

The next day, we returned to our primary mission of tracking al-Awlaki. We backed off to two CAPs to give maintenance time to catch up. The Task Force, unusually quiet, didn't press us for more.

CHAPTER 19

Tightening the Noose

I headed over to the Task Force to check in with the liaison officer.

"We've got a lead," Frog admitted.

That caught me off guard.

"We're getting close," Frog continued. "Problem is, the guys we want are hiding in the ungoverned region."

The ungoverned region was code for areas that al Qaeda dominated in Yemen. The Yemeni military was actively fighting Houthi rebels in the north along the Saudi Arabian border and al Qaeda to the east of Sana'a, the country's capital. Town by town, al Qaeda slowly pushed out government control and instituted Sharia, or Islamic law. Viewed by Muslims as the unfailing law of God, it governed everything from crime to moral choices like sex, diet, and etiquette. More often than not, the populace was ruled through threat and intimidation as these ancient laws were imposed on them.

It didn't help that Yemen didn't allow US troops into the country. We wanted to roll up key leaders from time to time. Capture was still the best option in the war on terror. A live prisoner provided real-time intelligence. Without the raid option, we were limited to air strikes only.

"What's the problem?" I asked.

"Naser al-Shadadi."

Al-Shadadi was a high-level facilitator key to al Qaeda in the Arabian Peninsula operations. He organized the attacks on government outposts throughout the region. He also protected al-Awlaki.

"We can't get a team in country to roll him up," Frog said. "So far, our only chance to neutralize him is to hit him at a meeting. Problem is, he operates in the city. The collateral is too high for an air strike."

My aircraft had already taken a couple of shots at al-Shadadi, one attack occurring just before Admiral Mullen's visit. Each time, al-Shadadi was in the open, either meeting informants or in transit. After each miss, he taunted the crews on the radio.

"You missed," he'd broadcast, knowing we were listening to his communications. "I'm still alive."

We all wanted him.

"When is he in the open?" I asked.

"Only when he drives between towns," he said. "And he goes fast."

"I have an idea," I said.

"What?"

"Moving target shot."

Frog considered it for a moment.

"They're not trained for that."

He was right. The 3rd Special Operations Squadron, like the conventional squadrons, had resisted advanced techniques developed by the 17th. It wasn't that the techniques were difficult; they were just time-consuming to learn. Most units spent the majority of their time on target with little or no time available for training.

"I'm not talking about the advanced techniques."

The advanced techniques taught by the new Predator Weapons School involved complicated computer programs processing numerous variables to include target speed, angle of intercept, timing, and others. Few crews were trained to this standard. When I was in the 17th, we came up with a simple way to make the shot.

"Here, let me show you."

I borrowed Frog's legal pad. I scribbled a crude picture.

"Look, here's what you need."

I drew the road and the car. I used the pen to symbolize a Predator.

"The striker comes in from the side and flies behind or beside the target after missile release."

I drew a set of cross hairs just in front of the car. Essentially, the sensor operator had to lead the car just a bit. Just before the missile hit, he eased pressure off the stick and the laser would track back to the target.

"Put your laser here and the car will run right into the frag."

Frog considered my diagram.

"Frog, any crew can do this," I said. "They can practice while en route to the target area. Pick a random car and fly practice runs. That's what the 17th does and why they don't miss."

Frog nodded. As a weapons school graduate, he understood the nature of what I proposed and the simplicity of the tactic. We didn't need advanced techniques. We just needed the right technique to achieve the objective.

"I'll talk to the JOC director about this."

I smiled. The JOC director was an aggressive guy. He'd like the tactic.

"Keep in mind, if a moving target is your only option," I said, tapping the diagram, "this is the way to go."

I hoped my aircraft would get a chance to shoot. Occasionally, a Predator would come home without its missiles. That raised morale, as a shot provided a tangible effect to show my troops we were making a difference in the war. The squadron thrived on the stress of maintaining a constant stare when they knew it mattered.

We launched.

We landed.

We surged additional CAPs.

But it was clearly *Groundhog Day* for months on end while enduring oppressive heat, smothering humidity, and the choking poison smoke of the burn pits. Frequent squadron cookouts or humanitarian trips to the local orphanages could no longer compete with the heat or the long hours. The squadron took pride in keeping the Predators in the air and on the hunt. But they needed that tangible feedback too. They needed an affirmation of their efforts. Nothing was better than empty rails under the wing.

A couple of days after my visit with Frog, the Task Force wanted our aircraft to sit alert. I was reticent to do this. They were looking for a daytime launch, and the ambient temperatures on the concrete or metal-based ramps soared upward of 140 degrees. At those temperatures, the avionics would overheat within minutes of being activated. Worse, the glues that bonded the carbon fiber composites in the wings could melt and result in structural failure in flight.

I didn't want to lose another aircraft.

———

Unfortunately, we lost two more in May. Kate, Tail 249, started autonomously after we received a new software update. She was parked on the ramp when the engine started. The maintainers shut it down, but they were puzzled because the ignition and the fuel lines were shut off. There was no physical way the aircraft could start with no power or fuel. The only explanation was a bug in the software update.

The bug was never found.

We were wary of Kate after that and kept an eye on the aircraft. It was kind of creepy having a Predator with a history of starting itself. The whole incident was a little too close to the Terminator movies. Someone started calling her Christine after the horror film.

Kate later crashed while Teflon was on the controls. A thick deck of clouds made for low visibility. Teflon was using the gauges to fly, but the navigation sensor read several hundred feet higher than he really was. His first indication of a problem was when a tree flashed through the screen. There was nothing he could do, and Kate, our squadron aircraft, buried herself in the ground like a lawn dart.

Even though she was totally destroyed, 249's engine was still running when emergency responders arrived almost an hour later.

We lost Tail 173 when the flight controls failed. We called General Atomics about the problem but received no new information. Jon and his men replaced the flight controls, but a couple of weeks later they became erratic and failed again. Tail 173 flipped out of control on final approach and flew straight down into the water. It looked like a duck getting shot out of the sky. The Predator smashed into the ocean about a mile from shore. The engine separated and skipped along the water, landing closer to shore. Navy rescue divers from the base recovered the big bits of wreckage. The smaller bits washed ashore over the next few months.

I also had to deal with storing the Hellfire missiles while the Predators were on alert. Under Navy direction, the missiles couldn't sit on the ramp. I dreaded going up to the N-3 office to make the request for a waiver. Worm had finally rotated out, but I didn't know the new lieutenant commander. I didn't know whether I should expect more of the same.

"I'm Cruiser," the new lieutenant said when I introduced myself in the headquarters building.

His office was a smallish space in an old French building. The plaster walls needed repair. The cold ceramic-tile floor was slippery with dust, dirt, and atomized plaster. I noticed he wore a tan flight suit as he stood.

"What did you fly?" I asked.

"F-18s."

Cruiser was a carrier pilot with experience flying over both Iraq and Afghanistan. He knew what a ship on combat alert really meant. He understood what was at stake. I relaxed.

"I need some help."

"What's up?"

He was on guard. I wondered what Worm had told him about us.

"I need to stage missiles on the ramp."

"Can't do that," he said.

I expected the response. I was sure Worm had poisoned the well. But I was betting on Cruiser's understanding of combat and the need to be ready.

"Look, I've got three birds on alert," I said. "They have to launch as soon as our customer calls. I can't do that with the missiles in the ASP."

The ASP was the ammo supply point, an ammo dump located outside the base. My weapons loaders had to sign out of the base, pass through security, ask the ASP personnel to deliver the weapons, and then reverse the process to get back to the flight line. It took at least half an hour on a good day. We needed to go when the Task Force called.

Cruiser eyed me while he considered the request.

"Okay."

Okay? Really?

"Thanks, Cruiser," I said. "I owe you a beer."

"You can't store them out there, you know."

"I know," I said. "I only ask for the duration of the alert."

He nodded.

I walked back to the compound, pleased. Cruiser had a clue how combat ops were supposed to be run. It was my first bureaucratic victory and a huge weight lifted off the squadron. With the Task Force getting more leads on al-Awlaki, I was confident we'd be ready when the call came.

The call came down later that day. The crews rushed to the aircraft and raced to beat the late morning heat. I tried to get to the JOC to watch the mission but couldn't get there. Hours later, the Predators returned without missiles. I called over to Frog, but the news wasn't good.

"Cannon missed the shot," he said. "They managed to stop the car and kill most of the occupants. The lead crew barely missed the vehicle. The cross hairs ended up in a deep ditch on the side of the road. The blast scared the driver into crashing, but that was it.

I sighed.

Frog said shortly after the strikes that they heard the now familiar "You can't kill me" over the radio. Al-Shadadi had survived the strike. He was the only one who ever did. A hundred missiles could be fired at a hundred and one terrorists and this guy would be the one who got away each time.

The Task Force was still as unforgiving of mistakes as they had been during the infamous "23 seconds" incident when we missed al-Zarqawi.

A manned aircraft working with the Task Force attempted a strike a few days later. I'm not sure who flew it and I knew the Task Force wasn't going to tell me. The aircraft shot a Griffin missile, which is smaller than a Hellfire but carries an equivalent punch. This shot missed for the same reason. I felt somewhat vindicated that the miss wasn't a case of lack of talent in the RPA community. The tactic was a challenge for everyone.

Al-Shadadi went into hiding after the missed Griffin strike.

He would surface a couple of months later. This time, the 3rd didn't miss. The sensor led the car with the cross hairs until a moment before impact, then relaxed his grip. The laser spot shifted to the hood of the car. A moment later, the missile struck the engine block and disabled the vehicle. The survivors bolted. None got far. This time al-Shadadi didn't get a chance to taunt us.

I visited the operations center the next day.

"The shot worked out," Frog said.

I nodded. "That's all we needed to do."

"It needs to be better for the next target," Frog said.

I looked at Frog. "Which is?"

"We got a lead on number one," he said.

Number one was al-Awlaki. The entire purpose of our mission had just surfaced. I didn't know how he'd been detected. It didn't matter. All I knew was we had to be ready. But just when I felt like the squadron was getting ahead, we faced a new challenge.

The weather was changing again. We still battled the heat, but summer thunderstorm season brought issues we hadn't expected. Near the equator, convection sucked moisture from the Red Sea and Gulf of Aden to build massive cells over the Ethiopian plains. The storms quickly exploded to the size of Iowa, towering up to sixty thousand feet, almost twice the height of American thunderstorms. In the air, the storms tossed hail more than twenty miles. Ice pellets the size of peas blasted the Predators and shredded their fragile skin.

On the ground, we struggled with the rain. Downpours turned the parched landscape into a flooded quagmire. The hard-packed dirt, so long deprived of moisture, could not absorb the rain, leaving many roads washed out. Any patch of dirt not covered by crushed rock slowly soaked and softened into a mudhole.

Then there were the winds.

A massive cell erupted in Ethiopia several hundred miles away. The outflow of energy funneled through the mountains, intensifying into a hellish blast aimed at Djibouti. A wall of forty-knot gusts tore in from the south, slamming into the compound.

Gordon was arriving for its scheduled landing. The fuel tanks were nearly dry as the Task Force eked out every minute of target time. I stepped out of the ops tent into a maelstrom. The maintainers not out at the ramp were struggling to close the hangar doors. The security forces tent strained against its tie-down. One of the security forces troops was hammering at a peg as the other grabbed sandbags to weigh it down. I rushed over to the GCS. I knew they were taking control of Gordon.

The night shift pilot, MaDrawers, was in the seat. He was another young lieutenant who worked his way through the fighter track before getting an assignment to Predator. He was of Pakistani descent, which led to his call sign, a knockoff of *Saturday Night Live*'s Gulf War–era I-Zheet M'Drurz character.

He had already taken control of Gordon and held it in orbit at the northern holding point.

"How much gas do you have?"

"It's min fuel," he said.

The aircraft had just enough fuel to attempt a couple of approaches and then land or ditch.

"So what's the weather?"

I had an idea, but I wanted to know what the forecasters in the control tower were saying. MaDrawers called the weather shop from a phone in the GCS.

"Twenty-one hundred scattered, five thousand overcast," he said, hanging up. "A scattered cloud deck at twenty-one hundred feet above ground level and a solid deck at five thousand feet."

"The winds?" I asked.

A blank look.

"Call back."

He spoke on the phone for a few minutes and hung up again.

"Fifteen knots."

"What's the predominant direction?"

Another blank look.

"Call back."

He made his third call to the tower.

"Variable, though predominantly from the south."

"Okay," I said. "Does the wind outside feel like fifteen knots?"

"No, sir."

I looked at him. He caught the clue and called the Task Force weather desk. Those guys had better meteorological sensors than the Djiboutian air traffic control.

"What're the winds?" I asked.

"Task Force weather is calling forty knots from the south," he said.

"How long will they last?"

"A couple hours," he said.

That was problematic. The max wind we could land with in any direction was thirty knots. The max crosswind for our current weight was slightly more than sixteen knots, but Gordon didn't have enough gas to wait.

"I'll take the plane," I said.

"Sir, I can do it."

"Have you landed in crosswinds this strong before?"

"No, sir."

"Then I will do it."

I signaled him to get out of the seat. More than four thousand flight hours and fifteen years of aviation experience had taught me how to land with this kind of crosswind. I had suffered through this type of landing before in an E-3, a Boeing 707 converted into a radar platform. Then, with a highly experienced crew, we had almost ripped an engine off the aircraft at touchdown.

MaDrawers climbed out of the seat. He looked as if I had kicked his cat.

"Don't worry," I said. "I trust you, but I'm not going to make you land in conditions like this. Anything happens, we can say the most experienced aviator was in the seat. I'll take the hit." He deserved to hear that. MaDrawers was an excellent pilot in whose flying skills I held great confidence. My replacing him wasn't like pulling Jantz out of the seat before a shot. I hoped to protect him from an awful situation, one I could manage—to an extent.

I sat in the seat and immediately took control.

"Tower, Gordon Four Zero, ready for descent. Request runway two seven."

The French-Arabic voice came back.

"Gordon, winds are calm. Descend to one thousand feet, cleared visual approach to runway zero nine."

I chuckled. The wind still howled around the GCS. We could hear it above the noise of the HVAC coolers. I didn't accept the clearance. I didn't want to chance a crash on the civilian side of the airport or in a residential area. I wanted to stay over the water and land on the military end of the field.

"Gordon Four Zero, request runway two seven."

After a moment, the controller let me have my way. I was the only aircraft in the airspace. The tower controller had the luxury to grant me any wish at that point.

I dropped down and leveled off over the blackness of the Gulf of Aden. I turned to start my approach. The lights of the base and the city rotated into view and then slid sideways. The tracker display showed the Predator virtually flying sideways to the north, though it was pointing west.

Winds calm, my ass, I thought.

The little pink aircraft icon inched its way toward the final course. I turned to start my momentum back to the base. The icon

"S" turned about the course until I figured out the winds. Like a boat, planes had to point into the wind to counter a crossing force in order to hold a course.

Our ground speed read only twenty knots at most. Most of our engine power was spent fighting the wind. I had to keep the power high to maintain my glide path or else I would drop too soon. I knew I was close to the runway when I saw our parking ramp slip into view. At the end of the runway and well clear to the side, I would never have seen the parking ramp at this point on a normal approach. Tonight, I looked right at my horrified maintainers as the airplane flew sideways toward the runway, crabbing a full forty-five degrees off runway heading.

"You're about ten feet, sir."

The lights marking the edge of the runway were in view. I could see the ground rushing at us.

It was time.

I kicked the rudder to twist the nose around to line up with the runway. I rolled the wings to the left toward the wind so the lift in the wings could replace some of the thrust into the wind I had just lost. The painted stripes of the center line came into view. The wheels skipped a couple of times and the aircraft settled onto the runway. I shoved the stick over to keep the left wing from lifting and pressed the nose down, risking a bounced nose gear, a surefire way to destroy the plane.

The aircraft slowed to taxi speed and allowed me to relax. The taxiway was below the flight line fence and was somewhat sheltered from the gusts. Even so, the little bird bucked all the way back to the ramp as it tried to flip over. I had to "fly" her by making constant adjustments to the flight controls to counter the winds until the maintainers could tie her down.

Back in the compound, Jon dropped by the ops tent.

"Sir, we didn't think you were going to land when we saw the airplane pointing at us."

I didn't either, I thought.

"Did I scrape anything?" I said.

"Not a thing, sir."

The next night we were faced with the same weather conditions. This time, we brought the aircraft back with more fuel. I let MaDrawers attempt the landing. Three times he tried. Three times he forgot to adjust the wings enough and the Predator got pushed over the French Air Force's Mirage 2000 ramp. I made him go around, climb back to altitude, and try again. After the third attempt, I let another pilot try. The winds died down to a less challenging level and he managed to skip it home.

The landings were tricky, but so was the hunt for al-Awlaki. Mapping a target's pattern of life was a painstaking process. But it was harder because al-Awlaki was aware of how the United States tracked terrorists. Predators were in the news and it was widely known that we could track a cell phone signal.

The Task Force relied on the Predator during the early days of hunting al-Awlaki, but they quickly realized that we could not provide the coverage necessary. Africa Command (AFRICOM), which oversaw US forces on the continent, decided to deploy Reapers to the region to help the operation.

Since the Reaper had joined the hunt for al-Awlaki, the Task Force wanted my maintainers to upload bombs and then relaunch the aircraft. The only problem was space at Camp Lemonnier.

Anything that staged out of Camp Lemonnier would stay on the ramp overnight, and there wasn't enough room for the Reapers.

To figure out a work-around, the AFRICOM Air Expeditionary Group sent Mike, now a deputy group commander, out to coordinate. I hadn't seen Mike for years. After our time at Creech, he'd bounced around before becoming the first pilot from the RPA community to command a squadron. Mike did a short stint as a squadron commander before he deployed to stand up this new group for AFRICOM. He had to move part of his flying squadron to Camp Lemonnier to set up the forward staging area. After all, we were going after the same targets.

I met him in front of our two hangars.

"Squirrel," he called out, stepping from a gator.

He had driven the flight line to access the compound instead of coming through the gate.

"Mike," I said. "Welcome to Djibouti."

We shook hands as he looked around.

"Place looks good on you," he said.

"Let's get out of this heat," I said, guiding him toward the ops tent. "So what's it like being the second-best Predator pilot at your base again?"

"Ahhhh." He laughed and hit me on the arm. "I don't fly Preds anymore."

"Ha," I returned. "They're all Preds."

In fact, the official General Atomics nomenclature for the MQ-9 was the Predator B. Only the Air Force called them Reapers.

Mike laughed.

We spent the next week discussing how to make his move happen while sitting on a T-barrier wall that circled my compound. The barriers, constructed of concrete, resembled massive eight-foot inverted "T's."

One night, Mike and I sat on the barriers talking as we had done for days. We alternated between watching the operations on the parking ramp and watching the occasional airplane on the runway.

"We've got to find a way to fit in here," he said.

"I need the space for all my aircraft," I said. "Besides, you'll just use this place as a lily pad."

Mike eyed me.

"You know that isn't the endgame."

I sighed. I knew it wasn't. It was the special operations way. Take. Don't give.

"Yeah, you guys will find a way to make your stay permanent."

"We gotta make it work," he said.

I looked up at the night sky. Brilliant stars peeked through the glare of the camp's streetlights. It would never get dark enough on base to see the Milky Way, something I had hoped to witness on this expedition. At least the light southerly breeze was somewhat fresh. The burn pits were inactive that night.

"I know."

"We should be discussing this on the golf course."

I laughed. The national course was a couple of miles down the road. The caddies carried a square patch of Astroturf they could lay down when you teed off. There were no greens or fairways. It was just rocks on top of other rocks. The pins were your only indication you were hitting in the right direction.

I could fight the move and win, at a great cost to my political capital. I would lose face with the Task Force. That effectively left me with one option.

"I'll give you half a hangar," I offered.

"Thanks," he said.

He was genuine.

"It is what it is," I said. We both knew I was getting screwed.

I followed one of my Predators as it taxied out and took off, its low hum the only sound in Africa for a few moments.

"No, I mean it," he insisted. "Thanks."

"Look," I said. "You need to know that if we weather recall, we can't go anywhere else. I need that space if all our birds are on the deck."

I couldn't fit all my aircraft in only one hangar.

"I know," Mike said.

"I can't have an MQ-9 in the hangar when that happens."

The Reaper took up the space of three Predators.

"We'll fly it out if it comes to that," Mike assured me. "We have the legs to get around the storms."

No airplane in our hangars would launch in a storm. We both knew that. Still, I appreciated the gesture. I quickly changed the subject.

"You know we won a safety award?"

"Really?" Mike said. "Congrats."

It was no small feat, considering our beginning. We had been accident-free for nearly four months. Flight discipline was so high that my young and very inexperienced lieutenants were saving previously unlandable aircraft. My aviators were vindicating themselves. I was very proud of what they had become.

Mike and I stood on the barrier and watched the airfield. Every pilot I know can watch an airfield for hours. It is second only to Pred porn. From the top of the barrier, I could watch our aircraft circle above the field while they struggled to gain altitude before heading north to the target areas. Out of the corner of my eye, I saw the flashing strobes of a Predator descending toward the single runway at Djibouti-Ambouli International Airport. It was flying in the wrong direction. It was supposed to head north.

The engine didn't sound right either.

"Excuse me, Mike," I said. "I think we are about to lose an aircraft."

"Go," Mike said quickly. He recognized the signs too.

I burst into the GCS. Ponis was in the seat. He was frozen at the controls, his sensor operator unsure what to do.

"What's going on, Ponis?" I asked.

"The engine's coming apart," he said. "I'm trying to land."

I looked at the tracker. He wasn't going to make the runway.

"Turn toward the airfield," I ordered.

"I don't know where it is."

The most important thing when flying a single-engine aircraft is to know the location of the closest runway. We train pilots to know where their landing field is and immediately turn toward it if the engine malfunctions. But he was faced with a possible third accident, and he lost track of where he was.

His first incident had been when a Predator came apart in flight over Iraq. The plane was gone before he could react. His second was Tail 173, and he had no control when the aircraft flipped itself over on its back. Now he had full control. The aircraft and runway were clearly depicted on the tracker. He just couldn't think enough to focus on it. All he could do was stare straight ahead at the HUD.

There wasn't time to yank him from the seat and take over. I leaned down so I could speak directly into his ear.

I went calm like I did when I killed.

"Turn right," I said.

Mechanically, he started a turn. The nose tracked around until the more familiar landscape around the airfield came into view.

"Stop turn," I said.

He rolled out. I used the same commands he had heard while practicing radar approaches in the T-38, a two-seat, supersonic jet trainer. I hoped the familiar language would break through his haze.

"Aim for the end of the runway."

He turned a little. A Djiboutian Air Force hangar came into view. This hangar housed the president's personal plane. I checked our glide path and it looked like we might hit the hangar.

"Give me a little left rudder."

The rudder pedal squeaked as he pressed down. The aircraft started tracking to the left. The right wing rose as the aircraft rolled.

"That's enough."

The hangar grew large very fast. I held my breath and hoped the Predator still had enough lift to get over the building. The hangar filled the whole screen and then disappeared. The video remained, which meant we were still airborne.

"Turn back to brick one."

"Brick one" was the first foot of landable runway. Ponis started to turn. The Predator was about twenty feet off the ground. If it sank any lower, he risked digging the right wing into the dirt and cartwheeling the aircraft down the runway.

"Roll out," I ordered.

"But . . ."

"Roll out," I repeated evenly. "Use your rudder for alignment now."

The rudder pedal protested with a loud metallic screech as Ponis pressed down hard. Usually, cockpit noise was sufficient to drown out the movement of the spring that centered the rudder pedals. The noise grated like fingernails on a chalkboard.

The nose tracked to the right and rolled out slowly. The side runway marker was centered underneath us. Our left wheel was within five feet of being in the pockmarked dirt. Ponis stayed on the rudder and the nose tracked more to the right, starting to drift back to the center of the runway.

"Start your round out."

Without flaring, the nose wheel would hit first and break under the stress of a heavyweight landing. Ponis eased back on the stick and the nose tracked up. Seconds later, the aircraft slammed onto the runway and pulled to the right.

The impact shook the last of the cobwebs from Ponis's mind. He centered the rudder and kept the aircraft from bolting off the edge of the runway. The engine was still running enough for him to taxi back to the compound. The last thing the Djiboutians wanted was for us to close their only runway again.

I patted Ponis on the shoulder.

"Good job," I said. I meant it.

Maintenance would later discover shards of metal in the oil filter. The pistons had shattered in the engine block and torn themselves apart. Miraculously, the engine was able to keep spinning long enough for Ponis to land safely.

I put him in for a safety award. Instead of being faced with a total loss, we had only to change the engine. We didn't have aircraft to spare. If Ponis had failed, we couldn't have kept up our ops tempo, and al-Awlaki might have eluded us.

We were close. Each air strike for the next two months eliminated his immediate subordinates and their replacements. Morbid jokes began flying through the squadron. Someone posted a Help Wanted sign in the operations tent: "Wanted, Facilitator, long work hours, lots of time in the field, job just vacated."

After another successful mission, one of the weapons loaders summed it up perfectly.

"One day, AQ is going to realize they are volunteering for jobs with a life-span of two weeks."

He was right.

We were issuing pink slips to al Qaeda on a pace close to that. Still, we were missing target number one.

Our break came in August. A source said al-Awlaki traveled in a pair of SUVs or trucks. Most operatives used only one truck, but his personal bodyguards and aides rode in a second truck.

Al-Awlaki was a cautious man. He was the face of al Qaeda propaganda worldwide. His loss would be a serious blow to the credibility of his English-language magazine, *Inspire*, as well as recruitment efforts in the West. The extra security was in place to protect al-Awlaki against a raid. The source said al-Awlaki expected to be captured and tried in the United States.

Ultimately, this precaution would prove to be his downfall.

The Predators and Reapers providing the coverage for the Task Force converged on his suspected location. We knew he operated around Al Jawf, but now the pilots were on the lookout for the pair of trucks.

Temperatures soared in the summer, despite the high altitude. Daytime activities across the region slowed after noon, only to resume again after the heat broke for the day. Al-Awlaki drove to meetings in the afternoons, when few people were outside. We found him during these off-peak times.

A convoy of two four-by-four trucks, both extended king cabs, worked from village to village, racing on the highways, driving cautiously in the cities. They stopped occasionally outside houses. Sometimes the trucks' occupants got out and walked into the buildings. Other times, the locals walked up to the trucks to chat.

Each time, we had difficulty gaining a positive identification on al-Awlaki. We flew at a distance to avoid detection, and that affected our optics enough that the few face shots we got weren't conclusive. The target was basically the right height, but the bearded face resembled everyone else in the region.

It wasn't enough—until a second source confirmed the two-truck convoy with a date and time for a meeting. We camped out over the house and waited. The trucks arrived at the appointed hour. They were the trucks we had been following.

The noose was tightening.

CHAPTER 20

Al-Awlaki

The Task Force was ready to take action against al-Awlaki by mid-September.

The right cues had been met to trigger direct action. In this case, enough pattern of life had been collected that the analysts could positively identify al-Awlaki in the convoy. We set up the alert aircraft as we had before. The Reaper and one Predator would share time above the target. That would be sufficient to maintain a constant stare while the two other birds stood ready to launch with a full load of missiles. I kept a third in reserve under the sunshade.

We set up the constant stare near Al Jawf. Al-Awlaki would be easy to identify. The American terrorist rode in the passenger seat wherever he went. The others in the car deferred to him through their body language. That, and they were armed with AK-47s.

Al-Awlaki wasn't.

The second car carried additional security. At each stop, they typically got out of the truck and moved in a coordinated manner to scout the perimeter of the meeting location or to discreetly position themselves to watch avenues of approach.

We had to maintain additional missiles on the ramp. I went to tell Cruiser.

"Cruiser," I said. "I'm surging again."

He smiled.

"You seem to do that a lot."

We had surged about 170 days since my arrival.

"Yeah," I continued. "This one's important."

"Aren't they all?" he said.

He was right. Anything with the Task Force was advertised as important or critical. Nothing was ever routine.

"This one especially so," I said. "Can you help out?"

He regarded me a moment.

"What do you need?"

I could see he was on guard.

"We are keeping three on alert," I said. "I need missiles on the ramp for all of them."

"You know you can only have two."

I didn't budge. The Air Force said I could have around 150 missiles. Only the Navy put the restrictions on me.

"I get that," I said, "but going to the ASP takes too long. Any delay and we miss the window."

Cruiser just looked at me. I pressed.

"I need six missiles."

Cruiser looked down at his pad as he scribbled down my list. He considered the text a moment, nodded as if making a decision, and then looked up at me.

"You got it."

My next stop was the maintenance tent. It was decidedly cooler than ops since the ops tent AC had melted down. One of the maintenance troops was sitting in the 120-degree sun trying to rewire it. She'd already fixed half the squadron's ACs that summer.

The old Gulf War–era units chugged loudly. A canvas tube wound down from the ceiling and aimed at a bank of handheld radios. The blast of air that greeted me at the door felt truly arctic compared to outside.

I walked up to the status board in the back of the tent. This was a large dry-erase whiteboard on which were written the seven aircraft tail numbers and the maintenance status.

"'57 Chevy," "Marissa," and "Kate II" stood ready.

Z-man looked up from his desk. He was a fiery master sergeant from Holloman. While Jon oversaw all of the maintainers, Z-man still worked on the aircraft side by side with the other wrench turners. I had grown to respect his ethic and inherent capacity to herd the maintenance cats. I was sorry to hear he would be retiring upon his return home in a week.

"Sir, when did you come in?"

Maintenance never seemed to hear me walk into their tent. Their space was no louder than any other. For some reason, they just never seemed to notice until the last minute. The other maintainers instantly stood. I waved at them to sit back down. I wasn't there to disrupt their work.

"Just practicing my HUMINT [human intelligence] skills, Z."

He stood and joined me at the board.

"Everything is still green, sir," he said. "Any leads?"

"Not that they've said."

"We've had to move the birds."

I noticed that our three alert birds were no longer out on the parking ramp.

"And?"

"The heat is too much," he explained. "We can keep them on the ramp for part of the day, but the afternoon is brutal. We put them back in the hangar to get them out of the sun."

"Okay."

It was a prudent move. When the call came, maintenance could roll them out to the parking ramp, load the weapons, and launch them. Until then, the Predators waited in the cooler tents.

"We'd like to keep them in there," Z said.

"How long will that delay a launch?"

Z-man considered his response.

"Thirty minutes max for the first," he said. "No change for the others."

The target area lay at least three hours away. A decision to launch would occur well in advance of a strike. The most likely scenario in my book was the Task Force would want to have aircraft overhead for at least an hour before a potential strike. We'd already have at least one other aircraft out there covering any gap the delay caused.

"Okay."

"Want me to tell Task Force?"

"No," I said. "The less they know, the less they'll hold against us later."

Thirty minutes wouldn't matter in the end.

With limited sorties, we kept enough crews on hand to immediately launch the strikers when the call came down. I knew the Task Force would be jumpy when the time came. A couple of weeks back, they had changed the configuration of a mission six times while it tried to launch.

I ordered a third alert bird just in case. It was a blank canvas in the event that the Task Force decided to change anything as we launched.

We were ready. All we could do now was wait.

The pilots milled around the ops tent crew lounge waiting. "Hurry up and wait" became the order of the day while the Task Force tracked al-Awlaki. Movies and video games replaced work in the ops cell. Notification would happen via phone call so we stayed close. Every so often, Jose, one of the sensor operators, checked the chat rooms for an update.

Jose was of Mexican descent. An avid bodybuilder, he had thick arms and a barrel chest. When he wasn't working or in the gym, he was doing boneheaded stuff. He was a smart guy with a penchant for blond moments, which made him the target of our practical jokes.

One constant was his ability to lose his ID card. It was almost a habit, which was a problem because the card was required in order to gain access to the chow hall, gym, and even work computers.

"Hey, where's my ID?" Jose called out as he went over to check the chat room for an update.

The crews paid no attention. Everyone was watching an episode of *The Walking Dead* on the Xbox.

"Well?" he said.

No one looked in his direction. Someone sniggered. With a huff, Jose stomped back into the computer room and dug through papers on one of the desks. I could hear him tear through a second desk.

"Seriously, guys, I need that ID," Jose said.

"Isn't it about *time* you kept track of that thing?" someone said from the crew lounge.

Jose paused and then slowly looked at the tent's door. Above it, at the apex of the rounded ceiling, was a little clock caked in black diesel residue. It had fallen at one time, cracking the glass and leaving an opening into which we could fit his ID.

"Oh, come on, guys."

The ID was resting at the bottom of the clock, covering the six. The clock was too high to reach without help. The office chairs rolled and were too unsafe to stand on. Jose looked for the stepladder behind the large wooden stand that held the computers and Internet servers for the GCS and squadron.

It wasn't there.

He rushed out of the ops tent and made a beeline for maintenance. Surely, they had ladders for everything.

"Sorry," the supply tech said, scrolling through his laptop. "All the ladders are checked out. Not sure when they will be back."

"Who checked them out?"

The tech gave a name.

"He's not even on shift," the sensor said. "Wasn't he required to turn them in before leaving?"

"Yes," the tech said. "It's strange."

"Can you help me find them?"

"I'm sorry, I can't leave the tent," he said. "I have to maintain positive control of the tools."

The tech's face remained neutral.

Frustrated, the sensor operator stalked out of the tent. It took Jose the better part of an hour before he found a chair without rollers. We all watched as he climbed up on the chair and reached for the clock. His fingers brushed the face.

Someone stifled a laugh.

Jose spent several minutes working the clock off its mount. He sat on the chair and monkeyed with the glass. When he finally freed his ID, the ops cell burst into laughter.

As soon as he recovered the ID, we started planning another prank. We debated freezing it in a block of ice or letting it fly a sortie by sticking it in a Predator. We knew there would be a next time with this kid.

Finally, the phone rang in the squadron operations center and I immediately picked it up. It was the private line direct to the JOC.

"Squirrel here," I said.

"Launch."

It was the Predator LNO.

"How many?" I said.

"All three."

The line clicked dead.

All three aircraft meant we had al-Awlaki. The LNO couldn't tell me more over the phone. The line wasn't secure enough to pass target information. But I knew one thing as I hung up the phone.

Today, the Pirates hunted.

We were going after the target like German U-boats tracked convoys in World War II. Attack en masse. Attack like a wolf pack.

"Fire up the GCS," I told the watch pilot as I left the ops cell.

I had two crews on shift today. MaDrawers was due to rotate out and his replacement had already assumed his night shift. He ran out to help. I stopped in the maintenance tent. Z-man had already gotten the call.

"We're pushing the first one out now," Z-man said.

"Anything I can do to help?"

As we spoke, several maintainers were pushing the first bird out of the hangar. She crouched under the full load of gas, dragging her tail. The plane looked eager to launch.

"I could push," I said.

"Not a chance, sir," he said. "We can't let you do that."

I nodded. Maintenance regulations were quite specific. Only certified personnel could move the aircraft on the ground. As much as I wanted to help, I couldn't.

"All right, how much time do you need?" I asked.

Z-man had the answer ready.

"Thirty minutes for the first, and then every thirty minutes after."

"Okay," I said. "Crews will be ready."

Two crew chiefs positioned the first aircraft just outside the hangar. A tech driving a small forklift lifted a pallet of tools, then backed up to the Pred. The crew chiefs attached a tow bar and the first bird started her quarter-mile journey to the launch ramp.

As the plane trundled to the compound entrance, the crew chiefs raced into the hangar and pushed the second Predator out into the sun. Another tug had materialized in position to receive her. The Reaper squadron offered their tug next. They had little to do, with their one aircraft already in the air.

Within minutes, we had our Predators being towed in column toward the ramp. Navy maintainers working on the P-3s and troops working on the taxiways pulled into the dirt and silently watched the procession. Predators didn't do "elephant walks." Bombers did. The "walks" were common in World War II as numerous bombers taxied and launched all at once.

Predators went out solo, so it was strange to see three going out at the same time.

The weapons loaders waited on the ramp. They drove a truck

ahead of the column and pulled up to a metal Sea-Land container where they kept the missiles out of the sun. They started loading the hundred-pound Hellfires the moment the crew chiefs chocked the Predators in place.

The chiefs ran their checklists and called ready. The crews eight thousand miles away in the United States scrambled to their cockpits, sitting at consoles in air-conditioned quarters in Cannon Air Force Base in New Mexico. I knew the feeling. Part of me wanted to be one of the crews on the hunt, but there would be no glory for them if the Predators never got off the tarmac.

As the aircraft started to spin up, I checked the thermometer hanging next to the ops tent. Outside, the temperature hovered at ninety-five degrees. We were in the "heat window," the time when ambient temperatures could overheat the delicate electronics within the Predators. The temperatures would rise sharply now that the sun was approaching its zenith. I hoped the breeze would keep the ramp cool enough.

The planes taxied as individuals. I didn't have enough maintenance crews or cockpits to launch them all together. The first two planes taxied minutes apart. The crews were still loading the third aircraft when I heard the familiar whirring of the Rotax motor of the first Predator.

Standing on a T-barrier, I could see the little gray aircraft start its roll. It was slow at first and then accelerated to a new stage of slow. The Predator looked as if it was moving fast, but it still took well over a minute to pass me. Almost reluctantly, the aircraft lifted off the ground. It hovered inches above the runway, engine straining to gain speed.

Over the water, the plane hit cooler air and climbed a little better. The landing gear started to retract as the Predator turned to the south to get out of the airport's traffic pattern. I watched until the last bird disappeared in the distance. The sun had baked me. The temperature was now 110 degrees. I went inside to cool off as the planes flew across the Gulf of Aden and joined the Reaper over Al Jawf. I made a note of the time and made plans to head over to the Task Force to watch the mission.

The mission unfolded on the six fifty-inch plasma screens that lined the walls around the JOC commander's podium.

"That him?" I asked the Predator LNO.

"We confirmed he was active about five hours ago," Frog said, not looking away from the monitors showing the Predators' video feeds. "We are still looking to get eyes on him right now."

On the monitor, I saw the feed shift to Al Jawf, a small village near Sana'a. The aircraft monitoring the communications picked up al-Awlaki's signal and realized that he was on the move. Two trucks pulled up outside a house in the village. They were white Toyota HiLuxes, king cab trucks like Tacomas that sat about five.

"The target's active," one of the Army officers in the operations center said. "We are seeing indications he's on the move."

The officer gave the coordinates and I checked the Predators' feeds. The two trucks sat very near the given coordinates. The Predators were close enough to count them as on target.

Suddenly, eight figures spilled out of a nearby house and quickly climbed into the trucks. The doors had barely shut before the driver took off. The other vehicle followed a moment later.

"Stay on them," the JOC commander said.

Gordon took the lead and followed al-Awlaki out of the village and onto a highway. The road's straightaway was the most logical place for the shot. The vehicles would maintain a constant speed on a predictable course. There were few ridgelines to block the missile or the targeting laser.

We all waited for the green light. Finally, the JOC director nodded and the JTAC transmitted the 9-Line. Gordon was ready to shoot.

"Copy, cleared hot," the pilot in Cannon said.

Thirty seconds passed. The two HiLux trucks grew larger in the camera's field of view.

"Laser on," Gordon said.

A black icon reading "LRD Lase Des" flashed on the screen. The lead truck ferrying al-Awlaki grew to fill the screen. The picture twitched as the proximity made the controls hypersensitive.

The second vehicle was no longer in sight.

"In three, two, one . . ."

The familiar double-click overrode the audio as the fire signal interrupted the satellite signal. A moment later, the HUD went blank as the blinding white flash of the missile's exhaust plume washed out the sensitive IR picture.

Immediately, the Predator banked to the right. On the computer monitor, the little blue icon for Gordon rotated until it paralleled the road. At that magnification, the aircraft looked as if it was on top of the road.

My mind wandered to the diagram I had drawn of the moving shot. So far, the crew was following it perfectly. The Predator flew parallel to the trucks to make it easier for the sensor to keep the laser on target. The sensor's cross hairs pulled off the target after the rollout but quickly adjusted and placed the cross hairs about twenty yards in front of al-Awlaki's truck. The vehicles didn't swerve or even change speed. Al-Awlaki continued down the road as if unaware of the threat.

In my head, I started checking off my mental checklist as if I was flying. I knew the short two-second burn of the Hellfire engine accelerated the missile to nearly 1.4 Mach, creating a sonic boom. This intense acceleration subjected the missile to ten times the force of gravity. When the missile's sensor detected enough g-forces, the warhead armed. The infrared eye opened and then looked for the laser spot.

I knew the missile used its fins to keep the reflected laser energy in its field of view. It constantly tweaked its course to keep the spot centered on the seeker head's glass.

"Ten seconds," the pilot said.

The Predator floated alongside al-Awlaki's truck. Had he looked up, it would have been entirely possible that he would have seen the aircraft as the pilot eased a little rudder to pull the nose away from the target. Distance at this point determined stability for the sensor. Too close and the cross hairs would wobble. A couple of miles out, the angle down wouldn't be so steep and the cross hairs would remain stable.

At five seconds, the missile slowed below the speed of sound, causing a second sonic boom. The shock wave coursed in all directions, loudest in the direction of the missile's travel. The boom washed over the two trucks. These were not large booms and would have been hard to hear if the radio was on or the window was open causing the wind to howl into the cab. The trucks sped forward.

"Five, four, three . . ."

The sensor relaxed his grip a mite. The cross hairs drifted toward the lead vehicle. The pilot paused to let the sensor focus on his cross hairs. A black streak entered the picture from above, raced downward, and slammed into the hood of the truck. It hit right where the sensor had placed the cross hairs.

Smoke mushroomed out of the hood and debris shot out of the engine in all directions. The truck skidded awkwardly, spun sideways, and rolled to a stop. The truck containing the security team frantically hit the brakes and swerved to miss the first vehicle. Bong was trailing behind. He rolled in, cleared by the Task Force JTAC, and put a missile into the hood of the second truck.

Months of tracking ended in a matter of seconds. There was little reaction in the operations center. No cheers. No high fives. The Task Force was too professional for that. Frog and I shook hands. He was smiling. We were one team. We'd earned a victory, evident by the trucks smoldering in the monitor.

Two of the Predators started the journey back to Djibouti. The third lingered for a while watching for survivors. There was no ground team to verify the kill. We had to wait for other sources. He would be missed at his next meeting and someone would think to send out a team to find him.

Verification that al-Awlaki had died came within hours.

Abdullah al-Jumaili, a tribal sheik from Al Jawf Province, later told the *New York Times* the truck was nearly destroyed and it was hard to recognize bodies. He was "100 percent sure" al-Awlaki was killed. We also saw message traffic from the enemy about his death almost as fast as CNN announced the air strike.

"The death of Awlaki is a major blow to al Qaeda's most active operational affiliate," President Obama said a few days later.

I walked back to my compound and stepped onto the T-barriers to watch the first aircraft, Bong, approach. Colonel Jay Bickley, my group commander, was touring the base and joined me.

"We had a mission success today," I told him.

I watched the transmitter tower as it panned the sky. It maintained a position where it could best transmit to the airplane as it rotated around to point at final approach.

"Here it comes, sir," I said.

"Where is it?"

In the distance, a speck emerged from the late afternoon haze. At first, it was a dot. Then wings sprouted. Only inside a mile did we recognize it as a Predator.

We could hear nothing.

The little plane glided toward the runway, flared, and touched down with two little white puffs of rubber smoke. The bird, devoid of missiles, rolled past us en route to the taxiway that would take it to parking.

"That's it?" Bickley asked.

"It's more exciting in the cockpit."

We walked to the GCS to recover the last bird. I took the seat and Bickley sat behind me on an office chair. The Gulf of Aden slipped below us. We clipped the north shoreline of Djibouti and entered the Gulf of Tadjoura. My flight path took me around to the west of Djibouti City, where I would land pointed at the sea.

The sun was setting over Ethiopia. The large orange ball sank low to the horizon, making the shadows long. I had wanted to see a famous African sunset for my entire year in theater. So far, I had not been treated, as most of our sunsets had been shrouded by distant thunderstorms or haze. Today, we watched from the Predator's cameras.

The Predator, nicknamed "'57 Chevy," touched down as gracefully as it could and rolled down the runway, slowing to taxi speed. I marveled, as I always did, at the empty rails of the aircraft. We flew so often with weapons that we often forgot how the aircraft looked unarmed. I knew the maintainers wouldn't miss the empty rails as the Predator taxied from the runway to the ramp. In combat, empty rails meant we had done more than just watch our prey grow old. We were no longer vultures.

We were birds of prey.

EPILOGUE

The October sun still baked the flight line in Djibouti. The heat had broken and the temperatures slowly dropped to the low hundreds. The strong summer blast from the west had diminished to the doldrums as the prevailing winds started their shift to the east.

We gathered in the shade of a hangar. My operators, maintainers, and security forces assembled under the wing of an MQ-9 to meet the JOC commander. The JOC wanted to thank the troops and to offer them feedback. This was a first for us.

Predator squadrons never got feedback from the units we supported. We only got complaints. Nobody liked failure, no matter how trivial. In our world, the lack of feedback always meant we were doing our jobs.

I approved the meeting more out of curiosity than anything else.

I stood to the side while the commander talked. He spoke about the mission and its impact. He congratulated the team on their hard work and the success it garnered. And I tuned out all of it.

Instead, I marveled at the airmen arrayed around the JOC. They were a mix of airmen from numerous backgrounds and specialties. They didn't clump into groups, but integrated themselves like equals. After nearly a year, they had become a seamless team, a family. They had suffered together through physical, mental, and spiritual deprivation. They had stood together and carried those who felt the effects of isolation from their friends and families.

The 60th Expeditionary Reconnaissance Squadron was not a unit I had ever expected to see, let alone command. Nor did I ever anticipate that the aircraft they flew would revolutionize modern warfare and intelligence gathering.

Times had changed significantly since I had joined the program.

Following the Facilitator shot, I had an epiphany while drinking that martini on my buddy's balcony. It occurred to me that the Air Force had just entered a great transformation as significant as that seen following World War I.

In 1916, artillery was the only way to hit your enemy from long range. The aircraft was a new invention flown by the aristocracy in combat as a novelty. Initial missions were essentially reconnaissance only. Pilots waved like gentlemen as they passed each other over the trenches. Then the war bogged down and the slaughter mounted. Someone threw a wrench in frustration. Then someone fired a pistol. Then someone mounted a machine gun. The ensuing arms race heated up the skies of Europe. By 1918, the aircraft had superseded artillery as the principal long-range threat, leaving behind its surveillance-only mission set.

World War II brought with it greater destruction and loss of life. General Henry Arnold and the US Army Air Corps (or USAAC) looked for alternatives to the increasing casualty rates incurred through their precision daylight bombing campaigns. Project Aphrodite experimented with remotely controlled aviation. Its major project became a radio-guided B-17 to be flown kamikaze style into difficult targets. The USAAC intended to hit the sub pens at Lorient, which had proven impervious to aerial bombardment. The war ended before the technology could be used in combat.

It would take nearly fifty years until research truly delved into RPA technology.

In the 1990s, the first-generation Predators flew in Kosovo and Southwest Asia, providing limited imagery to an unappreciative, and at times hostile, community. Predators were a novelty, much like aircraft were in 1916.

The years following September 11 saw a nearly exact replication of World War I. The new Predator with advanced avionics and its AGM-114 Hellfire missile deployed. Droopy's shot fired in defense of friendly forces ushered in a new era of weapons development reminiscent of biplanes evolving from surveillance to full-scale fighters.

RPAs of all kinds, from the small hand-tossed Ravens to the gargantuan Global Hawks, appeared. Some only looked over hills to detect possible ambushes; others collected strategic intelligence by flying high above their targets. Each year of the war, manufacturers introduce dozens of new platforms in an effort to meet the ever-increasing demand for intelligence.

Now remotely piloted aircraft dominate the theaters and the news.

The Air Force no longer calls them drones. The very word invokes fear and misunderstanding. Lack of information about how the aircraft operate has led vivid imaginations to envision James Cameron's Terminator rampaging around the countryside, killing anything that moves.

The technology controlling the Predator and Reaper is anything but robotic or autonomous. Real pilots control these aircraft. They follow the Federal Aviation Administration's regulations when in the United States and comply with the International Civil Aviation Organization's rules when operating overseas. In Djibouti, not only did we prove that we could operate safely in a high-traffic area with both civil and military aircraft, but we also helped develop the airspace plans to make it a routine occurrence.

The incident with the Air France Airbus spurred me to approach the State Department and request permission to directly engage the Djiboutian government. I proposed special procedures to help de-conflict our aircraft. I also invited them into our compound to see us fly from the cockpit. The incident was both eye-opening and wildly successful for us. The Djiboutian air traffic controllers had a ball waving at themselves from the ground and watching their images on the cockpit HUDs.

If anything, they learned that we flew like real pilots. Push stick forward, cows get big. Pull stick back, cows get small. We had complete control, just like any other aircraft in the world. The only difference between the Predator and a manned aircraft was that our cockpit was not physically connected to the aircraft. Despite that, we were just as capable as any professional aviator out there.

We did lose four aircraft during my year in country. Some losses were preventable; some were not. One was a new experience for the whole community. I would later learn from sources at Air Combat Command and Air Force Special Operations Command that the results of all four safety investigations had been thrown out. Both ACC and AFSOC determined the investigations had tainted conclusions.

The only parts of the reports to survive the purge were the

recommendations for improvement. These recommendations would serve only to make the community stronger and safer in the increasingly congested airspaces around the world.

And flying safer was our goal.

In 2011, the Air Force flew more than five hundred thousand hours in combat with the Predator alone. In comparison, all the fighters and bombers in the Air Force flew approximately forty-eight thousand hours worldwide, not just in combat. Despite that heavy load, Predators lose an average of only thirteen aircraft a year. That number remained stable, or dropped, while our hours flown expanded exponentially over the decade. We became safer as we flew over the years, eventually achieving the status of having the lowest accident rate in the Air Force. Our crashes, like those of airliners, make good headlines, though that is rarely the whole story.

But the RPA's main moral issue is its use to kill.

Amnesty International and other organizations cry foul when an RPA kills an al Qaeda operative or helps ground forces do the same. They never complained when F-117s dropped bombs on the Baath Party headquarters in an attempt to kill Saddam Hussein on the first night of Operation Iraqi Freedom. They didn't complain when an F-16 dropped a bomb on al-Zarqawi, even though a Predator had followed the same legal procedures the day prior. Each strike involves a pilot pulling a trigger in full compliance with the Law of Armed Conflict.

We never flew autonomously.

The Predator is a remotely piloted aircraft, with a human in the link at all times. Nothing can occur without a human first commanding it. The plane cannot shoot without a pilot pulling the trigger. A kill cannot be made without the pilot's first complying with a lengthy string of rules before a strike clearance is issued.

I wrote this book in part to tell the incredible story of the Predator's surge to prominence as a valuable tool to combat terrorism. I never intended this book to decide or define the legal and moral arguments the lawmakers and philosophers must decide. I wrote it to showcase the manner in which the Predator revolutionized warfare.

The al-Awlaki mission marked a noticeable shift in American military operations. Osama bin Laden had been killed only five months before, using scores of SEALs, helicopter pilots, and a few other assets. Tracking had taken nearly two decades, with little to show for it other than frustration, significant loss of treasure, and a string of terror attacks that propelled the United States into an ugly war. Mission failure would have been a national nightmare, with dead or captured men paraded on foreign televisions.

We saw that in the failed hostage rescue in Iran.

RPAs revolutionized the hunt for terrorists by removing risk to the human element. There were no choppers to be shot down, no men to be wounded or killed. The capabilities RPAs brought to the fight both augmented and superseded human limitations in a way that allowed us to find al-Awlaki more quickly without committing the whole of America's conventional and special forces to the task. More important, this evolution in warfare gave us the hope that we might live in a world without another UBL holding the world hostage for years.

In the eight years of flying the Predator covered in this book, I've seen our combat air patrols increase more than twentyfold to fight terror worldwide. In the year we hunted al-Awlaki, the 60th flew more than nine hundred missions, encompassing more than seventeen thousand hours of combat. In that time, we explored new missions including sea interdiction and antipiracy. We also fulfilled the president's priority mission.

When I think of iconic images of past wars, I think of the trenches in World War I, the P-51 and B-17 in World War II, Huey helicopters and napalm in Vietnam, and the M1A1 Abrams tank and A-10 in the Gulf War. The MQ-1 has become an icon, along with the SEALs, of the global war on terror that will characterize this past decade.

The young men and women standing on the tarmac listening to the JOC commander were the ones to do it. Their actions have changed the face of war forever. They remain anonymous by choice. They fiercely defend one another, their communities, and the nation while watching over our heroes on the ground. They ask for no reward beyond the simple acknowledgment of their contributions to our overall war effort.

I marveled at how farsighted General Arnold really was when he said, "The next war may be fought by airplanes with no men in them at all. . . . It will be different from anything the world has ever seen."

ACKNOWLEDGMENTS

The journey from concept to publication of this book was nearly twelve years long. When given an opportunity to present myself in public fashion, I usually pass and give way to those who prefer to bask in the spotlight. I would rather remain on the fringe of the crowd and observe the action. Being low-key feels comfortable to me.

Anonymity affords those in my line of work a means to live a normal life without enduring the scrutiny of a curious public. At times, this seclusion proves a benefit as we are able to celebrate our family life quietly and in relative peace. And in others, it frustrates us as we watch misinformation propagate through the media about our motives and actions. There's nothing worse than watching a story get "it" wrong.

When I met General Mark Welsh in Djibouti, he was still the commander of the United States Air Forces in Europe. It would be another year before he would assume the role of the Chief of Staff

Acknowledgments

of the Air Force. He had a reputation of encouraging airmen to tell their stories so the world could share in our collective experience. Upon our introduction, the local Group Commander relayed a laundry list of my accomplishments within the Predator program, most of which I had no idea he knew about. General Welsh considered me for a moment and then he told me I needed to write my story.

I sat on that idea for nearly two years, unsure if I should write the book or why my story was even worth the effort. I was loath to expose myself to the public eye. I was even more reticent to endure the sure-to-be-colorful commentary from the Predator community. They had been vicious with the other guys who had gone public.

After all, I'm not a hero; I just watch over the guys who are.

My position changed when I got a call from a friend. He sent me a link to an article in the *Washington Post*. The article identified me personally and discussed the al-Awlaki strikes in excruciating detail, a level of detail that should never have been released. I was shocked, since the Air Force has a policy not to release names of combat commanders until after a war ends. Yet there was my name in print, identified with a major operation.

It was only then that I seriously considered writing the story of the Predator.

I contacted Kevin Maurer to feel out the market for our story. He immediately jumped at the opportunity and wanted to shop it to his agent and publishers. That started a whirlwind journey through the exciting publishing process. He taught me how to write the way publishers want and guided me through pitfalls I hadn't even been prepared for. The rest is, as they say, history.

Since then, I have been blessed to work with an amazing team of professionals who've made the idea of this book into a reality. To

Acknowledgments

Scott, Ben, Christine, Amanda, Stephanie, and the rest of the staff at Dutton—thank you for believing in me. And to Mark: Your extraordinary effort pushed this book through a challenging review.

Most important, I want to thank my beautiful wife. Without her tolerance for my long hours poring over manuscripts, typing madly into the computer, and morosely researching details, I could not have completed a workable draft, let alone completed the whole book. I love you, sweetie.

ABOUT THE AUTHORS

LT. COL. T. MARK McCURLEY is a retired Air Force pilot and former intelligence operator. In 2003, he volunteered for the secretive Predator program, deploying five times to Iraq, Afghanistan, and other locations, where he has flown the MQ-1 Predator and the MQ-9 Reaper, accruing more than one thousand combat hours in flight.

KEVIN MAURER is an award-winning journalist and the best-selling coauthor, with Mark Owen, of *No Easy Day: The Firsthand Account of the Mission That Killed Osama bin Laden*. He has covered special operations forces for a decade.